Chile
& Easter Island
a travel survival kit

Alan Samagalski

Chile & Easter Island – a travel survival kit
2nd Edition

Published by
Lonely Planet Publications
Head Office: PO Box 617, Hawthorn, Victoria 3122, Australia

Printed by
Colorcraft Ltd, Hong Kong

Photographs by
Alan Samagalski
Front cover: Ahu Nau Nau, Easter Island

First Published
July 1987

This Edition
March 1990

National Library of Australia Cataloguing in Publication Data

Samagalski, Alan.
 Chile & Easter Island, a travel survival kit.

 2nd ed.
 Includes index.
 ISBN 0 86442 074 9.

1. Chile – Description and travel – 1981 – – Guide-books.
2. Easter Island – Description and travel – 1981 – – Guide-books.
I. Title.

918.30465

text © Lonely Planet 1990
maps © Lonely Planet 1990

The Author

Alan Samagalski's background includes a lengthy sojourn on the Indian subcontinent, a degree from the Melbourne University Genetics Department, and an illustrious career as the world's first Atomic Folk musician at Melbourne's legendary *Last Laugh*, *Comedy Cafe* and *Aberdeen Hotel*.

He started working at Lonely Planet several years ago. Excursions to distant parts of Australia were soon followed by a long foray into China from which emerged the voluminous *China – a travel survival kit*. Alan has also updated other Lonely Planet travel survival kits, is the author of *Argentina – a travel survival kit* and co-author of *Indonesia – a travel survival kit*.

Chile & Easter Island was his first book on a South American country, and recently he returned to Chile to research this new edition. He now lives in Adelaide. During the day he can be found near the top of an office building creating adventure-fantasy novels.

Islands. And to the many foreign visitors to Chile who wrote letters with update information, or accounts of interesting destinations.

Acknowledgements

More than a couple of words of thanks are due to the many people who helped in the writing of this book. First and foremost, I'd like to thank the amazing Verena Heidrich for her charming company and lively conversation as we stampeded around the Atacama desert.

Nor can I fail to thank Bobby Andrews of San Pedro de Atacama, a gold mine of information and proprietor of one of the best hotels in Chile. Another gold mine is Eduardo Scott, proprietor of the Hotel Austral in Puerto Natales.

Thanks also to a number of Chileans who translated, explained, filled me in on background, resolved various mysteries or pointed me in worthwhile directions. Also, thanks to Michael Buckley (co-author of Lonely Planet's *China – a travel survival kit* and *Tibet – a travel survival kit*) for allowing me to reuse his piece on Alexander Selkirk and the Juan Fernández

A Warning & A Request

This book covers Chile, Easter Island and a small part of Argentina. It is advisable not to extrapolate information about health requirements, crime, transport and almost everything else to other Latin American countries. Travel in Chile and Argentina can be very different compared to travel in other Latin American countries.

Things change – prices go up, schedules change, good places go bad and bad places go bankrupt – nothing stays the same. So, if you find things better or worse, cheaper or more expensive, recently opened or long since closed, please write and tell us and help make the next edition better!

Your letters will be used to help update future editions and, where possible, important changes will also be included as a Stop Press section in reprints.

All information is greatly appreciated and the best letters will receive a free copy of the next edition, or any other Lonely Planet book of your choice.

Lonely Planet Credits

Production Editor	Sharan Kaur
Maps	Ralph Roob
	David Windle
Design, cover design & illustrations	Margaret Jung
Typesetting	Ann Jeffree

Thanks to Hugh Finlay, Gillian Cumming and David Meagher for copy-editing; Lindy Cameron and Michelle de Kretser for editorial direction; and Sharon Wertheim for compiling the index.

From the Publisher

Thanks also to all the following people who wrote to us:

Juan Carlos Alvarez (Ch), P C Bayers (USA), Art Bloom (USA), Joyce M Bogner & Shun-Ring Chau (Ch), Struve & Cohen (USA), Breandian Delap (Ire), Barbara Fricova (Aus), Paul William Garger (USA), Giorgis Gustavo & C Robert Harberson (USA), Daniel Hays (USA), B R Heitzman & Thomas Hiutermann (Swz), Cynthia Hora (USA), Pauline Huddle (USA), Birger Husted (Dk), Nancy Kelley (USA), Angela Kuschelch & A J Lofgrew (USA), Susan MacCallum (Aus), Declan McCarthy (Ire), Lionello Morganti (It), Cristian Paghera (It), Angela Piccardo (It), Robert A Raguso (USA), Adrian Rainer (Ire), H Reinholt (Nl), I & R Reynolds (USA), Tim Sandberg (Can), M Spencer & Daniel Tormey (USA), J Veesau (Fr), Niels Willumsen (USA), Jill Yesko (USA).

Aus – Australia, Can – Canada, Ch – Chile, Dk – Denmark, Fr – France, Ire – Ireland, It – Italy, Nl – Netherlands, Swz – Swaziland, USA – United States of America

Contents

Introduction

Most people with any interest in Latin America know something of the politics of Chile and the events of 1973 when the communist president, Salvador Allende, was overthrown by a military coup.

Politically and economically Chile was – until the coup – an oddity in Latin America, if not the envy of many other Latin Americans. In comparison with other Latin American countries, Chile was a relatively industrialised, prosperous nation. It had also managed to maintain some semblance of a democratic tradition, despite several interventions by the military since it won independence from Spain in the early 19th century.

Few people know much else about Chile, however, or have much idea of what the country actually *looks* like. The traditional images which most westerners associate with Latin America have no place in Chile; there are no Aztec sundials,

no Mayan pyramids, no mysterious Inca ruins. The powerful images generated by the American Indian cultures which once ruled in Mexico, Central America and Peru have no place in this country, where the majority of people have far more in common with Europeans and North Americans than they do with the early Indian inhabitants.

Encompassing only the narrow strip of land between the Pacific Ocean and the high peaks of the Andes – approximately 180 km wide, but with a coastline stretching over 4300 km – Chile has one of the most varied landscapes in the world. It includes the almost waterless Atacama Desert in the north, the snow-covered volcanos, forests and tranquil lakes of the centre, and the wild and windswept glaciers and fjords of the far south. It has magnificent trekking country with several national parks where guanacos, rheas, seals, pink flamingos and penguins can be seen. It boasts some of the world's finest salmon and trout fishing. Just a few hours drive from Santiago, you can ski for no less than five months of the year on the slopes of the Andes, or swim year-round at the Pacific beaches.

Chile also has two Pacific outposts: Easter Island, with its giant stone statues, has long been a drawcard for explorers, adventurers, anthropologists, archaeologists and tourists; and the Juan Fernández Islands, famed as the home, for four years, of the Scotsman Alexander Selkirk on whose experiences Daniel Defoe based the novel *Robinson Crusoe*.

The country is a gold mine of undiscovered nooks and surprises – and its people, even by Latin American standards, are remarkably friendly and hospitable to foreigners. In the past, it's mostly been seen as a detour from Peru or Bolivia, but there's no reason why Chile couldn't be a destination in its own right!

Facts about the Country

HISTORY

The history of modern Chile begins with the invasion of the Spanish under Pedro de Valdivia, a conquistador, who led a small force into Chile from Peru, founded Santiago and several other Chilean cities, and became the first governor of the new Spanish colony. The subjugation of Chile was a bloody affair involving the massacre and enslavement of its Indian population. Valdivia met his own end at the hands of the Mapuche (Araucanian) Indians in the south. One version of the story has his head cut off and passed around on a pike. Another has him tied to a tree while molten gold, the metal which the Spanish spent so much energy and blood to acquire, was poured down his throat by his Indian captors.

The Indian Settlers

The ancestors of the Indians whom Valdivia subdued entered the American continent over 20,000 years ago when the Bering Strait between Siberia and America was dry land. By 1500 BC, after spending thousands of years as semi-nomadic hunters and gatherers, many Indian groups had adopted maize farming as the basis of their existence and had developed permanent settlements.

In Mexico, Central America and the northern regions of South America, sophisticated Indian civilisations developed. By 300 AD the Maya – a collection of culturally related but politically independent tribes – had arisen in Central America. Many other Indian groups developed their own distinctive civilisations, contributing to the heritage of the Aztecs, who made their appearance in Mexico around 1200 AD. The civilisations of the central Andes reached their zenith with the Incas, a tribe who made their first appearance in Peru in the 11th century AD.

The Spanish Conquest

It was primarily the Spanish and Portuguese who were responsible for bringing Central and South America under European control. A treaty in 1494 divided the world between Portugal and Spain, at that time, the two principal contenders for the discovery and conquest of overseas possessions. A line was drawn dividing the world in two, and all the land east of the line was granted to Portugal and all the land west of the line was granted to Spain. By chance, this placed the coast of Brazil (then unknown to Europeans) within the Portuguese sphere and the rest of America within the Spanish sphere.

It is difficult to grasp the speed with which the Spanish 'discovered' and subsequently conquered the New World. Christopher Columbus first landed in the Caribbean Islands in 1492. By 1550, the Spanish presided over an area which extended from the southern part of what is now the USA to central Chile. In the same time, they had founded most of what are now Latin America's largest cities, including Lima, Santiago, Asunción and La Paz.

This whole affair was carried out by a rabble of adventurers and men-of-fortune. Small in numbers, what they had on their side was determination, an exceptional ruthlessness, horses and firearms which terrified the Indians, the willingness of Indian tribes to ally with the Spanish against their Inca and Aztec masters, and the luck to enter Central and South America when the Indian empires were vulnerable to attack. The conquest of the Aztecs was achieved in two years by a force of just 550 men, under the command of Hernán Cortés. The conquest of the Inca Empire was achieved by 180 men, led by Francisco Pizarro.

The Conquest of Chile

Pizarro was assassinated in 1541. Just before his death he handed the task of conquering Chile to Pedro de Valdivia. Valdivia's expedition set out from Peru in 1540, crossed the desert, reached the fertile central plains of Chile in 1541, subdued the local Indians and founded the city of Santiago.

South of the Río Bío Bío, Valdivia confronted the Mapuche Indians, who had learnt to manage horses and devise combat tactics which were successful against the Spanish cavalry. The Indians killed Valdivia in 1554, and in the following years wiped out many Spanish settlements. However, enough survived to form the foundations of the modern Chilean state.

The first Spanish colonisers in Chile were soldiers, and, since they knew little about building, agriculture or mining, it was the Indians who had to do the work. A soldier would receive an *encomienda*,

Mapuchi fortune teller

17th century Spanish conquistadors

which meant that the Indians of a certain area were 'commended' or allotted to him, and he made them work.

The racial make-up of Chile also changed. Valdivia's expedition included only one Spanish woman, so his men married the local Indian women. Children of mixed Spanish and Indian parentage, mestizos, resulted from these relationships. After 50 years, there were more mestizos in Chile than 'full-blooded' Spanish.

Military campaigns against the Indians, the killing of troublesome Indians by the *encomenderos*, epidemics of smallpox, measles and typhus, forced labour, and further intermingling of the Spanish and mestizos, all helped reduce the size of the Indian population.

The Division of the Land

Valdivia also rewarded his soldiers with allotments of land. Some received whole valleys stretching from the Andes to the

Pacific. Others received more moderate grants but immediately began to enlarge them by taking over bordering land. The process went on until the large farm estate became the dominant unit of Chilean agriculture.

So long as the landowners faced problems in holding onto their forced labourers, the encomienda system was maintained, with the Indians remaining wards of their masters. But as the estates gradually consumed all the best land, and as the labourers found no alternative but to work on the estates, the system gradually changed.

From the old encomiendas and land grants arose the hacienda. The Indian labourer became the *inquilino* or tenant. The labourers and their families now worked for their master in exchange for certain rights. They were allowed to live in a hut on the estate, to pasture some animals, and to use part of the land to grow crops. In effect the *hacendado* reigned like a feudal lord presiding over Indian and mestizo serfs.

By the end of the Spanish colonial period, the hacienda (or *fundo*, as it's more commonly called in Chile) formed the basic unit of Chilean society. Even by the middle of the 20th century, the division of the land had not essentially changed, with a very large quantity of arable land still concentrated in the hands of a few owners.

Thus Valdivia, in allocating land to his soldiers, had established the basis of the Chilean landed oligarchy which would dominate the country's politics until the 20th century.

The Independence Movements

Within a few decades of Columbus landing in the Caribbean, Spain found itself with an empire twice the size of Europe. Yet the empire, which lasted for some 300 years, was suddenly swept away in the early years of the 19th century. In 1808, Spain controlled an area stretching from California to Cape Horn. Two decades later, she retained only Puerto Rico and Cuba.

There were many factors involved in the development of the independence movements in Latin America. One was the rise of a class of *criollos* (creoles), people of Spanish descent born in the Americas, who considered themselves American rather than Spanish.

More importantly, Latin American trade was primarily regulated in the interests of Spain and was under the rigid control of the Spanish government. To facilitate the collection of taxes, all trade had to pass through Porto Bello in Panama, or through Veracruz in Mexico. This was an extraordinarily cumbersome system and it hampered the economic development of Latin America.

Ironically, the influx of gold and silver from Latin America into Spain stimulated inflation and discouraged industry. Eventually, Spain could no longer provide the manufactured goods which the American colonies demanded. So, by the latter part of the 18th century, the colonies were becoming increasingly self-sufficient, maintaining their own administrations, defence forces and economies.

Spain also had to contend with interloping European nations. The British, Dutch and French all acquired minor bases in Latin America. By the 18th century the British, in the interests of advancing British trade in the region, were giving moral support to those who hoped to break the Spanish monopoly on Latin America.

The successful North American war of independence against the UK, the overthrow of the French monarchy at the end of the 18th century, Napoleon's seizure of Spain, which weakened links between Spain and America (allowing a period of temporary self-government for the colonies), and the influence of an enlightened intellectual trend of thought in Europe have all been cited as reasons for the sudden upsurge of Latin American independence movements from 1808 to 1810. The fact that the colonial armies were composed mainly of criollos and mestizos, and not Spanish troops, made it possible for the Latin Americans to fight Spain.

The Revolutionary Wars

Revolutionary movements rose and ferocious wars of independence were fought. From Venezuela, a revolutionary army fought its way to the Pacific side of the mountains and then marched south towards Peru. Another army, under the command of José de San Martín, set forth in 1817 from Argentina, marched over the mountains into Chile, occupied Santiago and then sailed northwards up the coast and entered Lima. By 1825, Spain had been completely ejected from all its Latin American colonies except Cuba and Puerto Rico.

The liberating army which marched from Argentina to Chile included Chilean refugees who had fled Chile when Spain reimposed her rule after the Napoleonic Wars. Spain had been unable to reimpose her rule in Argentina due to the presence of a strong criollo army, which had consolidated itself during the Napoleonic Wars. At the head of these Chilean contingents, San Martín placed a Chilean with the rather unlikely name of Bernardo O'Higgins, the son of an Irish immigrant who had become Viceroy of Peru under Spanish rule.

O'Higgins became head of the new Chilean republic, while San Martín pushed on to drive the Spanish from Peru, transporting his army in ships either seized from the Spanish or bought from British or North American owners, often with the aid of British and North American finance. British and North American merchants also financed the purchase of arms and ammunition, knowing that the removal of the Spanish would allow them to set up their own businesses on the continent. The command of the Chilean navy was given to the Scotsman Thomas Cochrane, a former officer in the British navy.

The Early Years of Independence

The Spanish administrative divisions provided the political framework for the new countries which emerged from the wars, and Latin America broke up into some 17 independent republics. When Chile became an independent state, it was but a fraction of its present size, with undecided boundaries with Bolivia in the north, Argentina to the east and the independent Mapuche Indians to the south of the Río Bío Bío.

Although other Latin American countries came out of the wars in a state of economic distress, Chile quickly achieved a degree of political stability which permitted rapid development of agriculture, mining, industry and commerce, all of which sought new areas in which to expand. The population was more homogeneous and less affected by the racial problems of other Latin American countries.

Old banknote showing the first President of Chile, Bernardo O'Higgins

O'Higgins dominated the Chilean government for the first five years after independence. A pragmatic 'enlightened despot', he was concerned about cultural and economic progress, tax reform, initiating immigration, improving transport and extending education to even the poorest Chileans. He concentrated power in his own hands in order to enforce reform in the face of vested interests. Possibly because his reforms threatened the wealth and power of the landowner class, he was overthrown in 1823 by a revolt supported by the army.

Latin America had won political independence but it had yet to undergo a social revolution. The essential structure of society remained the same, with the criollos and other members of the Latin American upper classes stepping into the shoes of the departed Spanish. Chile was dominated by the interests of the large landowners, who exercised great political power and sought to run the country like a big hacienda for their own benefit.

Following the overthrow of O'Higgins, a period of conflict ensued, including a civil war in 1830 which delivered Chile firmly into the hands of the landed gentry. In 1833, they secured a new constitution, which excluded the landless and illiterate (the majority of the population) from the franchise. Great power was granted to the president, who was, of course, the nominee of the landowners.

The Expansion of Chile

Having won independence from Spain and built a fairly strong and stable nation, the Chileans entered into their own period of imperialism. The last campaigns against the Indians in the south were fought and won in 1883. To the north, the War of the Pacific (1879 to 1883) ended in the victory of Chile over Peru and Bolivia and the annexation of the nitrate-rich Atacama Desert.

The victory sparked an economic boom, inspired confidence in the future (at least amongst the upper classes) and led to the belief that Chile was on the way to becoming one of the world's great powers. Situated on the trade and emigration route around Cape Horn, Chile was conveniently placed to establish close links with Europe and the USA.

Before the opening of the Panama Canal, Valparaíso and the ports of the nitrate mining centres in the north were major ports of call for international shipping. Chilean vessels visited Australia, Asia and Polynesia. Extremists even advocated the annexation of the Philippines, then in Spanish hands. Chile's first overseas possession, however, was a more humble one: Easter Island, annexed in 1888.

Reforms Under Balmaceda

Chile had emerged from the War of the Pacific considerably enriched with the annexation of the nitrate and copper-rich Atacama Desert. Nitrate was exported to fertilise the farms of Europe and the USA, with much of the money needed to finance the mining operations being provided by British investors. Nitrates alone were Chile's major source of income for some 40 years.

Expansion of the mining industries led to the development of a new working class and to the rise of a class of nouveaux riches, both of whom demanded a say in the running of the country. Political power still lay in the hands of the landowners, but as the urban working and middle classes grew, so did their demands for representative government and welfare legislation.

The first president to tackle Chile's uneven sharing of wealth and power was José Manuel Balmaceda, who was inducted in 1886. He proposed state ownership of the railways, spoke of breaking the monopoly of the British capitalists, of setting up Chilean-owned nitrate companies, and introducing tariff protection to aid the development of Chilean industry. Balmaceda began to carry out numerous public works – expanding the rail network, building new

Expansion of Chile

From Peru

Arica

Iquique

From Bolivia

Antofagasta

0   100   200km

Copiapó

PACIFIC OCEAN

ARGENTINA

Valparaíso   Santiago

Río Bío Bío

Temuco   *From the Mapuche*

Puerto Montt

Effectively occupied 1800

Territorial consolidation 1800–1880

Expansion 1882–1883

roads, telegraph lines, bridges, docks, water supply systems, hospitals and schools.

Such policies naturally met with a violent reaction from the British, who saw their economic interests being threatened, and from the Chilean upper classes, who objected to paying taxes to finance social services. In 1890 the Congress rejected Balmaceda's budget, voted to depose him and appointed a naval officer, Jorge Montt, to head a provisional government. Montt's troops occupied the northern mining towns while Balmaceda held out in the central valley. The inevitable civil war resulted in the death of perhaps 10,000 Chileans and the defeat of Balmaceda – who is said to have shot himself after months of asylum in the Argentine legation.

Election of Alessandri as President

The Chilean working class had to wait until 1920 for their next hope of social reform – the election of President Arturo Alessandri Palma. To break the power of the central valley aristocracy, he demanded greater self-government for the outlying provinces. For the relief of the government treasury he advocated an income tax on corporations and individuals, and a high tax on land. To aid the working class, he advocated laws which would increase wages, shorten hours and provide insurance against illness, accident, old age and death.

His reforms were not easily carried out. Blocked by the conservatives in Congress for four years, he succeeded in winning only one major reform. This was the introduction of a labour code which recognised the right of labour unions to organise freely with leaders of their own choice, restricted child labour and introduced a workers' health insurance plan.

Army opposition forced Alessandri to resign in 1924. For several years, the presidency was held by a dictatorial army officer, Carlos Ibáñez del Campo. Despite many initial successes, misguided or miscarried economic policies (coupled with the world depression) led to widespread opposition which forced Ibáñez into exile.

The confusion following Ibáñez' ousting resulted in the realignment of political groupings in Chile. Small socialist groups merged in 1933 to form the Socialist Party, of which future president Salvador Allende was a member. Splits between Stalinists and Trotskyists divided the Communist Party while splinter groups from existing radical and reformist parties created many new parties.

By now the large trade unions, such as the Chilean Workers' Federation (FOCH), had developed into militant organisations linking socialists, anarchists and syndicalists. Although internal power struggles reduced the union's membership, by the 1920s it was a major force amongst miners, maritime and tram workers, and some rural labourers. The anarchists and syndicalists became significant forces on the docks, and amongst construction workers and craftsmen. Aggressive labour movements grew up in Chilean Patagonia amongst the workers on the cattle and sheep ranches and in the meat and hide-processing plants.

Meanwhile, the influence of the USA in the Chilean economy was steadily growing. German influence had been eliminated after WW I, and the UK went into rapid decline as a debtor nation. The invention of synthetic nitrates during the war also reduced the UK's economic influence in Chile. In the first two decades of the 20th century, the USA gained control of the Chilean copper mines – by now the cornerstone of the Chilean economy.

Rural Problems
Although the unions had some influence in the countryside, in the 1920s up to 75% of Chile's rural workers were still largely isolated on large haciendas which controlled 80% of agricultural land in the central valley. The inquilinos remained at the mercy of the landowners for access to land, housing and daily needs. As a result, their votes belonged to the landowners, who used them to keep their seats in Congress and maintain the existing system of land ownership.

The Alessandri government helped maintain this system, partly in response to the demands of the urban leftist parties. These parties pressed for lower food prices and restrictions on the export of agricultural produce in order to counter rising food prices and shortages. Price controls and restrictions on food exports were introduced, and the price of agricultural produce was kept artificially low, passing the burden of price and export controls on to the producer. This kept the urban consumer happy, and the goodwill of the landowners was maintained because they were allowed to keep control over their land and workers. Many of the leftists had sold out the rural workers in the interests of political expediency.

As industry expanded and the government introduced new public works, employment opportunities increased and the lot of the urban worker improved. The lot of the rural worker, however, declined rapidly; real wages dropped, forcing many to migrate to the towns in search of work. The inquilinos suffered a decrease in the quality and quantity of their land allotments, supplies of seed, fertiliser and other help, as well as their rights to graze animals.

Most haciendas failed to introduce modern agricultural techniques, resulting in a decline in production and the increasing backwardness of Chilean agriculture. Police enforced evictions of rural workers, broke up newly formed rural unions and allowed the landowners to retain control of the countryside.

Elections: 1952 to 1961
In 1952, the former dictator General Carlos Ibáñez won the presidential election as an authoritarian but 'above politics' candidate. Under Ibáñez, reforms were introduced to curtail the power of the landowners in Chilean politics by eliminating their control over the votes of their labourers. The Law for the Permanent Defence of Democracy (which had been instituted in 1948 in order to ban the Communist Party) was also revoked.

The elimination of a law which banned the Communist Party allowed a new coalition of socialists and communists – the Popular Action Front (FRAP) – to contest the 1958 presidential elections with Salvador Allende as their candidate. Jorge Alessandri, the son of Arturo Alessandri, represented the Conservative

Party and the (inaptly named) Liberal Party coalition. Eduardo Frei represented the newly formed Christian Democrat Party, a moderate reformist party whose goals were very similar to FRAP's but whose philosophical basis was Christian humanism.

Alessandri won the election with just under 32% of the vote, to Frei's 21% and Allende's 29%. (Allende had managed only 5% of the vote in the 1952 election.) However, with the rural vote wrenched away from the conservatives by electoral reform, the 1961 Congressional election saw FRAP and the Christian Democrats out-poll the Conservative and Liberal parties.

Congress was now controlled by powerful opposition groups which were committed to real land reform. In 1962, Alessandri was virtually forced to adopt land reform programmes. This began a 10-year assault on the haciendas. Though not a great deal was actually done while Alessandri remained as president, the new laws did provide a legal basis for expropriating land from the large estates and transferring them to the farm workers.

The Christian Democrat Period

The 1964 presidential election saw a two-way battle. FRAP again supported Allende. The Christian Democrats, and the conservative groups (who viewed the Christian Democrats as the lesser of two evils), supported Frei. In the campaign that followed, both the Christian Democrats and FRAP promised agrarian reform, supported rural unionisation and promised an end to the hacienda system.

The right and centre of Chilean politics were united against Allende. The USA backed Frei and provided the Christian Democrats with large sums of money to help him win the election. Perhaps more than half his campaign was financed by the USA. A tremendous barrage of anti-communist propaganda was dispersed. Frei won the election with 56% of the votes to Allende's 39%.

The Christian Democrats were genuinely committed to social reform. Having won the election, efforts were made to control inflation, improve the country's balance of payments, carry out large scale rural reform, and improve public health, education and social services. Whatever the Christian Democrats did, however, threatened the privileges of the traditional elite – or the influence of the radical left. Fearful of losing their supporters to the Christian Democrats the FRAP parties urged faster and more extensive action.

The Christian Democrats had other problems. Rather than reduce dependence on foreign capital the Frei government sought to attract more. By 1970, over 100 US corporations had investments in Chile but their capital-intensive production failed to reduce unemployment. Too few jobs were created to cope with migration to the cities. The rings of shantytowns grew at an alarming rate.

The Christian Democrats were also faced with the often violent MIR (Left-Wing Revolutionary Movement). The MIR had joined with the Mapuche Indians in the south in organising land seizures, and had also spread its influence into the urban slums. The movement was led by André Pascal Allende, a nephew of Salvador Allende. Other leftist parties also gave support to strikes and land occupations by rural labourers.

Frei was unable to implement reforms fast enough to satisfy the leftists, and was obstructed in Congress by the National Party (formed by the merger of the Conservative Party and Liberal Party in 1965). He was also confronted by dissension within his own party over the pace and objectives of rural reform. Although his government had improved living conditions for thousands of rural workers and had made impressive gains in education and public health, increasing inflation, dependence on foreign markets and capital, and unequal distribution of wealth continued to be major problems. To a large extent, however, the Christian

Democrats had instituted policies which the forthcoming Allende government would implement more extensively.

Allende Comes to Power

As the 1970 presidential election approached, the coalition of leftist groups, now known as Popular Unity, once more chose Salvador Allende as their candidate. Popular Unity advocated radical changes. Nationalisation of banks, insurance companies and other key elements in the economy was proposed, and large agricultural estates would be expropriated.

The 1970 election pitted Allende against the Christian Democrat candidate, Radomiro Tomic, and the aged Jorge Alessandri, who stood as an independent. Alessandri appealed to the old elite and middle classes with the prospect of restoration of law and order, which they believed had eroded under the Christian Democrats. Barely a hair separated the candidates: Allende won 36.3% of the vote, Tomic 27.8% and Alessandri 34.9%.

Under the Chilean constitution, if the winner was short of an absolute majority of votes, Congress had to confirm the result and could in theory name the runner-up as president. By rights, Allende should have been confirmed as president, but since the Christian Democrats controlled the deciding votes in Congress they used their power to push through a number of constitutional amendments designed to limit the course of Allende's government. With no choice other than to lose the presidency for the fourth time, Allende backed down to their demands and was subsequently confirmed as president in October 1970.

The First Years of Allende

Allende had no revolutionary army to enforce his will. He headed a multiparty coalition which was still divided on the objectives of the new government. He faced a hostile Congress and an entrenched bureaucracy. He lacked a truly popular mandate to rule. As a leftist, he evoked the instant hostility of the US government under President Nixon and Henry Kissinger. Right-wing extremist groups called for his overthrow by violent means.

The short-term economic policies of the Allende government aimed at a massive redistribution of income, in order to benefit the poor. Wage increments to the urban and rural poor were made significantly higher than inflation. By coupling this with increased government spending, the government hoped to stimulate the demand for goods and encourage private enterprise to increase production. An increase in income and demand for goods, plus a reduction in unemployment, was expected to bring the country out of the economic recession inherited from Frei.

However, demands by farmers and workers for the expropriation of farms and factories, and the apprehension of private investors over the extent of the government's

President Salvador Allende

nationalisation policies, worked against any substantial private investment programmes. Instead of investing for the future, private business sold off stock or disposed of farm machinery and livestock. Wages and demand for goods increased, but production declined. That led to shortages of goods, rising prices and black markets. Inflation soared to over 300% by mid-1973, reducing the real income of workers to less than it was when Allende came to power. Agricultural production declined and the government had to use scarce foreign currency reserves to import food.

In an attempt to deal with shortages in the cities and towns, the government organised public companies to compete with private wholesalers and distributors. However, this directly threatened the viability of Chile's numerous retailers and helped turn them against the government. The activities of the MIR (which Allende could not, or would not, control) continued. Stories circulated about the development of armed communist workers' organisations in Santiago's factory belt.

The establishment of friendly relations between Chile and Cuba, and the expropriation of US copper companies and other foreign companies, provoked further hostility from the US government. Later hearings in the US Congress clearly indicated that President Nixon and Henry Kissinger played an active role in attempts to bring down the Allende government. The USA attempted to disrupt the Chilean economy by cutting off credit from international finance organisations, while providing both financial and moral support to Allende's opponents. It maintained friendly relations with the Chilean military and *increased* military aid while cutting off other aid.

Faced with these awesome problems, the government attempted to reduce the conflict by negotiating clearly defined limits on the extent of socialisation with the opposition groups. But neither the left-wing extremists, who believed that socialism could only be brought about by force, nor rightists, who believed it could only be halted by force, allowed the government any room to find a peaceful solution to the crisis.

The Right-Wing Backlash

In October 1972, the government was faced with a massive strike by shopkeepers, professionals, bank clerks, right-wing students, and even some urban and rural working class groups. The strike was brought about by the independent truckers' association, which demanded that the government scrap its plans to create a state-owned trucking enterprise. Supported by the Christian Democrats and the National Party, the strike quickly became a direct challenge to the Allende government.

With the possibility of a government collapse looming, the government declared a state of emergency. Ironically, this meant that the military was now responsible for maintaining law and order and for enforcing censorship on the opposition media. The army commander, General Carlos Prats, was invited to serve as Minister of the Interior. An air force general and an admiral were also included in the presidential cabinet. The truckers' strike was settled in November, with the government promising not to nationalise transport or wholesale trading, and to return private enterprises occupied by workers during the strike to their owners.

Despite the economic crisis, Popular Unity managed to poll 44% of the votes in the March 1973 congressional election – enough to prevent the Christian Democrats and National Party from gaining sufficient seats to carry out their plan to impeach Allende. It was obvious from the vote that popular support for Allende had actually increased significantly since the 1970 election.

In June 1973, there was an attempted military coup. This was unsuccessful but the pressure continued to mount. Absurd stories spread, claiming Popular Unity had a plan to kill all 100,000 members of the military. The extreme right was calling for the military to revolt and overthrow the government. Military units, under a gun control law passed in 1972, started going into the factories, shantytowns and government offices, ostensibly to search for guns, disarm workers and prevent a communist insurrection.

In July 1973, the truckers and other right-wing groups once more went on strike, supported by the entire political opposition. Prats resigned soon after, apparently having lost the support of the military. He was replaced by General Augusto Pinochet, whom both Prats and Allende thought was loyal to the principle of constitutional government.

The Coup

On 11 September 1973, General Pinochet led a military coup which overthrew the Popular Unity government and resulted in the death of Allende and thousands of his supporters.

The presidential palace in Santiago was bombed by air force jets. What happened to Allende, who was in the palace, is unclear. Some reports suggest he was killed by soldiers, while others suggest he committed suicide. Other parts of Santiago, including factories and working class neighbourhoods, were bombed and attacked by soldiers.

Thousands of leftists and suspected leftists were arrested. Many were herded into Santiago's National Stadium and Chile Stadium where brutal beatings and numerous summary executions were carried out. As happened under the Nazis during the 1930s, bonfires were made out of left-wing literature and government publications. A curfew was imposed and people were shot for being on the streets after hours. How many people were executed at the time of the coup and in the years after it is unknown; estimates range from as few as 2500 to as many as 80,000.

Hundreds of thousands of Chileans left the country.

The Chilean military claims it was necessary to use force to remove Allende because his government had brought about economic chaos and was planning, using clandestinely amassed weapons, to overthrow the democratic institutions of the country. The origins of the 'economic chaos' were to some extent the vague Popular Unity policies on the nationalisation of industry and farms, but it is too easy to say that Allende brought the coup upon himself. The real causes of the 'economic chaos' were the strikes of right-wing business people and professionals, artificially induced scarcities of commodities and food, foreign manipulation of the Chilean economy, and the creation of a black market. Had Allende been intent on murdering the military and civilian opposition leaders and imposing communism on Chile, he would have embarked on an armed rebellion rather than try to gain power legally by standing for election four times over a period of 18 years. When the coup came it was plain to see that all the guns were in the hands of the military.

Towards the end, Allende had decided to resolve the political crisis *peacefully* and *legally* with another election, but was prevented from doing so by the military coup. At the time of the coup, Allende remained in the presidential palace, refusing to surrender and flee the country while his supporters were left to be massacred by the military. In doing so he ensured his own death, but also manifested his own integrity and the integrity of the Popular Unity government. The last words belong to him; they are part of a radio address given just before the presidential palace was bombed:

My words are not spoken in bitterness, but in disappointment. They will be a moral judgment on those who have betrayed the oath they took as soldiers of Chile. . . They have the might and they can enslave us, but they cannot halt the world's social processes, not with

crimes, nor with guns. . . May you go forward in the knowledge that, sooner rather than later, the great avenues will open once again, along which free citizens will march in order to build a better society. Long live Chile! Long live the People! Long live the workers! These are my last words, and I am sure that this sacrifice will constitute a moral lesson which will punish cowardice, perfidy and treason.

For details on the history of Chile since the 1973 coup, see the Government section in this chapter.

GEOGRAPHY
Few countries as small as Chile can boast such a formidable variety of landscapes: Andean summits, snow-capped volcanos, valleys, deserts, fjords, glaciers, and countless lakes and beaches. For 4300 km, this narrow country runs along the south west coast of South America between the Andes mountains and the Pacific Ocean, yet it is only about 180 km wide.

The territory now occupied by Chile is the result of a number of military adventures, first by the Spanish conquistadors then by the Chileans themselves. Only at the end of the 19th century did Chile reach its present boundaries, extending from the city of Arica in the north to the islands of Tierra del Fuego and Navarino in the south. Chile also holds the Pacific islands of Rapa Nui (Easter Island) and Juan Fernández, and claims a large slice of Antarctica.

The country is divided up into a number of administrative regions. These, together with their capital cities, are as follows:

Region	Regional Capital
Tarapacá	Iquique
Antofagasta	Antofagasta
Atacama	Copiapó
Coquimbo	La Serena
Valparaíso	Valparaíso
Metropolitana	Santiago
Maule	Talca
O'Higgins	Rancagua
Bíobío	Concepción
Araucanía	Temuco
Los Lagos	Puerto Montt
Aisén	Coyhaique
Magallanes/Antartica	Punta Arenas

Geographically, the country has a number of fairly distinct divisions which roughly match these administrative regions. In the north, the great Atacama Desert stretches for some 1000 km from the Peruvian border towards central Chile. The area around Copiapó is often regarded as the desert's southern end. The only water is provided by river valleys and underground sources which sustain the scattered farming oases and river valley farming communities. Other than that there is no surface water, and some weather stations have *never* recorded any rainfall. In a sense, it is one of the most 'perfect' of deserts.

South of this desert, parts of the regions of Atacama and Coquimbo form a transition zone from desert to steppe land and then to the fertile central valley of Chile. The desert gives way to scrub and bush, which becomes richer as you approach the centre and rainfall increases. Like the northern desert, this is a region rich in minerals, and since there are a number of rivers cutting through the region it has been possible to establish large-scale agriculture and sizeable towns.

At the southern boundary of San Felipe de Aconcagua Province, the fertile region known as the Chilean heartland, or the central valley, begins. The heartland contains something like 70% of the country's total population and provides the lion's share of its industrial jobs. There are also copper mines in the provinces of Santiago, Valparaíso and O'Higgins. Here you find the capital of Chile – Santiago – containing almost a third of the country's population, as well as Valparaíso, which is Chile's major port. The heartland is Chile's chief farming region, ideal for orchards, vineyards, cereal crops and livestock.

Unfortunately, central Chile and the

adjacent provinces are amongst the world's most geologically unstable regions. Many of Chile's major cities (including La Serena, Santiago and Valdivia) are constantly under threat of damage or destruction by volcanic eruptions and earthquakes.

At the Río Bío Bío, the heartland gives way to what was once Chile's great frontier, the home of the Mapuche Indians and now a region of cereal and pasture lands. Although this is known mainly as a rural area, the majority of the population live in the towns and cities, of which Temuco and Concepción are the most important.

South of the Río Toltén lies the magnificent Lake District, a sprawl of snow-capped active volcanos, and lakes, covering the provinces of Valdivia, Osorno and Llanquihue. Apart from being a destination for overseas and domestic tourists, agriculture and timber are also important industries.

The land south of the city of Puerto Montt comprises about 30% of Chile's territory, but holds just a small percentage of the country's population. This is a land of heavy rainfall, storms and bitterly cold winds, lashed by rough seas. Offshore, Chiloé, Chile's largest island, comprises dense forest and numerous small farms. The mainland province of Aisén is made up of canals, lakes, islands and mountains, interspersed by grasslands which support a large sheep-grazing industry. This is Chile's last frontier and its isolated settlements are only now being joined by road.

The coastline further south is a maze of bleak fjords, where great glaciers slide down mountain slopes to meet the sea. In the far south of South America lies Magallanes Province, or Chilean Patagonia. The country's most southerly city, Punta Arenas, lies on the Straits of Magellan. Before the opening of the Panama Canal in 1914, this southern passage made Punta Arenas and Valparaíso major ports of call for international shipping. The prosperity of the south is now dependent on oil and gas.

Across the straits lies Tierra del Fuego, split between Chile and Argentina, where oil extraction and sheep-grazing are the main industries. Chile effectively comes to an end with the island of Navarino, separated from Tierra del Fuego by the Beagle Channel. Navarino is the site of Puerto Williams, the most southerly settlement in the world with a permanent population. Between Puerto Williams and Chilean Antarctica there is a scattering of small islands. On the southern flank of one of these islands lies the famous Cabo de Hornos, or Cape Horn.

As diverse as the country may be, there is one unifying feature – the Andes. In the far north at Lago Chungará, near the Bolivian border, the Andes are a string of awesome volcanoes. From Santiago's Santa Lucía, the mountains look like an invincible phalanx advancing on the city. In the Aisén region, they are barren peaks decorated with glaciers. Between Copiapó and the Río Bío Bío, the range occupies 30% to 50% of the country's width. The Andes contains some of the highest peaks in South America, some almost 7000 metres high. Though passable, this great mountain range made transport and communications difficult and generally isolated Chile from the rest of South America.

CLIMATE

Chile has formidable extremes of heat and cold. You bake in the Atacama Desert and freeze in Patagonia. You can cook to a crisp on Easter Island and die of exposure on Tierra del Fuego. Be prepared for these extremes, plus rapid changes from one to another, wherever you are.

Chile has several distinct climatic regions. In the north, the Atacama Desert is one of the driest, hottest places on earth. It can be searingly hot during the day but piercingly cold during the early hours of the morning. The coast tends to have higher humidity, more cloud and lower average temperatures. If you leave the desert and head towards Bolivia, you must cross mountain passes which are several thousand metres high, so while others are sunbathing on the beaches at Arica you can be up to your knees in snow.

The Chilean heartland (the area around Santiago and Valparaíso) has a Mediterranean climate, with temperatures averaging 28°C in January and dropping to an average of 10°C in July. Evenings and nights can be cold and you need some warm clothes even during summer. The rainy season in the Santiago area is from May to August. Though it is still warm and dry in the north of the country during this time, it is stormy and cold in the far south. It's worth remembering how narrow Chile is: in one or two hours you can drive from Santiago to ski resorts where there is skiing for no less than five months of the year.

Heading due south of Santiago brings you to the Lake District, the region roughly between Temuco and Puerto Montt. This area also has a pleasant Mediterranean climate during the summer months, although biting winds can suddenly sweep off the lakes and mountains. Windsurfing, swimming and sunbathing are popular on the many black-sand beaches of this area. Winter brings snow to the higher ground, around places like Petrohué, Puella, Lago Todos los Santos, and some of the hill resorts and chalets. During winter, some of the passes between Chile and Argentina may be blocked by snow, so ask before you set out. Generally speaking, you can expect sudden changes in the weather and you must be prepared for fog and stormy weather, even in summer.

Southern Chile is characterised by almost continuously cold weather. The one peculiar exception to the general rule is the region around the village of Chile Chico in the Región Aisén which has a warm microclimate similar to the Chilean heartland.

South of the 40th latitude, Chile has some of the stormiest weather in the world. Chiloé Island, the large island to the south of Puerto Montt, has fewer than 60 days of sunshine per year and up to 150 days of stormy weather. In summer, both the island and the adjacent mainland can have warm days but the nights are cold, and if you travel by ship you are whipped by icy winds.

Further south, in the Magallanes Province (southern Chilean Patagonia) and Tierra del Fuego, temperatures drop to a summer average of just 11°C, and to a winter average of about 4°C. Temperatures on Tierra del Fuego can drop very low and the chill is increased by cold, gusty winds which can occur even on sunny summer days. Rainfall is heavy – more so in the interior than on the coasts – and can be expected at any time of the year.

Puerto Williams, almost as far south as you can go in Chile without bumping into Antarctica, can have pleasant days of warm sunshine in summer, followed by days of rain and terrible cold. Rug up for crossing stretches of water in this region. Voyages can be stormy and terrifying year-round, even on the large vehicle ferries.

The best time to visit Patagonia and Tierra del Fuego is in the southern summer (December to February). Heavy snows set in from July. In the middle of the year in southern Patagonia and Tierra del Fuego there are just seven hours or so of daylight per day. The cold can be kept out but the wind pounds you day in and day out. You really need windproof clothing – particularly if you intend to trek, camp or hitch.

GOVERNMENT
Since the military coup of 1973, Chile has been headed by a junta made up of the commanders of the armed forces. After the coup, the junta dissolved the National Congress, banned the country's leftist parties, placed all other parties in an 'indefinite recess' and prohibited all other

political activities. In 1977, all the remaining political parties were banned, although they continued to operate. It was not until 1987 that the major political parties were once again allowed to operate legally.

The President

The head of the junta is General Augusto Pinochet Ugarte, who assumed the office of president in 1974 and has held it ever since. Unlike some other Latin American dictatorships which rest on the collective rule of the junta, Pinochet is very much a one-man show.

In October 1988, Pinochet actually held a plebiscite in which he asked the country to confirm him as president until 1997. He received a sound rebuff, with well over half the population voting against the continuation of his rule. Consequently, a multi-candidate presidential election was scheduled to be held in December 1989. Pinochet is unlikely to stand as a candidate and will step down from the presidency in March 1990.

Regardless of the outcome of this election, Pinochet will remain commander-in-chief of the armed forces. Although elections for a new National Congress will be held at the same time as the presidential election, one third of the new Senate will be comprised of members appointed by Pinochet, who will himself be a life member of the Senate.

Thus, barring his incapacitation or death, Pinochet (born 1915) will continue to be the real power in Chile for some years to come. In an effort to make himself more acceptable to the Chilean population, he has gradually taken on a more humane public image. He now tends to present himself as a fatherly elder statesman on whose continued influence the political and economic stability of Chile depends. Like President Suharto of Indonesia, he is also fond of portraying himself as the 'father of development' – embarking on lengthy tours of the country, opening new buildings, ports and other works.

The Army & Security Forces

Pinochet's power is based squarely on his command of the Chilean army. The total strength of the armed forces is about 100,000, of whom well over half are members of the army. As the man who controls the guns Pinochet is able, literally, to call the shots if the opposition gets out of hand. It is commonly believed that the Pinochet regime is an aberration in Chilean history, and that the Chilean army has normally been apolitical. In fact, since independence from Spain, Chile has had four civil wars, some 10 successful coups, and many uprisings and mutinies.

The Chilean army is very rigid, highly disciplined and obedient to its commanders. It owes its structure to foreign influence. In the late 19th century, a Prussian army officer, Emilio Körner, was contracted to reform the Chilean officer training academy. As head of general staff from 1891 to 1910, he introduced German instructors, uniforms, discipline and modern military equipment. Much of this has stuck, and even today Chilean soldiers in their parade uniforms look like they've marched down from a Nuremburg rally.

Underpinning the junta has been a system of repression, murder and torture. Torture of political prisoners by members of the Chilean security forces has been reported regularly since the junta seized power in 1973. Those detained and tortured because of their political activities come from a broad range of Chilean society, from doctors and lawyers right down to shantytown dwellers. Although torture and ill-treatment has been used by both the Carabineros (uniformed police) and Investigaciones (plain clothes police), it is the National Information Centre (Central Nacional de Informaciones, CNI) which is most frequently cited as torturing political prisoners.

The most common physical tortures described in testimonies to Amnesty International include beatings, electric

The 'parrot's perch' torture

shocks and burns to sensitive parts of the body, rape and sexual abuse of women, drugging, sleep deprivation and submerging the victim's head in water. Another common torture has been the 'parrots perch', where the victims are placed in a crouching position with their arms hugging their legs. They are then hung upside down from a pole which is slipped through the gap between their knees and elbows. They are then given electric shocks and have water squirted at high pressure into their mouths and noses.

International assassination has also been a forte of the Chilean security forces since the coup. General Prats was murdered in Buenos Aires a year after the coup. Bernardo Layton, a Christian Democrat leader, narrowly escaped being killed in a bomb attack in Rome in 1975. Orlando Letelier, Chile's foreign minister under Allende, was killed by a car bomb in Washington in 1976. All these acts have been attributed to Chilean agents or people associated with them.

Although the plebiscite of 1988 rejected Pinochet's plans to remain president until 1997, there is unlikely to be any real change in the status quo while he continues to command the police and armed forces.

Opposition Groups

The results of the 1988 plebiscite to some extent reflect traditional voting patterns amongst Chileans, with a large section of the population supporting conservative and extreme right-wing political parties. Certainly there are many Chileans who believe that Pinochet is the saviour of the country, and you meet Chileans who *implore* you to return home and tell people how good life is under the present government. Their reasons include bad experiences during the Allende years, a tremendous fear of communism, and a belief in the need for strong government and a stable society.

Opposing the regime is a range of left-wing, centrist and even some right-wing organisations and political parties. Since the introduction of new legislation in 1987, most opposition parties have operated legally. Opposition newspapers and magazines are widely available and carry many articles critical of the government. Since 1987, it has become a common sight to see offices of the various parties opening up in many Chilean cities. Many prominent exiles have also returned to Chile, including Allende's widow. The Roman Catholic Church and the trade union movement are also major focuses for dissent.

Ironically, some of the political parties supported the coup against Allende in the expectation that the military would hand back power to civilians as soon as the communists were deposed. The left-wing of the Christian Democrat Party opposed the coup. The right-wing supported the coup, but turned against Pinochet when it became clear he would not hand back power to civilians. The National Party largely supported the coup, though a number of

National Party leaders eventually spoke out against Pinochet. After the coup the Communist Party, once a moderate group which favoured an alliance with the Christian Democrats during the Allende years, began to advocate armed opposition to the Pinochet regime.

The union movement has been fraught with problems. Many of the older and more experienced leaders were killed at the time of the coup, or disappeared, were imprisoned, or forced into exile after it. Many of the unions appear to be bankrupt, and have neither paid, full-time organisers nor buildings from which to operate. With 30% to 35% unemployment and low wages it's difficult to rebuild the union movement. Strikes are declared illegal after 60 days duration. Picketing by strikers or soliciting money to help strikers' families is illegal. Employers are allowed to use non-union labour to break strikes.

The Future

Pinochet will not cease to be a political force in Chile until he is finally incapacitated or in the grave. Even then, another (and possibly even worse) general may take the opportunity to seize power.

The long term problems are complex. The history of Chile has been one of conflict between those who have attempted to better the lot of ordinary Chileans, and an economic and political order which has rested on the subjugation and coercion of the working class. It is probably not unfair to say that the Chilean working class has been reduced to the status of a servant class, with few options and little chance of bettering their lot by themselves.

A comment attributed to Diego Portales, who ruled Chile as a virtual dictator in the 1830s, captures the tone of Chilean politics in the 19th and 20th centuries: 'The cake and the stick... are the remedies with which any nation can be cured, however deep rooted its bad habits.' Ever ready to use the stick, Portales' autocratic rule spared Chile the anarchy that many other Latin American

Pinochet supporters brandish his photo

countries experienced after independence. But Portales failed to solve the country's internal problems, and passed them on to future generations to deal with. For many years to come, the Chileans will be faced with a number of old and seemingly insoluble questions: how do you make Chile a free country while maintaining political order? how do you achieve economic progress without exploiting the working classes? how do you maintain social order without the use of political repression? how do you keep the army out of politics?

ECONOMY

When the junta seized power its support for private enterprise and 'law and order' appealed to the right-wing business people and professionals who had opposed Allende. The junta promised to combat inflation, restore private property and purge the country of leftists.

Since the junta had little knowledge of economics or public affairs when it came to power, civilian advisers played the dominant role in determining policy. The junta opened the way for a group of economists who espoused a theory variously labelled as monetarism, libertarianism or new economic orthodoxy. Essentially, all of these terms refer to an extreme form of *laissez faire* economics, which advocates taking economic control out of the hands of government and leaving it entirely at the mercy of individuals and international market forces.

A group of right-wing economic advisers (the so-called 'Chicago Boys', who were either graduates of, or had links with, the University of Chicago) gained the ear of Pinochet. Their plan for restructuring the economy appears to have been worked out prior to the coup and given to high-ranking military officers and opposition politicians. If nothing else, it must have created the impression that *someone* knew how to cope with the economic chaos which would face Allende's successor.

When Pinochet took power, the Chicago

Boys were able to place themselves in key positions in the banks and government, and the military ensured that their policies were implemented. Prices were freed while wages remained frozen. Tariffs were reduced. Interest rates for savings were frozen by state-owned banks but raised by private companies, causing a flood of personal savings into private hands. Government spending was cut and indirect taxes were introduced. Many nationalised industries were broken up and sold off to private business. A new investment code was set up to attract foreign capital. The North American copper companies were compensated for the nationalised copper mines.

In the short term the rate of inflation fell, domestic demand shrank and imports decreased. The growth of 'non-traditional' exports helped to compensate for the decline in the price of copper on the world market. But the cost of this 'success' was enormous. Industrial production dropped and some industries disappeared never to be seen again. Wages continued to fall and unemployment increased to almost 20% of the workforce by the beginning of 1976. Chile's already ramshackle social security system broke down as firms going into bankruptcy defaulted on their social security insurance payments, and the government refused to pay unemployment benefits to those workers who were made redundant. In some urban shantytowns, unemployment rose to as high as 80% or more, and only the church-organised soup kitchens kept people from starving.

Faced with the collapse of their internal markets employers were forced to find markets abroad for their produce. 'Non-traditional' exports such as fruit, vegetables, wine and even basic consumer products like shoes flowed abroad. Yet, in keeping with the Chicago Boys' policies, tariffs were further lowered, even though Chilean industry was hardly surviving in its own markets.

As the banks were sold to private owners, the rate of interest they were allowed to charge was freed from government controls, and subsequently soared. Firms trying to borrow money to stave off bankruptcy found themselves in huge debt to private banks and finance companies. Not surprisingly, the financiers - sometimes the Chicago Boys using foreign loan money - were able to buy up Chilean industry at very cheap prices and develop their own personal business empires.

As inflation continued to fall, real wages and salaries began to rise again, increasing the demand for goods and services. Since the battered local industry was often incapable of responding, the demand was met by importing manufactured goods. Chile became a profitable market for foreign consumer goods which might otherwise have been locally manufactured.

Foreign investment in Chile also failed to eventuate in the quantity and form that was expected. Although wages were low, the size of the local market was too small to interest foreign companies who, in any case, could export goods to Chile's unprotected markets from better situated countries with equally cheap wages. Chile was, therefore, forced to depend on the export of primary products such as minerals, timber, fruit and seafood in order to earn foreign exchange.

Private enterprise borrowed large sums of money from overseas to finance expansion, but this was only sustainable so long as exports increased (as they did in the second half of the 1970s) and the money was invested productively. Problems began to develop after 1979 when the peso was tied to the US dollar. When the US dollar was revalued upwards the peso went with it. Consequently, imports were very cheap and prices of Chilean exports abroad were expensive, and this created a growing deficit in Chile's balance of trade.

The crunch finally came in the early 1980s, when the world recession hit the price of copper and other minerals which were still Chile's chief exports. The trade deficit grew as the fixed exchange rate forced up the price of exports on the contracting international market. Foreign lending continued however, and Chile's national debt (almost all of it created by foreign loans to private banks and firms) increased. By the end of 1981, loan repayments were eating up 75% of Chile's export earnings. Interest rates climbed, bankruptcies increased and unemployment soared.

In 1982, the government sought to counter the trend by devaluing the peso and by further reducing wages, but inflation soon wiped out any benefits which Chilean exporters may have gained. With interest rates rising both locally and internationally the banks' debt problems worsened. The peso was then allowed to float and immediately plummeted by 40% against the US dollar. With the Chicago Boys' policies in shambles the government was forced to backtrack. At the beginning of 1983 it took over direct management of key private banks and finance houses, revealing the massive foreign debts these businesses had accumulated.

However, in keeping with monetarist economic policies, and in order to gain quick windfalls to help pay off the foreign debt, the Chilean government has continued to sell its assets to private business. One of the more controversial sales occurred in 1988 when almost half the Chilean telephone system was sold to Australian businessman Alan Bond.

The cost of the Chicago Boys' policies has been high, especially for Chile's poor. The social security system, once the most extensive in Latin America and benefiting 70% of the population, has been gutted. Although the inflation rate is low in comparison to some other Latin American countries, this has been at the cost of producing massive unemployment. Perhaps 25% to 30% of the national workforce is unemployed, and in some poor districts and amongst the young the figure may be much higher. Wages are extraordinarily low, with the basic wage hovering at around US$50 to US$60 *per month*. A lot of Chileans live very close to the bone and how they continue to make ends meet is a mystery.

POPULATION & PEOPLE

Chile is a country of some 12 million people, the majority of whom are mestizos of mixed Spanish and Indian ancestry. Over the centuries, many distinctions have been made between the different mestizo groups. The 'pure blood' Spanish are set apart from the 'mainly white' mestizos, the 'Indian' mestizos, Indians, blacks, mulattos (with mixed black and European ancestry) and *zambos* (with mixed black and Indian ancestry).

Since there are few blacks in Chile, the most important non-European element in the population are the American Indians. Around 95% of Chile's population is Caucasian or mestizo, and about 3% are American Indian. About 90% of the population is Roman Catholic but there are also Lutherans, Jews, Presbyterians, Mormons and Pentecostals.

Unlike Argentina or Brazil, the growth of Chile's population in the 19th and 20th centuries did not rely on successive waves of immigration from Europe. At the end of the 19th century, only a small percentage of Chile's population were foreign born. After 1848, several thousand Germans settled in the south where, to this day, many people speak German as well as Spanish. Other immigrants included French, Italians, Yugoslavs (there is a large concentration of Yugoslavs in Tierra del Fuego), European Jews, and Palestinians.

Immigration from Europe did not change the structure of Chilean society, but it did add a non-Spanish element to the middle and upper classes. The old Chilean aristocracy (the original landed gentry) is mainly of Spanish Basque origin, but some of Chile's 'best' families have British or French names like Edwards, Lyon or Subercaseaux. Despite their small numbers, the European immigrants became very powerful in Chile's economy, owning a large share of rural estates and commercial and industrial establishments.

About 75% of Chile's population lives in the central valley, which covers 20% of the country's total area. About a third of the total population is crammed into Santiago and its surrounding regions, making it the fifth or sixth largest city in Latin America. Only 20% of Chile's population can be classed as rural and this figure is gradually decreasing, a trend found throughout Latin America.

HOLIDAYS

Chile has a number of public holidays:

1 January
   New Year's Day
March/April (dates vary)
   Easter
1 May
   Labour Day
21 May
   Navy Day
25 May
   Corpus Christi
29 June
   St Peter's & St Paul's Day
15 August
   Assumption Day
11 September
   National Liberation Day
18 & 19 September
   Independence Days
12 October
   Columbus Day
1 November
   All Saints' Day
8 December
   Immaculate Conception
25 December
   Christmas Day

LANGUAGE

Chileans, along with the majority of people in Latin America, speak Spanish. There are variations, however, between the Spanish spoken in different regions and countries, caused by variations in the original imported Spanish dialects and the influence of indigenous languages and immigrant groups.

Chilean Spanish is characterised by a relaxation of consonants to the extent that they can almost disappear. So 's' often becomes 'h' (for example *los hombres* is pronounced 'loh hombreh' and *las mamas* is pronounced 'la mama'), leaving the openness of the final vowel and the context of the sentence to distinguish plural from singular. Chileans tend to speak rapidly and somewhat lazily so that many phrases are hard to understand.

There are also significant differences between the Spanish spoken in Spain and that spoken in South America. In Spain 's' and 'c' before 'e' are pronounced 'th', but are 's' or 'c' in Latin America. Throughout Latin America, personal pronouns (I, you, he, she, we, they) are rarely used, being implied in the verb.

Even the vocabulary differs. In Central America, the word for 'matches' is *cerillos*, but in South America it's the mediaeval Spanish word *fosforos*. The word for 'toilet' is generally *servicio* or *baño*, but can also be *urinario*, *sanitario*, *retrete* or *excusado*. In Chile it is usually one of the first two, though toilets are often simply marked *hombres* or *señoras*. The definite article can also vary between Latin America and Spain: *el radio* becomes *la radio* for example.

'Ch' is considered to be a separate letter in the Spanish alphabet, and words beginning with it are listed in the dictionary after the words beginning with 'c'; 'll' and 'ñ' are also separate letters and words beginning with them are listed after 'l' and 'n' respectively.

The stress in a Spanish word is usually on the second last syllable unless there is a stress accent (/), in which case the accented vowel is stressed. Vowels accented for stress are not considered to be separate letters. Accents and stress can be sometimes important for distinguishing meaning. For instance, *papa* is potato, while *papá* is father.

Learning Spanish

To set off for Chile without some knowledge of Spanish is very short-sighted. At the most basic level, you *have* to know enough Spanish to cope with everyday problems. You could resort to a phrasebook, but life becomes a lot easier if you don't have to! You will also find that all through the country people will want to talk to you; if you don't speak Spanish your exchanges aren't going to get past a few limited clichés and you'll start to feel trapped in a linguistic bubble.

English is quite commonly spoken in Chile but not enough to allow you to get around easily. Fortunately, Spanish is a relatively straightforward language and it's easy to learn the necessary rudiments quickly. Before you leave, attend an evening course; buy a phrasebook and a grammar guide and learn from them; borrow or buy a record/cassette course (they can be quite cheap and well worth the investment); or, if you can, find someone from Latin America.

When you get to Latin America don't worry about making mistakes. Latin Americans are not snobbish about their language and don't look down on people who speak Spanish poorly. Communication is what they look for, not perfect pronunciation and grammar. Another advantage is that many words are similar to English or French – you can often figure out what they mean.

Pronunciation

The letters f, k, l, m, n, p, t, y and ch are pronounced as they are in English. The exceptions are listed below, but remember there will be variations from country to country.

Vowels

a	as the 'a' in 'cart'
e	as the 'a' in 'late'
i	as the 'ee' in 'feet'
o	either as the 'o' in 'rope' or in 'hot'
u	as the 'oo' in 'loot'

Consonants

b as in English, but between vowels it makes a sound midway between 'b' and 'v'

c as the 's' in 'sit' before 'e' and 'i', otherwise as the 'k' in 'kit'

d as the 'd' in 'dog' though less distinct – between vowels and at the end of a word more like 'th' in 'this'

g as 'ch' before 'e' and 'i', otherwise as the 'g' in 'go'

h is always silent

j as the 'ch' in the Scottish 'loch' – thus the word *bajo* is pronounced something like 'ba-ko'

ll as the 'y' as in 'yet'

ñ as the 'ni' in 'onion' or the 'ny' sound in 'canyon'

qu as the 'k' in 'kit'

r usually rolled, particularly at the start of a word

rr very strongly rolled

s as the 's' in 'sit', but in Chile it is usually, dropped if it appears at the end of a word – thus *las ciudades* becomes 'la ciudade'

v as the 'b' in 'bad', but not as distinct; between vowels it makes a sound midway between 'b' and 'v'

x as the 'x' in 'taxi', and as the 's' in 'sit' if before a consonant

y is regarded as a vowel when alone or at the end of the word. At these times it is pronounced like 'ee' in 'feet'

z as the 's' in 'sit'.

Some Basic Grammar

In the space available here it is impossible to give a full rundown on Spanish grammar, but this brief section will point out some things worth following up. You should buy a *small* Spanish-English dictionary and a comprehensive phrasebook which includes some grammar and pronunciation. The Berlitz *Latin-American Spanish for Travellers* tends to emphasise Mexico, but it's clear, concise, easy to use and very useful in Chile.

Nouns in Spanish are masculine or feminine. The definite article 'the' agrees with the gender and number of the noun. For example, the Spanish word for 'train' is *tren*, a masculine noun; so 'the train' is *el tren* and the plural is *los trenes*. The Spanish word for 'house' is *casa*, a feminine noun; so 'the house' is *la casa* and the plural is *las casas*. The indefinite articles (a/an) work in the same way: *un lapiz* (a pencil) is masculine singular, and *una carta* (a letter) is feminine singular. Most nouns that end in 'o' are masculine and those that end in 'a' are generally feminine. Normally, nouns that end in a vowel add 's' to form the plural, and those that end in a consonant add 'es'.

Adjectives also agree with the noun in gender and number, and usually follow it. Possessive adjectives (my/*mi*, your/*tu*, and so on) agree with the thing possessed, not with the possessor. For example 'his suitcase' is *su maleta* while 'his suitcases' is *sus maletas*. A simple way to show possession is to use the preposition 'de' which means 'of'. For example 'Juan's room' would be *la habitación de Juan* or literally 'the room of Juan'.

Comparatives are formed by adding *mas* (more) or *menos* (less) before the adjective. For example, *alto* is 'high', *mas alto* is 'higher' and *lo mas alto* is 'the highest'. Demonstrative pronouns are also affected by gender: *este* is the masculine form of 'this', while *esta* is the feminine form and *esto* is the neutral; forms for 'these', 'that' and 'those'.

There are polite and familiar forms of 'you' as there are in French. Personal pronouns are usually not used with verbs. There are three main categories of regular verbs: those which end in 'ar' such as *hablar* (to speak), those which end in 'er' such as *comer* (to eat) and those which end in 'ir' such as *reir* (to laugh); there are also a number of irregular verbs.

Greetings & Civilities

yes	*sí*
no	*no*

please	*por favor*
thank you	*gracias*
hello	*alló/hola*
good morning	*buenos días*
good afternoon	*buenas tardes*
good evening	*buenas tardes*
good night	*buenas noches*
goodbye	*adiós*

Questions

where?	*dónde?*
where is?	*dónde está?*
where are?	*dónde están?*
when?	*cuándo?*
what?	*qué?*
how?	*cómo?*
how much?	*cuánto?*
how many?	*cuántos?*

At the Hotel

hotel
   hotel, pensión, residencial,
room
   habitación
I'd like a ....
   Quisiera una ....
Are there ....?
   Hay ....?
Can you give me ....?
   Puede darme ....?
      single room
         habitación sencilla
      double room
         habitación doble

What is the price ....?
   Cuál es el precio ....?
      per night
         por noche
      for full board
         por pensión completa

That's too expensive.
   Es demasiado caro.
Is there anything cheaper?
   Hay algo más barato?

May I see the room?
   Puedo ver la habitación?

No, I don't like it.
   No, no me gusta.
      the bill
         la cuenta

Toilets

In Chile, the toilet is usually called *baño* or *servicio*, and is sometimes marked simply *hombres* or *señoras*.

Some Useful Phrases

I don't speak much Spanish.
   No hablo mucho español.
I understand.
   Comprendo.
I don't understand.
   No comprendo.

May I have?	*Puede darme?*
I'll have........	*Tomaré........*

Some Useful Words

and	*y*
to/at	*a*
for	*para/pan*
in	*en/dentro*
with	*con*
without	*sin*
before	*antes*
after	*después*
soon	*pronto*
already	*ya*
now	*ahora*
immediately	*immediatamente*

Getting Around

bus	*bus*
ship	*barco, buque*
train	*tren*
plane	*avión*
car	*carro* or *car*
taxi	*taxi*
bicycle	*bicicleta*
motorcycle	*motocicleta*

I'd like a ticket to ....
   Quiero un billete para ....
What's the fare to ....?
   Cuál es el precio a ....?

When does the next plane leave for ....?
Cuándo sale el próximo avión para ....?
When does the train leave for ....?
Cuándo sale el tren para ....?
When does the first train leave for ....?
Cuándo sale el primero tren para ....?
first/last/next
primero/último/próximo
first/second class
primera/segunda clase
single/return (round-trip)
ida/ida y vuelta
sleeper coach (train)
coche cama

Canada	*Canadá*
France	*Francia*
Great Britain	*Gran Bretaña*
Holland	*Holanda*
Israel	*Israel*
Italy	*Italia*
Japan	*Japón*
New Zealand	*Nueva Zelanda*
Norway	*Noruega*
Peru	*Perú*
South Africa	*Sudáfrica*
Switzerland	*Suiza*
Sweden	*Suecia*
United States	*Estados Unidos*
West Germany	*Alemania Occidental*

Around Town

post office
(la oficina de) correos
Tourist Information Centre
Centro de Información Turística
airport
el aeropuerto

Post & Telecommunications

letter	*carta*
parcel	*paquete*
postcard	*un tarjeta*
stamps	*estampillas/francos*

I want to send this by ....
Quiero mandar esto ....
air mail
por correo aéreo
registered mail
certificado

I want to place a personal (person to person) call.
Quiero hacer una llamada personal.
reverse charges
cobro revertido

Countries

Australia	*Australia*
Austria	*Austria*
Argentina	*Argentina*
Belgium	*Bélgica*
Bolivia	*Bolivia*

Numbers

1	*uno*
2	*dos*
3	*tres*
4	*cuatro*
5	*cinco*
6	*seis*
7	*siete*
8	*ocho*
9	*nueve*
10	*diez*
11	*once*
12	*doce*
13	*trece*
14	*catorce*
15	*quince*
16	*dieciséis*
17	*diecisiete*
18	*dieciocho*
19	*diecinueve*
20	*veinte*
21	*veintiuno*
22	*veintidós*
23	*veintitrés*
24	*veinticuatro*
30	*treinta*
31	*treinta y uno*
32	*treinta y dos*
33	*treinta y tres*
40	*cuarenta*
41	*cuarenta y uno*
42	*cuarenta y dos*
50	*cincuenta*

60	*sesenta*
70	*setenta*
80	*ochenta*
90	*noventa*
100	*cien*
101	*ciento uno*
102	*ciento dos*
110	*ciento diez*
120	*ciento veinte*
130	*ciento treinta*
140	*ciento cuarenta*
150	*ciento cincuenta*
160	*ciento sesenta*
170	*ciento setenta*
180	*ciento ochenta*
190	*ciento noventa*
200	*doscientos*
300	*trescientos*
400	*cuatrocientos*
500	*quinientos*
600	*seiscientos*
700	*setecientos*
800	*ochocientos*
900	*novecientos*
1000	*mil*
1100	*mil cien*
1200	*mil doscientos*
2000	*dos mil*
5000	*cinco mil*
10000	*diez mil*
50000	*cincuenta mil*
100000	*cien mil*
1000000	*un millón*

Days of the Week

Monday	*lunes*
Tuesday	*martes*
Wednesday	*miércoles*
Thursday	*jueves*
Friday	*viernes*
Saturday	*sábado*
Sunday	*domingo*

Time

Telling time follows a logical pattern. For example, 10 o'clock is *las diez*, 11 o'clock is *las once*, 11.05 is *las once y cinco*, 11.15 is *las once y cuarto* and 11.30 is *las once y media*. Then, after the half-hour has passed, 11.35 is *veinticinco para las doce*, 11.45 is *cuarto para las doce* and 11.55 is *cinco para las doce*; 12.10 is *las doce y diez* and so on. Some useful terms to know are:

in the morning
  por la mañana
during the day
  durante el día
in the afternoon
  por la tarde
in the evening
  por la tarde
at night
  por la noche
yesterday
  ayer
today
  hoy
tomorrow
  mañana
the day after tomorrow
  pasado mañana
next week
  la semana próxima

Facts for the Visitor

VISAS

Visas are required by very few people. Most West European nationalities and citizens of Britain, Canada, the USA and Australia do not require visas. The only essential document is your passport. New Zealand passport holders *do* require a visa. Most people are given an entry stamp on arrival which allows for a stay of up to 90 days, and this can be renewed for an additional 90 days. If you need a visa, don't turn up at the border without one – you could easily find yourself tramping back to the nearest Chilean Consulate.

You do not need an International Health Certificate. It is advisable to go for a medical checkup before you embark on your trip.

Visa Extensions

If you want to stay longer than six months, it's probably simplest to make a short trip to Argentina or another adjoining country, then return and start your six months all over again.

Other South American Visas

The adjoining South American countries of Argentina, Bolivia and Peru all have embassies in Santiago and consulates in several other Chilean towns. Argentina has an embassy in Santiago and consulates in Punta Arenas, Puerto Montt, Arica and Antofagasta. Peru has an embassy in Santiago and a consulate in Arica. Bolivia has an embassy in Santiago and consulates in Arica and Antofagasta.

CUSTOMS

There are no restrictions on the import and export of local and foreign currency. Your duty-free allowance includes 400 cigarettes or 50 cigars or 50 grams of tobacco, 2½ litres of alcoholic beverage, and perfume for personal use.

Negotiating customs is usually straight-forward. Officials usually only check your bags for fruit, which is strictly prohibited in order to prevent the spread of diseases and pests. It's also illegal to transport fruit from northern Chile and there are numerous checkpoints along highways in the Atacama Desert where all baggage is searched.

MONEY

The unit of currency is the Chilean peso (Ch$). Notes come in denominations of 500, 1000 and 5000 pesos. Coins come in denominations of 1, 5, 10, 50 and 100 pesos.

There are two sets of coins in circulation. There are silver-coloured 1, 5, 10 and 50 peso coins which are gradually being phased out and which you rarely see now. These have been replaced with smaller copper-coloured 1, 5, 10, 50 and 100 peso coins.

The peso has been floating against the US dollar and is falling in value. The exchange rate, at the time of writing, was around US$1 = Ch$250. The rate of the Chilean peso's devaluation is mild by South American standards, but it is hefty enough to make it worth quoting prices in this book in US dollars.

There is no limit on the export or import of local currency but you will probably find your Chilean pesos useless outside Chile, except in a few border towns in adjoining countries.

Changing Money

US dollars are the best currency to take with you to Chile. US cash can be changed almost anywhere. You can change pounds sterling, Australian dollars, yen, deutsch-marks and other strange currencies at banks (*banco*) and change houses (*casa de cambio*) in Santiago, but elsewhere you may as well roll them up and use them as cigarette papers.

Take the bulk of your money in

Contemporary 1000 peso banknote

travellers' cheques from a major company like American Express, Thomas Cook or Citibank. Cheques from small banks are impossible to change. Even in fairly large towns it can sometimes be difficult finding a bank which will change travellers' cheque from a major company.

Apart from cheques, you should take some US cash with you since it's *not* possible to change travellers' cheques in small places or when the banks and moneychangers are closed. Take some US\$20 and US\$50 cheques, or small notes, to avoid ending up with large amounts of excess currency when you leave the country.

If you have money sent from home, have the bank send a draft to you. If the money is transferred by cable it should reach you in a few days. Chilean banks will give you your money in US dollars if you ask.

Black Market

There is a black market for US cash and travellers' cheques which is very open – especially in Santiago where you'll be approached by dealers along Huérfanos, Agustinas and Ahumada in the city centre. The rate is about 10% above the official rate. The black market, or so-called parallel dollar, rate is listed daily in the newspapers.

If you have travellers' cheques in US dollars, it's probably better to convert these to cash and then change the cash for pesos. If you have American Express cheques you can convert them to US dollar cash at the American Express office in Santiago. You can often get the street rate at hotels, or in shops which sell imported items such as electronic goods and pharmaceuticals.

Credit Cards

Credit cards, particularly those which allow you to withdraw cash or to buy cheques (American Express and Visa), can be very useful in Chile. They're also useful if you are required to show 'sufficient funds' before you enter another South American country.

Bargaining

Usually the only things you have to haggle over are long term accommodation and purchases from markets such as handicrafts. Otherwise, prices for hotel rooms are almost always fixed, and displayed in the foyer.

GENERAL INFORMATION
Postal Rates

An ordinary letter costs about US\$0.08 to send anywhere in Chile. An airmail letter costs US\$0.40 to the USA and US\$0.50 to anywhere else in the world. Aerogrammes are US$0.40 to anywhere. Allow quite a bit of time for letters and postcards to get through – some may take several weeks.

Sending Mail Unlike in some Latin American countries, sending parcels is a straightforward process in Chile, although you may have to have the contents inspected and passed by a customs officer before they can be accepted by a postal clerk. All the requisites for wrapping parcels can generally be bought from the vendors outside large post offices.

Receiving Mail Have letters sent to you c/o Lista de Correos, followed by the name of the city you want the letter to go to. Mail addressed in this way will always be sent to the main post office in that city.

The American Express office in Santiago has a mail service for customers. Some embassies will also hold mail for their citizens.

To collect mail from a post office (or from Amex or an embassy) you need to produce your passport as proof of your identity. Uncollected mail is sent back to the country of origin.

If you're not getting expected letters ask them to check under every conceivable combination of your initials, not forgetting they might also be under 'M' (for Mr, Ms, etc) or 'S' (for Señor, Señora). The confusion arises because of the naming system in Latin countries. If you were called Juan García Moreno, for example, Juan would be your first or given name, García your father's name, and Moreno your mother's name. A post office employee would file such a letter under 'G'. In a non-Latin country, of course, it would be filed under 'M'. To avoid this confusion, address a letter in block capitals, leave out all titles (Mr, Mrs, Señor, etc) and underline the surname.

Telephones
International and domestic long distance telephone calls can be made from offices of ENTEL or from the Compañia de Telefonos de Chile.

Approximate charges for domestic calls from Santiago are: to Valparaíso, US$0.40 for the first three minutes and US$0.10 for each additional minute; and to more distant places, US$0.70 for the first three minutes. Local calls from public telephone boxes are US$0.10 for five minutes.

Approximate international call charges are: to the USA and Canada, US$9 for the first three minutes and US$3 for each additional minute; to Europe and Australia, US$10.50 for the first three minutes and US$3.50 for each additional minute; to other Latin American countries, US$8 for the first three minutes and US$2.70 for each additional minute.

International telephone charges tend to go up quite rapidly, usually every month. However, lines are usually good and it generally takes only a short time to put your call through.

Telex & Telegraph

Telexes and telegrams can be sent from the offices of TELEX Chile.

Telexes to Australia are US$5.60 per minute; to the USA and Europe US$4.20 per minute. Telegrams to Australia are US$1.70 per word; and to the USA and Europe US$0.80 per word.

HEALTH

Travel health depends on your pre-departure preparations, your day-to-day health care while travelling and how you handle any medical problem or emergency that does develop. While the list of potential dangers can seem quite frightening, with a little luck, some basic precautions and adequate information few travellers experience more than upset stomachs.

It is advisable to go for a medical checkup before you start travelling.

Travel Health Guides

There are a number of books on travel health:

The Traveller's Health Guide, Dr Anthony Turner, Roger Lascelles, London, 1979. A good health guide, particularly if you intend doing some far-ranging travel in South America.

Backpacking in Chile & Argentina, Hilary Bradt & John Pilkington's, Bradt Enterprises, 1980. A useful guide which gives a rundown on problems faced by trekkers and campers in Chile.

Staying Healthy in Asia, Africa & Latin America, Volunteers in Asia. Probably the best all-round guide to carry, as it's compact but very detailed and well organised.

Travellers' Health, Dr Richard Dawood, Oxford University Press. Comprehensive, easy to read, authoritative and also highly recommended, although it's rather large to lug around.

Where There is No Doctor, David Werner, Hesperian Foundation. A very detailed guide intended for someone, like a Peace Corps worker, going to work in an undeveloped country, rather than for the average traveller.

Travel with Children, Maureen Wheeler, Lonely Planet Publications. Basic advice on travel health for younger children.

Vaccinations

Vaccinations provide protection against diseases you might meet along the way. No vaccinations are required to enter Chile, and the country is free of malaria and yellow fever. Typhoid, polio, tetanus, and hepatitis immunisation are recommended.

Typhoid protection lasts for three years and is useful if you are travelling for long in rural areas. You may get some side effects such as pain at the injection site, fever, headache and a general unwell feeling.

A complete series of oral polio vaccines or a tetanus-DPT vaccine are considered essential if you hadn't had them before. In addition, a tetanus-DPT booster should be taken every five to 10 years.

You should also have a gamma globulin shot as a precaution against infectious hepatitis. Gamma globulin is not a vaccination but a ready-made antibody which has proven very successful in reducing the chances of hepatitis infection.

All vaccinations should be recorded on an International Health Certificate, which is available from your physician or health department.

Pre-Departure Preparations

Travel Insurance A travel insurance policy to cover theft, loss and medical problems is a wise idea. You may never need it but if you do it's worth a million. There are a wide variety of policies and your travel agent will have recommendations. The international student travel policies handled by STA or other student travel organisations are usually good value. Make sure the policy includes health care and medication, covers the money you lose for forfeiting a booked flight, and includes a flight home for you and anyone you're travelling with, should your condition warrant it.

Medical Kit Medical supplies and drugs are available from pharmacies in Chile, but it is advisable to carry a small, straightforward medical kit. A possible kit list includes:

1. Aspirin or Panadol – for pain or fever.
2. Antihistamine (such as Benadryl) – useful as a decongestant for colds, allergies, to ease the itch from insect bites or stings or to help prevent motion sickness.
3. Antibiotics – useful if you're travelling well off the beaten track, but they must be prescribed and you should carry the prescription with you.
4. Kaolin preparation (Pepto-Bismol), Imodium or Lomotil – for stomach upsets.
5. Rehydration mixture – for treatment of severe diarrhoea; this is particularly important if travelling with children.
6. Antiseptic, mercurochrome and antibiotic powder or similar 'dry' spray – for cuts and grazes.
7. Calamine lotion – to ease irritation from bites or stings.
8. Bandages and band-aids – for minor injuries.
9. Scissors, tweezers and a thermometer – mercury thermometers are prohibited by airlines.
10. Insect repellent, sunblock, suntan lotion, chapstick and water purification tablets.

Health Preparations Make sure you're healthy before you start travelling. If you are embarking on a long trip make sure your teeth are OK. There are lots of places where a visit to the dentist would be the last thing you'd want to do.

If you wear glasses, bring a spare pair and your prescription. Losing your glasses can be a real problem, although in many places you can get new spectacles made up quickly, cheaply and competently.

If you require a particular medication, take an adequate supply as it may not be available locally. Take the prescription, with the generic rather than the brand name, which may not be locally available, as it will make getting replacements easier. It's a wise idea to have the prescription with you to show you legally use the medication; it's surprising how often over-the-counter drugs from one place are illegal without a prescription or even banned in another.

Drinking Water
Chilean cities have a decent, chlorinated water supply and you can drink from the tap. On Easter Island, the water is rather strong-tasting bore water and takes some time to get used to. If you're trekking in the Chilean mountains draw your water from springs or small streams; if you have any doubts about the purity of the water boil it or use iodine-based water purifying tablets. The only trouble with iodine is that it makes the water taste foul – but this is a small price to pay.

Medical Problems & Treatment
Generally speaking, as far as health is concerned, Chile presents only three real problems: altitude, extremes of climate, and a change of diet.

Altitude Sickness Although you are more likely to be affected by altitude on the Altiplano of Ecuador, Peru and Bolivia (average height 3000 to 4000 metres), you can experience altitude sickness crossing some of the high mountain passes from Chile into Bolivia and Argentina. There are also popular tourist destinations, like Lago Chungará, which lie at very high altitudes – in this case 4500 metres above sea level.

Altitude sickness goes under a variety of names, including mountain sickness and *soroche*. Acute Mountain Sickness (AMS) can be fatal, and is unpredictable. Athletes can suffer from it, and even people who have had no problems at high

Volcán Osorno

altitude before can suddenly come down with it.

You start to notice altitude sickness at around 3000 metres. If you make a sudden ascent to a high altitude you have to take it easy for three to four days or even longer. The best thing to do is to reduce your level of activity, drink lots of fluids, stop smoking and don't drink alcohol. In the meantime your body will start producing more red-blood cells so that it can absorb more oxygen from the rarefied air. Until this happens – and it takes at least a month until you're fully adjusted – the heart and lungs must work harder to compensate.

Since the brain absorbs 40% of the blood's oxygen intake, you get headaches if not enough oxygen is coming through. The mild symptoms of altitude sickness include headaches, general weakness, loss of appetite, shortness of breath and irregular breathing, insomnia, mild nausea, dry cough, slight loss of co-ordination and concentration, and puffy face or hands in the morning. These symptoms should clear up after a few days. If they don't, or if they get more severe, then you should get down to a lower altitude as soon as possible. The only cure for altitude sickness is get down to a lower altitude *immediately*.

Severe altitude sickness can be fatal. It can cause pulmonary oedema (in which the lungs fill with fluids), or a cerebral oedema (fluid collects on the brain) which is fatal within two days. Symptoms of severe altitude sickness include marked loss of co-ordination, dizziness, walking as if drunk, severe headaches, serious shortness of breath even after mild activity, severe nausea and vomiting, extreme lassitude, abnormal speech and behaviour, reduced urine production, bubbly breath, persistent coughing spasms that produce watery or coloured sputum, and a loss of interest in food, conversation and self-preservation. Delirium and coma also occur.

There's no cure for altitude sickness

except for descent to lower altitudes. Oxygen can provide temporary relief, and a painkiller for headaches and an anti-emetic for vomiting will help relieve the symptoms. Make sure you drink as much as you can, even if you have to force it down. Loss of appetite can wear down your resistance so try to eat as well. Carbohydrates are supposed to be good for countering altitude sickness.

In South America, the traditional relief for altitude sickness is *mate de coca* – tea made from coca leaves. You can get this in Peru and Bolivia. The leaves also find their way down into northern Chile. If you chew the leaves you have to add ash or some bicarbonate of soda (mild alkalis) so the cocaine will leach out of the leaves.

Heat Exhaustion & Sunburn In hot climates – like the Atacama Desert and Easter Island – you sweat a great deal and lose both water and salt. Drink enough liquid and add enough salt to your food to make up the losses (a teaspoon of salt a day is sufficient). Otherwise you may suffer from heat exhaustion and cramps. Heat can also make you impatient and irritable. Good sunglasses are an absolute necessity on Easter Island and in the Chilean desert. Sunburn is a *real* problem in these places and you need a powerful sunblock, some headgear which shades your whole face and neck, and a light long-sleeved shirt to cover your arms. Make no mistake about how formidable the Easter Island and Atacama sun can be!

Hypothermia At the other end of the temperature scale, hypothermia is a simple but effective killer, usually referred to as 'exposure'. Basically, the body loses heat faster than it can produce it and the core temperature of the body falls. It's deceptively easy to fall victim to it through a combination of wind, wet clothing, fatigue and hunger, even if the air temperature is well above freezing. Hypothermia's symptoms include a loss of rationality – so people can fail to recognise their own condition and the seriousness of their predicament.

Symptoms of hypothermia are exhaustion, numb skin (particularly toes and fingers), shivering, slurred speech, irrational or violent behaviour, lethargy, stumbling, dizzy spells, muscle cramps and violent bursts of energy. This can progress to collapse, unconsciousness and death. Anticipate the problem if you're cold and tired, and recognise the symptoms early. Immediate care is important, since hypothermia can kill in as little as two hours.

The first response should be to find shelter from wind and rain, remove wet clothing and replace with warm dry clothing, drink hot liquids (not alcohol) and eat some high calorie, easily digestible food. These measures will usually correct the problem if symptoms have been recognised early. In more severe cases, it may be necessary to place the patient in a sleeping bag insulated from the ground, with another person if possible, while they are fed warm food and drinks. Do *not* rub the patient, place them near a fire, give food or drink if they're unconscious, remove wet clothes in the wind, or give them alcohol.

You could face this problem if you're trekking, day-walking or hitching anywhere in southern Chile. Be prepared for cold, wet and windy conditions. Get under cover before you get soaked, keep your sleeping bag dry, and if you're day-walking and don't have the proper gear, turn back if the weather looks threatening. Warm, waterproof clothes are essential. These should retain their insulating qualities when wet so use wool and various synthetics – *not* cotton. They should also protect all parts of the body, including hands, feet, neck and head. Solid shoes are also essential. Thermal underwear – at least a thermal top – is a good investment.

Diarrhoea & Dysentery Montezuma's Revenge, the Inca Two-Step and other endearing terms describe an experience you'll have sooner or later, so accept it as inevitable and know how to deal with it. Although Chile and Argentina are much more hygienic than some of their northern neighbours, the problem can arise from a change in food – it doesn't necessarily mean you've caught something. Amongst other things, oily food, seafood saturated in vinegar, and strange creatures you're not used to eating can bring on diarrhoea.

Avoid rushing off to the pharmacy and filling yourself with antibiotics at the first signs. The best thing to do is eat nothing and rest, avoid travelling and drink plenty of liquid (tea or *mate* without sugar or milk). Many cafes in Latin America serve camomile tea (*té de manzanilla*) which is excellent for this. Otherwise, drink mineral water (*agua mineral*). About 24 to 48 hours should do the trick. If you really can't cope with starving, keep to a diet of yoghurt, lemon juice and boiled vegetables.

After a severe bout of diarrhoea or dysentery, you will probably be dehydrated and this often causes painful cramps. Relieve these by drinking fruit juices or tea into which a small spoonful of salt has been dissolved. Maintaining a correct balance of salt in your bloodstream is important.

Lomotil or Imodium can be used to bring relief from the symptoms, although they do not actually cure it. Only use these drugs if absolutely necessary. For children, Imodium is preferable, but do not use these drugs if you have a high fever or are severely dehydrated. Antibiotics can be very useful in treating severe diarrhoea, especially if it is accompanied by nausea, vomiting, stomach cramps or mild fever. Ordinary 'traveller's diarrhoea' rarely lasts more than about three days. If it lasts for more than a week you must get treatment, move on to antibiotics or see a doctor.

Sexually Transmitted Diseases Sexual contact with an infected sexual partner spreads these diseases and while abstinence is the only 100% preventative, use of a condom is also effective. Gonorrhoea and syphilis are the most common of these diseases and sores, blisters or rashes around the genitals, discharges or pain when urinating are common symptoms. Symptoms may be less marked or not observed at all in women. The symptoms of syphilis eventually disappear completely but the disease continues and can cause severe problems in later years. Treatment of gonorrhoea and syphilis is by antibiotics.

There are numerous other sexually transmitted diseases for most of which effective treatment is available. There is no cure for herpes and there is also currently no cure for AIDS which is most commonly spread through male homosexual activity but also common amongst some heterosexuals. Using condoms and avoiding certain sexual practices such as anal intercourse are the most effective preventatives.

AIDS can also be spread through infected blood transfusions, most developing countries cannot afford to screen blood for transfusions, or by dirty needles – vaccinations, acupuncture and tattooing can potentially be as dangerous as intravenous drug use if the equipment is not clean. If you do need an injection it may be a good idea to buy a new syringe from a pharmacy and ask the doctor to use it.

Women's Health
Gynaecological Problems Poor diet, lowered resistance due to the use of antibiotics for stomach upsets and even contraceptive pills can lead to vaginal infections when travelling in hot climates. Keeping the genital area clean, wearing cotton underwear and skirts or loose-fitting trousers will help to prevent infections.

Yeast infections, characterised by a rash, itch and discharge can be treated with a vinegar or even lemon juice douche or with yoghurt. Nystatin suppositories are the usual medical prescription. Trichomonas is a more serious infection with a discharge and a burning sensation when urinating. Male sexual partners must also be treated and if a vinegar-water douche is not effective medical attention should be sought. Flagyl is the prescribed drug.

Pregnancy Most miscarriages occur during the first three months of pregnancy so this is the most risky time to travel. The last three months should also be spent within reasonable distance of good medical care as quite serious problems can develop at this time. Pregnant women should avoid all unnecessary medication, but vaccinations and malarial prophylactics should still be taken where possible. Additional care should be taken to prevent illness and particular attention should be paid to diet and nutrition.

THEFT
Things *can* get stolen in Chile. People *can* get mugged in Santiago. But of all the South American countries, Chile rates as one of the safest.

You have much less chance of coming up against bag-slashers or pickpockets than you do in Peru or Colombia. You can fall asleep on buses and trains and your bags will still be where you left them when you wake up. I wouldn't leave bags lying around bus terminals, but you don't have to watch them like a hawk when you pull into a roadside stop.

It's still a good idea to get some baggage insurance before you leave home. Valuables such as passports and air tickets can be conveniently carried in a light jacket or vest with one or two zip-up or button-up pockets. Money belts or pouches hung round the neck are popular alternatives, but not so comfortable.

Do *not* leave valuables in a hotel room. A lot of Chilean hotel rooms have only token locks, and in the south many don't have any locks at all. Nobody's going to steal your faded old jeans but travellers' cheques and money have a very good chance of wandering off. Likewise, don't leave valuables on a beach while you go for a swim. Theft is not as great a problem as in some parts of South America, but a certain amount of discretion is advisable.

ACCOMMODATION
You can often get a roof over your head for around US$2 to US$5 per night. Obviously, a great deal depends on what you're satisfied with in terms of comfort and cleanliness, how much searching you're prepared to do when you land in a place, and whether you're in a city or a small town. Prices for all accommodation have risen sharply in the last few years and if you intend travelling on a rock-bottom budget then you'll often have to accept rock-bottom standards. Low-budget accommodation can be quite good value, but in many places if you want something decent you'll have to pay more.

Hospedajes & Residencials
The cheapest places go under the title of *hospedaje* or *residencial*. Distinctions are somewhat academic, but a hospedaje is usually a family house with a room or two for rent. These are often excellent value; they have hot water and you share the lounge with the family. Hospedajes are sometimes permanent affairs but are often only temporary. Some of these places are mentioned in this book. Others can be found by asking at the tourist offices or, especially in the small towns, by walking around the streets and looking for signs in the windows.

A residencial is a small permanent hotel with a number of rooms to rent, often run by a family who also lives in the same building. They're usually fairly basic, providing only a bed, table and chair in an otherwise bare room. Usually clean sheets and blankets are provided. Some of them have heating units in the rooms, some don't; some have rooms with attached bathrooms, but usually there are shared toilets and showers. Most have hot water, particularly those in the south, though you often have to pay extra for it. Places in the north, and sometimes in Santiago, often only have cold water.

Although they're always quite basic and often spartan, the quality of the hospedajes and residencials varies quite a bit. Some of these places, especially in Santiago, have windowless rooms resembling solitary confinement cells. Some are just large rooms divided up with paper-thin masonite into separate compartments. Others have friendly managers and decent little rooms, but bathrooms and toilets that look like they haven't been cleaned since the colonial era. Others are bright, clean and comfortable, with hot water included in the price or at an extra charge of US$0.50 to US$1.

On the whole the managers and owners of most of the cheaper places are friendly to foreigners, even if you don't speak much Spanish. Some have a safe in which you can leave your valuables. Many cheap hotels, residencials and hospedajes either have no locks for the rooms, or token locks as a statement of intent. Although theft is not as common in Chile as it is in some other South American countries *don't* leave valuables lying around your room. Give them to the manager if you think he or she can be trusted, if not carry them with you.

The price of rooms in residencials and hospedajes often includes breakfast. In the very cheapest hotels and residencials, it's often just a cup of coffee and maybe a piece of bread with butter or jam. If you pay more, your breakfast may well be a whole buffet consisting of fruit juice, bread, butter, jam, biscuits, eggs and a pot of coffee.

Hotels & Pensiones
Hotels and *pensiones* are generally more expensive than residencials and hospedajes though the distinction is often obscure. Most pensiones tend to have slightly better facilities, and services of a higher standard. For a few dollars more than you would pay in an hospedaje you will probably get a private bathroom. Quite a

few have their own restaurant, as do some residencials.

The term hotel is usually applied to mid-range and up-market places. At the bottom end of this price bracket are hotels which provide you with a small room, attached bathroom and toilet, hot water, private telephone and TV, and occasionally even a small refrigerator. These places usually have a restaurant which is fairly inexpensive.

Beyond this there's not much variation until you get to places like the Holiday Inn Crowne Plaza in Santiago which is an international-standard, five-star hotel with luxury rooms, swimming pool, room service, shopping arcades and so on. You can always find excellent mid-range hotels in the larger towns right through Chile, though international and luxury-standard hotels are largely restricted to Santiago, Valparaíso and Viña del Mar.

Chalets
Look out for some of the fine mid-range hotels found in the Lake District, usually located on the shores of the lakes or by thermal springs in the mountains. These are often run by people of German descent, are built like European chalets, and have mineral water swimming pools, hot therapeutic baths and their own restaurants.

Youth Hostels
Youth Hostels in Chile are something of a mystery to me. They seem to cater mainly to Chilean school children and teenagers on organised holidays, and are in places like sports stadiums, camping grounds, schools and educational institutions. In some instances, there is conflicting evidence as to where the hostel is actually located, and most only seem to be open during the holiday season in the first two or three months of the year. They usually charge only a dollar or two per night for a dormitory, which makes them just about the cheapest accommodation in Chile, except for camping grounds. There does

not, however, appear to be any 'youth hostel' network like those run by the International Youth Hostel Association in Australia, Europe or the USA.

Camping & Refugios

The tourist office in Santiago has a free pamphlet called *Camping* which lists campsites throughout Chile and gives details of their facilities. You can pitch a tent at campsites in the national parks and in other places for a dollar or two per day per tent. Apart from the campsites, there are also *refugios* which are huts set up in the national parks to provide shelter for walkers and trekkers.

FOOD

From battling soroche (altitude sickness) with coca leaf tea on the border with Bolivia, to holding down sea urchins in the stormy climes of Punta Arenas, such are the delights of eating in Chile. Eating does not have to be an endless succession of *empanadas*, the simple baked pastries stuffed with meat, vegetables or cheese.

If empanadas are as far as you get with Latin American food then you really are missing out on an extraordinary variety of cuisines which have been influenced by the original Indian settlers, the Spanish invaders and colonisers, and later European and African immigrants. The influence has also worked the other way – even the humble tomato was unknown in Europe before the Spanish conquest of Latin America.

Each Latin American country has developed a distinctive cuisine. Corn-based food like tortillas, and soups and beans are the backbone of the Mexican diet. In Peru, it's potato with corn. In Argentina the going thing is meat, from a grilled cow dished up with a pile of chips to elaborate meat stews and *matambre arrollado* – rolled beef stuffed with spinach, onion, carrots and eggs. Chile has something of everything to offer, with some fine seafood as its own contribution.

Places to Eat

In Chile, you can eat cheaply from many small restaurants in the towns and cities. A sign of a good restaurant is locals eating there – restaurants aren't empty if their food is good and cheap. There is usually at least one large covered market in the central district of Chilean cities, which provides a roof for many small, cheap restaurants.

Eating places fall into a number of categories: bars serve snacks and both alcoholic and non-alcoholic drinks; *cafeterías* and *hosterías* are straightforward restaurants; *confiterías* are primarily cake shops but also serve coffee, tea and other drinks; snack bars sell fast food and the English words are used to describe them; and finally, the fully fledged *restaurantes* are distinguished by their quality and service. The distinctions are never exact and restaurante can be applied to everything from the simplest to the most illustrious establishment.

Almost all eating houses serve alcoholic and non-alcoholic drinks. Except in places run and worked by families it is customary – and expected – that you tip waiters 10% of the bill. The menu is *la carta*; the bill is *la cuenta*.

Many cafes put on a cheap set meal (*comida corrida*) both for lunch (*almuerzo*) and dinner (*comida* or *cena*). Breakfast (*desayuno*) is rarely a set meal and you generally order whatever you like. Following the European custom you will often find that you get exactly what you ask for. If you ask for chicken and rice that's exactly what you get. Salad is *ensalada*; vegetables are *verduras*.

Some of the most common dishes are listed here, but it's impossible to mention all the possibilities. You need a dictionary and a phrasebook with a good food section.

Snacks

Empanadas are similar to Cornish pasties; they're stuffed with vegetables, or combinations of vegetables, meats and cheese. Two or three of these with a coffee should set you up for the morning. Empanadas can be fried (*fritas*) or baked (*al horno*). In some other South American countries empanadas are known as *saltenas*.

Humitas is better known in western cookbooks as 'seasoned puréed corn' – corn kernels and milk mashed into a thick pulp. This is found in one form or another in every Latin American country. It is frequently wrapped in corn husks and steamed; when served this way it is known as *humitas en chala* – a tasty change from empanadas.

There are various types of bread worth trying. *Chapalele* is a bread made with potatoes and flour and boiled in hot water. *Milcao* is another type of bread made with potatoes. *Sopaipa* is a bread made from wheat flour and fruit, but is not baked; it's recognisable by its dark brown exterior.

For breakfast, the usual eggs and bread rolls are the main alternatives to empanadas. *Huevos fritos* are fried eggs, *revueltos* are scrambled, and *pasados* or *a la copa* are boiled or poached. As far as the last two are concerned, *bien cocidos* means well cooked and *duros* means hard. *Tostadas* is toast, and *pan* is bread; eat these with *mantequilla* (butter), *mermelada* (jam), *jamón* (ham) or *queso* (cheese).

Main Courses

Lunch can be the biggest meal of the day. The only trouble with comidas corridas (set menus) is that they tend to be almost exactly the same wherever you are. They generally consist of a thick soup, usually of potato or maize with some meat, a main course of rice with chicken or a slice of grilled meat, and a dessert.

For the biggest standard meal in Chile ask for *lomo a la probe*. An enormous slab of red meat decorated with two fried eggs, hemmed in by chips and buried in a truck load of rice descends on your table – or at least it should if the restaurant is worth its weight in cholesterol.

Popular places for meat dishes are the *parilladas* or steak houses and grills, which cook everything from steak to sausages over charcoal fires. They're wonderful if you like meat and a complete loss if you don't. Ordinary restaurants usually serve up chicken; common dishes include *pollo con papas fritas*, which is chicken with fried potatoes, and *pollo con arroz*, chicken with rice.

Seafood

Good seafood is always available in the coastal towns. The richest dish you'll probably ever come across is *curanto*, a combination of seafood, chicken, pork, lamb, beef and potato. Curanto is eaten with chapalele and milcao bread and is a speciality of Chiloé Island and the southern regions of Chile.

Soup is *caldo* or *sopa*. Popular soups are *sopa de mariscos*, which are delicious fish soups found in both Chile and Argentina, or *cazuela de mariscos*, which are fish stews. Fish soup is *sopa de pescado*. Try the soups using the conger eel (*congrio*) and abalone (*locos*).

Try the eating places at the fish markets in the large coastal towns like Puerto Montt. Be warned that some of these dishes require a cast-iron stomach and a blast-furnace digestive system. There is some good seafood to be found in Chile, particularly the seafood soups and stews, but a lot of it requires some getting used to.

A few seafood terms worth knowing are:

fish	*pescado*
shrimp	*camarones*
prawns	*camarones grandes*
crab meat	*carne de cangrejo*
mussels	*mejillones*
oysters	*ostiones, ostras*
shellfish	*concha*
clams	*almejas*
sea urchin	*pilluelo, erizo*
squid	*calamares*
octopus	*pulpo*

Desserts

Dessert (*postre*) is commonly ice cream (*helado*). *Helado de fresa* is strawberry flavoured and *helado de chocolate* and *helado de vainilla* require no further explanation. Also try rice pudding (*arroz con leche*) and cakes (*tortas*).

Ethnic Food

Santiago has a large selection of 'ethnic' restaurants. There are eight pages of restaurants and bars listed in the Santiago yellow pages. Seek out Brazilian restaurants for boiled black beans (the famous *feijao*), grilled or barbecued meats and manioc flour. There are also Indian (Asian, not Mapuche) curry houses, Italian pasta specialists, Chinese noodle shops, and Mexican tortilla dispensaries, amongst many others. There are many Chinese restaurants in the towns of the Atacama Desert, such as Iquique and Arica. These are known as *chifas* and are generally cheap, good value, and offer a pleasant change from South American food.

Vegetarian Dishes

Vegetarianism is a growing movement in South America. There are some vegetarian restaurants in Santiago, and you might find some in other large towns. If you tell the waiter at an ordinary restaurant that you don't want meat they'll often put something together for you. Ask for a meal *sin carne* (without meat).

Every town has a market with a wide variety of fruit and vegetables for sale – the Chilean heartland is a fine fruit-producing region and its produce is exported to the southern regions of the country. Remember that it is absolutely forbidden to carry fruit from northern Chile to the centre, or to import it from foreign countries.

Fast Food

Santiago also has the largest number of fast-food restaurants. These are mostly poor imitations of Kentucky Fried Chicken or McDonalds. There are other fast-food chains around which serve a variety of food including rather bland pizzas. The Dino's group is common in the towns south of Santiago and on the whole they're not bad places to eat.

DRINKS

Top of the list and easy to consume in great quantities (before it strikes you down like a whack over the head with a dead guanaco) is a powerful spirit called *pisco*. It's a grape brandy, served with lemon juice or syrup. Pisco sour is served with ginger ale (*chilcano*), or with vermouth (*capitán*).

Gol is a translucent alcoholic drink made with butter, sugar and milk and then left for two weeks to ferment. It's drunk in the south of the country but you probably won't find it in the restaurants.

Yerba mate is herbal tea. *Yerba* is the name of the herb, *mate* is the cup from which it is drunk and *bombilla* is the pipe with which the tea is sucked from the cup. The herb is a greenish colour, ground to about the size of ordinary tea leaves. It is mixed with hot water and drunk through the bombilla, which has a filter at the end to prevent the leaves being sucked up. A proper *mate* is roughly spherical with a small hole in the top. When the liquid is finished more hot water is poured in. This drink is consumed in both the north and south of Chile, but is much more common in Argentina. If you can't find it in the restaurants then buy it in small packets from the shops and supermarkets.

Guinda is a cherry-like fruit used to make a drink called *guindado*. The fruit is bottled with water and allowed to ferment for two to three months into a dark red alcoholic liquid. New guindado is an orange colour. Again, you probably won't find it in restaurants.

Bars and restaurants commonly sell draught beer (known as *chop* and pronounced 'shop'), which is cheaper than the bottled beer (*cerveza*) and often just as good.

Fine wines – some world class – are produced in Chile. *Vino tinto* is red wine, *vino blanco* is white wine; *seco* is dry, *dulce* is sweet.

Other drinks available include *jugos* or fruit juices, and these include *naranja* (orange), *toronja* (grapefruit), *piña* (pineapple), *mora* (blackberry), *maracuya* (passionfruit), *sandía* (watermelon) and *limón* (lemon).

All your favourite multinational soft drinks like Sprite, Coca-Cola and Fanta are sold in Chile. Sprite is pronounced 'essprite' for some reason.

Café con leche means coffee with milk but is literally milk with coffee; a teaspoon of coffee is scooped into your cup which is then filled with hot milk. Likewise, *té con leche* is milk with tea that tastes like muddy water. *Café con agua* or *café negro* is coffee with hot water only. If you don't want milk with your tea it will be served black, probably with sugar and a slice of lemon.

BOOKS

Before you start to read about Chile it's worth reading about South America, since it's impossible to understand how modern Chile has developed without some understanding of early Indian settlement and the Spanish and Portuguese conquest.

Latin America

A good starting point is the *History of Latin America* by George Pendle (Penguin, 1973), a pocket-size account of the period from the Spanish conquest to the mid-1970s; it's very readable, though it contains hardly anything about South America prior to the Spanish invasion.

The story of the South American independence wars is told in John Lynch's *The Spanish-American Revolutions 1808-*

1826, which gives a detailed account of the wars against Spain.

The most bitter account of the consequences of economic imperialism in South America, and the social and political struggles of the continent following independence from Spain, is Eduardo Galeano's *Open Veins of Latin America: Five Centuries of the Pillage of a Continent* (Monthly Review Press, New York & London, 1973).

Chile

Probably the best overview of Chilean history and politics from the time of the Spanish conquest to the late 1970s is *Chile: The Legacy of Hispanic Capitalism* (Oxford University Press, New York, 1979) by Brian Loveman. The book gives an intelligent, no-holds-barred account of the struggle of the Mapuche Indians and the Chilean working classes against the Spanish and Chilean elite.

The Allende years and the subsequent coup, with so many political parties and conflicting interests, has produced an awesome number of books describing the events from every conceivable angle.

A very readable account of the Allende years is given in *Allende's Chile* (International Publishers, New York, 1977) by Edward Boorstein, a US economist who worked for the Allende government.

For a first-hand account of what happened in the countryside during the Allende years read *Agrarian Reform Under Allende: Peasant Revolt in the South* (University of New Mexico Press, Albuquerque, 1977) by Kyle Steenland, who lived in Chile's Cautín Province from 1972 to 1973.

For background on the USA's involvement in the campaign against Allende read *The United States & Chile: Imperialism & the Overthrow of the Allende Government* (Monthly Review Press, New York, 1975) by James Petras & Morris Morley.

Amongst the people murdered by the military at the time of the 1973 coup was the Chilean folk singer Victor Jara, something of a South American Woodie Guthrie if comparisons need to be drawn. His story is told by his English wife Joan Jara in *Victor: An Unfinished Song* (Jonathan Cape, London, 1983). It's also a very personal account of life in Chile during the 1960s and early 1970s.

Orlando Letelier, former ambassador to the United States under President Allende, was killed by a car bomb in Washington in 1976. A remarkable account of the investigation into Letelier's murder is given in *Labyrinth* (Penguin, 1983) by Taylor Branch & Eugene Popper.

US citizens Frank Teruggi and Charles Horman were killed at the time of the 1973 coup, and the US Embassy in Santiago was later accused of being implicated in the death of Horman. The story was recounted in a book by Thomas Hauser, which became the basis for the 1982 film *Missing*. The US ambassador to Chile at the time, Nathaniel Davis, includes his side of the story in his book *The Last Two Years of Salvador Allende* (Cornell University Press, 1985).

The Chilean military regime's official account and explanation of the coup is the *White Book* (*Secretaría General de Gobierno*), which is available in both Spanish and English. Another is *Hoy y Ayer* (*Today & Yesterday*), which is available in Chile in Spanish.

Chile: The Pinochet Decade by Phil O'Brien and Jackie Roddick (Latin America Bureau, London, 1983) covers the first years of Pinochet's rule, concentrating on the economic policies devised by the so-called Chicago Boys. From the same organisation and written by a number of contributors is *The Poverty Brokers: The IMF & Latin America*, which includes a discussion on Chile.

If you have any doubts about the brutality of the Chilean military government then try to see the documentary *Chile: Hasta Cuándo?* by Australian film-maker David

Bradbury (who also made *Nicaragua: No Pasarán*).

Easter Island
There is a voluminous literature available about Easter Island, spanning the 250 years since the first Europeans landed on the island. A number of books are listed in the Easter Island chapter.

Patagonia & Tierra del Fuego
The most comprehensive and readily available account of the far south of Chile and Argentina is *Tierra del Fuego* by Rae Natalie Prosser Goodall, first published in Argentina in 1970. It tells you everything from how many Indians were wiped out by measles epidemics to when the first lifts (elevators) were installed. It's printed in both Spanish and English and can be bought from bookshops in Chile and Argentina. Two popular traveller's accounts of southern Chile and Argentina are Paul Theroux's *The Old Patagonian Express* (Penguin, 1980) and Bruce Chatwin's *In Patagonia* (Pan Books, London, 1979).

Travel Guides
Lonely Planet's *South America on a shoestring* is an overview of the entire continent designed for low-budget travellers. The book is written by, or drawn from the work of, the various authors who have written Lonely Planet guides to individual Latin American countries. If you intend going to other Latin American countries, then check out Lonely Planet's other guides to the continent. These include guides to Argentina, Bolivia, Brazil, Columbia, Ecuador, Mexico and Peru.

The South American Handbook (Trade & Travel Publications, Bath, UK) is generally regarded as the standard guide to the continent. It is a book of exceptional detail, listing everything from saunas in Potosi to manzanilla trees in Willemstad.

If you can read Spanish, one of the most useful guides to Chile is the *Turis Tel* guide, published by the Compañi'a de

Telefonos de Chile. It's orientated to people who are travelling by car, and provides very comprehensive maps and background information on all parts of Chile. The latest edition is divided into three separate books: North, Central and South Chile. Even if you can't read Spanish you may still find the maps useful.

Trekking Guides

For trekkers, there's a series of guidebooks on South America written by UK-based Bradt Enterprises, including the very amusing and informative *Backpacking in Chile & Argentina plus the Falkland Islands*. Their *South America: River Trips* includes a description of rafting down Chile's Rio Bío Bío.

Phrasebooks

The Berlitz phrasebook, *Latin-American Spanish for Travellers*, is a good one to bring with you. It's oriented to Mexico but is clear, concise, easy to use and it works well in Chile. A dictionary is also worth bringing. One that has been recommended is the paperback *University of Chicago Spanish-English, English-Spanish Dictionary*, which has many more entries than most pocket-sized dictionaries and also contains words used in Latin America but not in Spain. Lonely Planet's forthcoming *Latin-American Spanish Phrasebook* would be available sometime in December 1990.

MAPS

There are two good maps of Chile which can be bought from kiosks and newspaper stands in the main towns and cities. These are the *Gran Mapa Caminero de Chile* published by Informaciones Unidas Para América Latina, and the *Atlas Caminero de Chile* published by Silva & Silva Ltda. Both are very detailed, clearly labelled and quite cheap. They're also stocked by some specialist shops in the USA.

For even more detailed maps go to the retail office of the Instituto Geográfico Militar de Chile at O'Higgins 240, near the Holiday Inn Crowne Plaza in Santiago. They sell the most detailed maps of the country available to the general public. They're particularly useful if you intend trekking in Chile.

Street maps of Chilean cities and towns are available throughout the country; look in kiosks, newspaper stands and ask at the local tourist offices.

There are a number of maps for Easter Island, most of them very poor. For details see the chapter on Easter Island.

WHAT TO BRING

Travel light. An overweight pack or carrier bag will quickly become a pain to carry, particularly in hot weather. If you need something – from windsurfers, skis and trekking gear to everyday necessities – you can buy it in Chile.

Personal preference largely determines the best way to carry your stuff. A large zip-up bag with a wide shoulder strap is easy to get on buses and easy to put down and pick up, but it's hard to carry for long distances and throws you off balance if its heavy. A backpack is most convenient if you have a lot of walking to do. There is no prejudice about backpacks and their owners – Chileans and Argentines all travel with backpacks, so you just blend into the crowd. A very useful type is one with an internal frame and a cover which zips over and protects the straps so they don't get snagged when the bag is stowed in the bowels of buses or planes.

After that, what you take largely depends on what you want to do and where you want to go. If you intend to camp or trek keep the difficulties of Chile's climate in mind. In the far south of Chile, the wind blows almost unceasingly and a stove will be useless unless it has a wind shield. Likewise your tent needs to have flaps that can be well secured so they don't keep you awake flapping in the wind.

I generally found that even the cheapest places in Chile provided sufficient blankets and gave me more if I asked for them, so sleeping bags are not essential. Camping gear will, however, give you extra freedom of movement.

Clothing which copes with extremes of climate is essential if you intend travelling extensively – see the section on Climate in the Facts about the Country chapter and the section on Health in this chapter – to give you some idea of what you'll need. If you're travelling right through Central and South America you can keep the weight of your pack down by initially taking clothes for hot and temperate climates and buying things like pullovers when you need them, in places like Ecuador, Peru, Bolivia and Chile. Warm jackets, socks, solid footwear and gloves, scarves and headgear are all essential! Thermal underwear, at least a thermal underwear top, is a good investment. In the far south your clothing must be wind and waterproof.

Don't forget small essentials like a combination pocket knife or Swiss Army knife, needle and cotton, a small pair of scissors, contraceptives, sunglasses, swimming gear and so on. All the usual stuff like toothbrushes, paste, shaving cream, shampoo, and tampons can be bought in Chile. The only places you may have difficulty getting certain items are remote towns, small villages and isolated places like Easter Island.

Getting There

Chile is expensive to get to. If you're doing an extended overland journey through Latin America then Chile is just one more border to cross. If you want to go directly from the USA, Australia or Europe then it's a long and expensive way to fly although some discount air tickets are available.

AIR
Discount Air Tickets
There are a number of different types of discount air tickets available. The main ones are:

Advance Purchase These are advance purchase tickets which must be bought 14 days to two months in advance. They are usually only available on a return basis. There are minimum and maximum stay requirements, no stopovers are allowed and there are cancellation charges.

Excursion These tickets are priced midway between an advance purchase fare and a full economy fare. There are no advance booking requirements but a minimum stay abroad is often obligatory. Their advantage over advance purchase tickets is that you can change your bookings and/or stopovers without surcharge.

Point-to-Point This is a discount ticket which can be bought on some routes in return for the passenger waiving their rights to a stopover.

ITX These are Independent Inclusive Tour Excursion tickets. They are often available for popular holiday destinations. Officially, they are only available as holiday package deals which include hotel accommodation. But many agents will sell you one of these and issue you with phony hotel vouchers in the unlikely event that you're questioned at the airport.

Economy Class This is indicated by 'Y' on the airline ticket and is the full economy fare. Tickets are valid for 12 months.

Budget These tickets can be booked at least three weeks in advance but the actual travel date is not confirmed until seven days prior to travel. There are cancellation charges.

MCO This is a Miscellaneous Charges Order. This is a voucher which can be exchanged with any IATA airline for a flight of your choice. Its principal use is as a flexible alternative to a specific onward ticket.

Standby This can be one of the cheapest ways of flying though advance purchase fares may be even cheaper. You simply turn up at the airport or at an airline's city terminal, without a ticket, and if there are spare seats available you can get them at a considerable discount.

RTW These are Round-the-World tickets, which can be a cheap way of travelling. There are some excellent deals available and you may well pick up one of these for less than the cost of a return excursion fare. You must travel round the world in one direction and you cannot backtrack; you are usually allowed five to seven stopovers.

Bucket Shops
In addition to the official ticket structure there are unofficially discounted tickets available through certain travel agents – known in the UK as 'bucket shops'.

Generally, bucket shop tickets are lower in price than advance purchase tickets, and without the cancellation penalty requirements. Some agents do have their own penalties for cancellation. Most bucket shops are well established and scrupulous, but it's not unknown for fly-by-night operators to set up office, take money and then disappear before they've given you a ticket.

In Europe, two of the best places for buying cheap tickets are London and Amsterdam. In both places, there are numerous bucket shops and their services and prices are well advertised. In Australia, there are a number of travel agents which offer cheap air tickets. In the USA, deregulation has made it much easier for travellers to find cheap air tickets, and there are a number of discount outlets in Canada.

TO/FROM THE USA & CANADA

To find cheap tickets look through the travel sections of the Sunday papers for likely looking agents – the *New York Times*, *San Francisco Chronicle-Examiner* and the *Los Angeles Times* are particularly good.

American Student Council Travel (SCT) and Student Travel Network (STN) sell cheap tickets and interesting routes, and you don't have to be a student to use their services. SCT has offices in New York, Los Angeles, San Diego, San Francisco, Boston and Seattle. STN has offices in Los Angeles, San Diego, San Francisco, Honolulu and Dallas.

Travel Cuts is Canada's national student travel agency and has offices in Vancouver, Victoria, Edmonton, Saskatoon, Toronto, Ottawa, Montreal and Halifax. Again, you don't have to be a student to use their services.

LAN-Chile has several flights a week from New York, Miami, Los Angeles and Montreal. The normal one-way economy fare from Santiago to Miami is US$934, from New York US$1057, and from Montreal US$1120. Connections can also be made to other US and Canadian cities. Ladeco also flies from Santiago to the USA and Canada.

Rather than land in the centre of the country at Santiago, you could fly to Lima (in Peru) or to Arica (in northern Chile),

and then go overland from there. One possibility is the Bolivian airlines, Lloyd Aéreo Boliviano, which has flights from Miami to Arica. The return fare is US$600. Aero Perú flies the same route for US$525 return.

TO/FROM THE UK & EUROPE

London and some European capitals are excellent places for picking up cheap air tickets.

In the UK, there are a number of magazines which are very good for information about cheap air tickets. These include *Business Traveller*, *Trailfinder*, *TNT* (The News & Travel Magazine), and perhaps the best known ones, *Time Out* and *LAM* (London Australian Magazine).

Two reliable London bucket shops are Trailfinders and the Student Travel Association. One company which specialises in cheap fares and tours to Latin America is Journey Latin America, also in London.

Similar fares to those from London are available from other European cities. Paris, Amsterdam, Brussels and Antwerp are all good places for picking up cheap tickets. Another route which has become quite popular is from East Berlin to Lima via Cuba using cheap Aeroflot or Interflug flights.

The bucket shops have great deals if you want to fly direct from the UK and Europe to Latin America. From London the cheapest places to fly to are generally Bogotá in Colombia and Caracas in Venezuela. There are also direct flights from London to Buenos Aires, Lima and Santiago. From almost any Latin American country you can catch LAN-Chile, Ladeco or some other airline to Santiago.

TO/FROM AUSTRALIA & NEW ZEALAND

There are a number of agents offering cheap air tickets out of Australia. Student Travel Australia (STA) is very good and you don't have to be a student to use their services. They have offices in Melbourne,

Hobart, Sydney, Adelaide, Perth, Canberra and Brisbane. Another company which offers cheap air tickets is the Flight Centre, with offices in Sydney, Melbourne and Adelaide. Also check out the advertisements in Saturday editions of newspapers like the *Age* or *Sydney Morning Herald*.

There are two ways of flying direct from Australia or New Zealand to Chile. The first option is to fly to Santiago via Tahiti and Easter Island. Qantas or UTA flies you to Tahiti, where you pick up the LAN-Chile flight to Santiago, via Easter Island. A discount ticket from Sydney or Melbourne to Santiago costs around A$2200 return. A regular flight from Sydney or Melbourne to Santiago, via Tahiti only, costs around A$2600 return.

Another possibility is to take the Air New Zealand and Aerolíneas Argentinas Round-the-World ticket. This flies you from Australia to New Zealand, Buenos Aires, Europe, South-East Asia and back to Australia. It includes a return flight from Buenos Aires to Santiago. The ticket costs about A$2700 and is great value if you want to combine Latin America with Europe.

TO/FROM PERU

There are two ways of entering Chile from Peru. One is by road from Tacna, in the far south of Peru, to the northern Chilean city of Arica. The other is on the Lima/Santiago flight.

The Tacna to Arica route is the only overland crossing between Peru and Chile. There is a choice of *taxi colectivo*, bus, or daily train. For details, see the Arica section in the Atacama Desert chapter.

The Peruvian airline, Aero Perú, has flights from Lima to Santiago four days a week. The fare is US$262 one way. They have daily flights from Lima to Tacna for US$79 one way.

TO/FROM BOLIVIA

There are three ways of entering Chile from Bolivia: by road or rail from La Paz to

Arica; by rail from La Paz to Calama; or by air from La Paz to Santiago or Arica.

On the La Paz to Arica route you can take either a train, bus or *ferrobus*. The ferrobus is a sort of bus on train bogeys. There is only one ordinary train on this route twice a month, and departure dates vary each month. Buses and ferrobuses are more frequent. For details, see the Arica section in the Atacama Desert chapter.

You can only go from La Paz to Calama by train. There are normally weekly trains between the two cities, though at the time of writing the service had been suspended. For details, see the Calama section in the Atacama Desert chapter.

The Bolivian airline, Lloyd Aéro Boliviano, has twice weekly flights from Santiago to La Paz. The fare is US$175 one way. LAN-Chile also flies this route. The Bolivian airline flies from Arica to La Paz and the fare is US$85 one way.

TO/FROM ARGENTINA

All train services to Argentina have been suspended so the only way to get between the two countries is by road or air. There are a number of crossing points; the main ones are from Santiago to Mendoza, various routes through the Lake District, and various routes between Chilean and Argentine Patagonia and Tierra del Fuego.

There are a number of flights between Chile and Argentina. Aerolíneas Argentinas flies five days a week from Buenos Aires to Santiago. The fare is US$187 one way. Ladeco has daily flights from Santiago to Mendoza, and the fare is US$87 one way.

The small airline, Aeroregional SA (ASA), has flights three days a week from Puerto Montt to Bariloche. The fare is US$21 one way.

Antofagasta or Calama to Salta

There are buses at least once a week between Antofagasta and Salta in Argentina. See the Antofagasta and

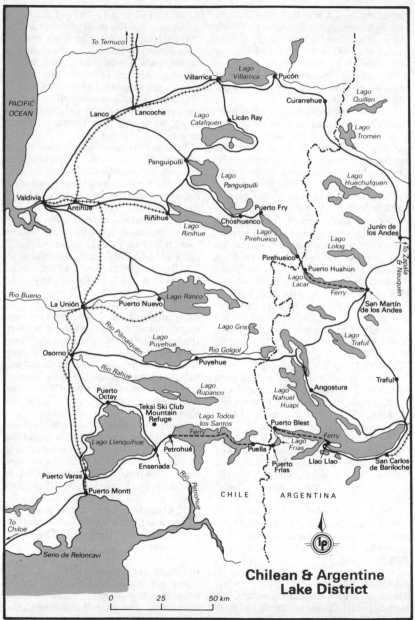

**Chilean & Argentine
Lake District**

Calama sections in the Atacama Desert chapter for details.

Santiago to Buenos Aires & Mendoza
There are several bus and taxi colectivo companies which cover the route from Santiago to Buenos Aires and Mendoza. The road is now open all year. For more details, see the Santiago chapter.

Puerto Montt to Bariloche via Todos los Santos
There are four routes across the Lake District to or from the Argentine side. Three of them terminate at Bariloche (full name: San Carlos de Bariloche). The other route ends at Zapala or Neuquén from where there are trains and buses to Buenos Aires.

The most popular route is from Puerto Montt to Bariloche via Lago Todos los Santos. This has the most spectacular scenery and involves a variety of trips on buses and boats.

There are two ways of doing this trip. One is with a through ticket with one of the bus companies operating out of Puerto Montt or Puerto Varas. However, the better way of doing this trip is in stages, with overnight stops at Ensenada, Petrohué or Puella. In winter, the roads can sometimes be blocked with snow. The first stage takes you from Puerto Montt by bus to Petrohué, from where you catch a ferry to Puella at the other end of the lake. From Puella, a bus takes you over the border to Puerto Frías in Argentina. The next step is by boat from Puerto Frías to Puerto Allegre, by bus from Puerto Allegre to Puerto Blest, by boat from Puerto Blest to Puerto Pañuelo, and then by bus to Bariloche.

Osorno to Bariloche via the Puyehue Pass
This is an all-road journey which passes beside four lakes. There are daily buses from Osorno and Puerto Montt to Bariloche, which enter Argentina via the Puyehue Pass. There are buses several days a week to Zapala, Mendoza and Buenos Aires via this route, which is sometimes blocked by winter snow.

Valdivia to Bariloche via Lago Panguipulli, Lago Pirehueico, Lago Lacar & San Martín de los Andes
The first step of this journey is by bus from Valdivia to Panguipulli, from where you go by bus to Puerto Fry (sometimes spelt Puerto Fuy or Puerto Fui). The third step is the ferry across Lago Pirehueico to Pirehueico. From there you take a bus to Puerto Huahun, where Argentine customs is cleared. The next step is from Puerto Huahun to San Martín de los Andes via Lago Lacar. There is a ferry across the lake between the two towns, and these connect with the buses from Pirehueico and Puerto Huahun. From San Martín de los Andes there are daily buses to Bariloche.

Valdivia to Bariloche via Lago Calafquén
From Panguipulli there is an alternative route into Argentina via Lago Calafquén and the Carirriñe Pass.

Villarrica to Junín de los Andes
This road route between Chile and Argentina goes across the Tromen Pass, which can be blocked by snow for four months of the year. The first step is to go by bus from Valdivia or Temuco to either Villarrica or Pucón. From Villarrica, take a bus to Curarrehue. Between Curarrehue and Junín de los Andes there is no public transport so you have to hitch.

Coyhaique to Comodoro Rivadavia
There is a road between Coyhaique and Comodoro Rivadavia served by a regular bus. See the Coyhaique section in the Aisén chapter for details.

Coyhaique to Caleta Olivia
The Coyhaique to Caleta Olivia journey involves bus and ferry. The first step is to take a bus or taxi colectivo from Coyhaique to Puerto Ibáñez on the shores of Lago Carrera. Next take a ferry across

the lake to Chile Chico. From Chile Chico hire a jeep or ford an unbridged river to the Argentine township of Los Antigos (also spelt Los Antiguos). You then bus or hitch to Perito Moreno, where you catch a bus to Caleta Olivia on the coast.

Puerto Natales to Río Gallegos
This is a relatively quick and convenient means of crossing from Argentina to Chile. Daily buses from Río Gallegos take you to Río Turbio, from where you catch one of the frequent local buses over the mountains to Puerto Natales.

Punta Arenas to Tierra del Fuego
There are daily ferries and planes from Punta Arenas to Porvenir, the small town in Chilean Tierra del Fuego. From Porvenir there are buses twice a week to Río Grande in Argentina, and from Río Grande there are daily buses to Ushuaia.

Getting Around

Travel in Chile is easy. The main roads are generally good, there are fast and punctual bus services, reasonably cheap flights and a number of useful passenger shipping services. It's also easy to work out an itinerary for this long, narrow country as you can start at one end and work your way through to the other with hardly any substantial backtracking or detours.

AIR

Because of the enormous distances in Chile, you may want to take the occasional flight if your time is limited. A flight can also save tedious backtracking. For instance, you can overland through Chilean and Argentine Patagonia to Tierra del Fuego and fly from Punta Arenas back to Santiago or Puerto Montt. The flight back will probably be no more expensive than a combination of bus fares and accommodation.

There are two national airlines: LAN-Chile and Ladeco. Both have domestic and international services. There are also some smaller airlines. These include DAP, which connects Punta Arenas with Tierra del Fuego.

Domestic fares around Chile are shown in the airfare chart in this chapter. Airfares from Chile to neighbouring South American countries are also shown.

LAN-Chile Air Pass

LAN-Chile offers a 21-day air pass known as the Visit Chile Pass. The cities you can fly to include Arica, Iquique, Antofagasta, Santiago, Puerto Montt, Coyhaique and Punta Arenas. Easter Island is also included.

The price depends on the route you choose. For example, the US$520 pass allows you to fly Santiago/Puerto Montt/ Punta Arenas/Santiago/Easter Island/ Santiago.

The passes must be bought outside Chile. They can only be used by foreigners and non-residents of Chile. They are valid for a maximum of 21 days, but there is no minimum restriction. Intermediate stops can be omitted.

Reservations

Both Ladeco and LAN-Chile have a computerised booking service so you can book domestic and international flights from their offices anywhere in the country.

Airport Departure Tax

The airport departure tax for international flights is US$12.50. For domestic flights it's about US$1.30.

Airport Transport

Often LAN-Chile and Ladeco provide a bus between the town centre and the airport – either their own bus or one run by a local company. The cost of the bus is sometimes included in your air ticket, sometimes not. In some places you have to use public transport or taxis to get to the airport. The best thing to do is to ask about arrangements when you buy your ticket.

BUS

All the main roads are surfaced and only in the rural or 'outback' areas do you come across dirt and gravel roads. All the buses on the main roads are comfortable (some of the them are luxurious), well maintained, fast and punctual. They generally have a toilet and often serve coffee and tea on board. When you consider the distances from one city to another they're a real bargain by European or North American standards.

Bus Terminals

Most Chilean cities have a central bus terminal where all the bus companies are

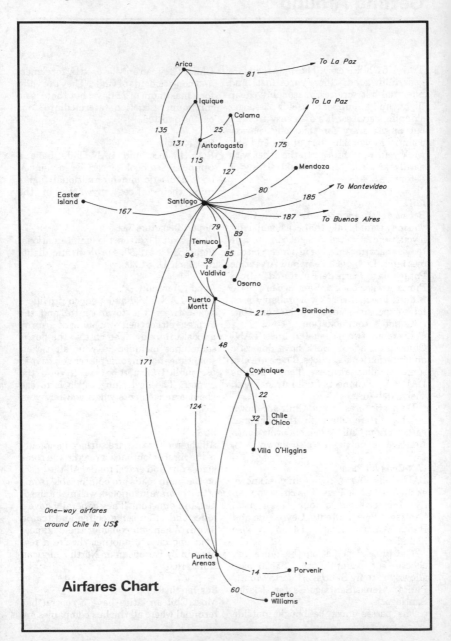

Arica

81 To La Paz

Iquique

Calama

To La Paz

135

131

25

175

115

Antofagasta

127

Mendoza

80 To Montevideo

Easter Island

167

Santiago

185

187 To Buenos Aires

79

89

Temuco

94

85

38

Valdivia

Osorno

Puerto Montt

21 Bariloche

48

171

124

Coyhaique

22

32

Chile Chico

Villa O'Higgins

One—way airfares around Chile in US$

Punta Arenas

14 Porvenir

60

Puerto Williams

Airfares Chart

gathered, although in some cities the bus companies have their own separate terminals. At the central bus terminals, the individual bus companies all have their own offices. The terminals are well organised and even if your Spanish isn't up to much it's a breeze finding the right ticket office since schedules and fares are always prominently displayed.

Reservations & Fares
You rarely need to book a ticket more than a few hours in advance. On really long trips, like Arica to Santiago, or on minor rural routes which are serviced by a single company (in the Lake District, for instance) it's a good idea to book seats in advance.

Fares vary from one company to the next and there are often promotion deals (ofertas) which can cut the normal fare in half. Student reductions of around 25% off the regular price are sometimes available. Fares between important destinations are listed throughout this book.

On weekends, public holidays and during the Chilean holiday season (around January and February) buses can be packed out – both on the main routes and the back roads. Sometimes the bus company will let you stand in the aisle if there are no seats available, but this depends on the company and the route.

Types of Buses
There are ordinary buses and sleeper buses. Sleeper buses (bus cama) have extra legroom, and reclining seats with calf and footrests similar to sleeperettes in 1st class on aircraft. These cost about twice as much as ordinary buses. The sleeper buses go on long hauls like Arica to Santiago, or Santiago to Puerto Montt and usually depart at night. Although the ordinary buses on these long routes are very comfortable, the sleeper buses are worth considering.

Things are a bit different on the back roads. Although the main roads and many of the minor roads are surfaced, that still leaves about 70,000 km which are gravel or dirt. Transport on these back roads is slower, the buses are less frequent, older and much more basic. You might get one or two buses a day between some small rural towns and they'll be packed like sardines with Mapuche Indians and their baskets of fruit and vegetables.

TRAIN
With the exception of the Arica to La Paz and Calama to La Paz lines which take you from Chile to Bolivia, there are no passenger services on the railways north of Santiago. The lines you see marked on maps of the north of the country are either goods lines, or disused lines which once linked the nitrate mining towns and ports.

The trains of interest to visitors are those from Santiago to Puerto Montt via Concepción and Osorno. There used to be regular passenger trains running from Santiago to Valparaíso, but at the time of writing these appear to have ceased.

Trains are worth considering if you're doing a long haul, but for short trips you'll generally find the buses much more frequent and convenient.

Santiago to Puerto Montt
The trains from Santiago to Puerto Montt run via Talca, Chillán, Temuco, Valdivia, Osorno and Puerto Varas. All trains going south from Santiago start from the Estación Central.

Tickets for these trains can be bought at the Estación Central and the ticket office is open daily until 10.30 pm. They can also be bought at the Venta de Pasajes Informaciones, in the Galería Libertador, Alameda O'Higgins 851; look for the yellow sign. This office is open Monday to Friday from 9 am to 6 pm, and on Saturday from 9 am to 1 pm.

Classes The trains have three classes: salón, economía and cama. Cama refers to 'sleeper' class, which has upper and

Distances by Road from Santiago

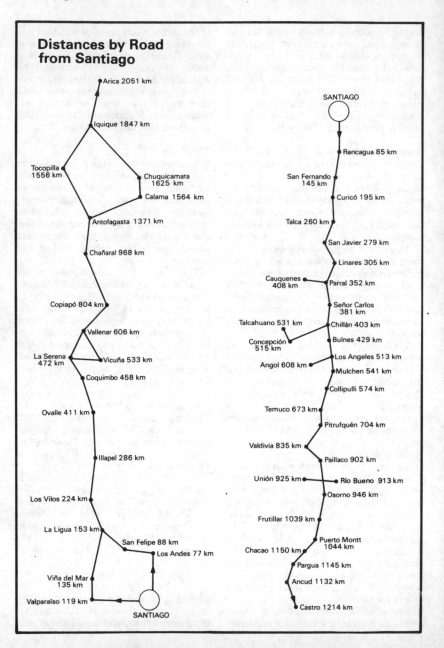

Arica 2051 km

Iquique 1847 km

Tocopilla 1556 km

Chuquicamata 1625 km

Calama 1564 km

Antofagasta 1371 km

Chañaral 968 km

Copiapó 804 km

Vallenar 606 km

La Serena 472 km

Vicuña 533 km

Coquimbo 458 km

Ovalle 411 km

Illapel 286 km

Los Vilos 224 km

La Ligua 153 km

San Felipe 88 km

Los Andes 77 km

Viña del Mar 135 km

Valparaíso 119 km

SANTIAGO

SANTIAGO

Rancagua 85 km

San Fernando 145 km

Curicó 195 km

Talca 260 km

San Javier 279 km

Linares 305 km

Cauquenes 408 km

Parral 352 km

Señor Carlos 381 km

Talcahuano 531 km

Chillán 403 km

Concepción 515 km

Bulnes 429 km

Los Angeles 513 km

Angol 608 km

Mulchen 541 km

Collipulli 574 km

Temuco 673 km

Pitrufquén 704 km

Valdivia 835 km

Paillaco 902 km

Unión 925 km

Río Bueno 913 km

Osorno 946 km

Frutillar 1039 km

Puerto Montt 1044 km

Chacao 1150 km

Pargua 1145 km

Ancud 1132 km

Castro 1214 km

Destination	Salón	Economía	Cama lower	Cama upper
Temuco	$10	$13	$28	$20
Valdivia	$11	$15	$28	$20
Osorno	$12	$16	$30	$22
Puerto Montt	$13	$17	$30	$22

lower bunks available. Lower bunks are more expensive than upper bunks. See the above table for approximate fares (in US dollars) from Santiago for these three classes.

It's worth getting a bunk on long overnight journeys. Santiago to Valdivia, for instance, takes 17 to 20 hours. Sleeper class is like something out of an old Hollywood movie, with wide bunks and thick blackout curtains. Very comfortable.

Timetable Departure times from Santiago may change so check an official timetable. There are a number of trains which go only as far as Chillán or Linares. Not all trains stop at every station. Train timetables are roughly as follows:

Train	Destination	Departure
Salón	Concepción	daily, 8.30 am
Expreso	Concepción	daily, 9 am
Salón	Concepción	daily, 1.30 pm
Expreso	Chillán	daily, 4 pm
Salón	Concepción	daily, 5.30 pm
Rapido	Puerto Montt	daily, 6.30 pm
Rapido	Valdivia	daily, 8 pm
Rapido	Temuco	Friday, 9 pm
Expreso	Puerto Montt	daily, 9.15 pm
Rapido	Concepción	daily, 10.30 pm

Approximate journey times from Santiago are:

Concepción	9 hours
Temuco	13 hours
Valdivia	17 hours
Osorno	18½ hours
Puerto Montt	20-22 hours

Auto Tren Fares
There are car trains which transport private cars. These are called *auto tren*. The cost of transporting a car from Santiago to Puerto Montt is about US$90.

BOAT
A road is currently being constructed which runs south from Puerto Montt and will eventually extend as far as Villa O'Higgins. There are now buses operating the stretch between Puerto Montt and Coyhaique. However, until the rest of the highway is finished you cannot get much further south than Coyhaique except by sea or by air. There are several useful sea routes along the Chilean coast. These are run by three main companies: Empremar, Navimag and Transmarchilay.

Puerto Montt to Puerto Chacabuco
Ships from Puerto Montt to Puerto Chacabuco (the jumping-off point for the connecting bus to Coyhaique) are run by Empresa Marítima del Estado (Empremar). For details of schedules and fares, see the Puerto Montt section in the Lake District chapter.

Empremar also has a tourist ship, the *Skorpios*, which takes sightseers to the Laguna San Rafael glacier. For details, see the Puerto Montt section in the Lake District chapter.

Inter-Island Ferries
Puerto Montt to Punta Arenas Ships from Puerto Montt to Punta Arenas are run by Naviera Magallanes (Navimag). These ships depart Puerto Montt about three times a month and take three days to get to Punta Arenas. For details of schedules and fares, see the Puerto Montt section in the Lake District chapter.

Chiloé Island to the Mainland There are

three connections between Chiloé Island and the mainland.

The first is with the Cruz del Sur ferries which operate between Chacao, at the northern tip of the island, and Pargua, across the straits on the mainland. For details of fares and schedules, see the Chiloé chapter.

The second and third connections are made by the Transmarchilay ferries which operate between Chiloé and Puerto Chacabuco and Chaitén. For details of fares and schedules, see the Chiloé chapter.

Patagonia & Tierra del Fuego There is a daily ferry link between Punta Arenas and Porvenir, the small town in Chilean Tierra del Fuego. For details of fares and schedules, see the Punta Arenas section in the Magallanes chapter.

DRIVING
The advantages of driving include freedom from timetables, the ability to stay wherever you like (particularly, if you bring camping equipment), the opportunity to get off the beaten track and the chance to stop when you see something interesting. In some places – like Easter Island – a car is definitely the best way to get around.

The chief disadvantages are expense and the difficulty of arranging safe garaging – particularly if you go trekking. Some people say that you isolate yourself by having a car because you don't have the opportunity to meet people on public transport. However, I have found that by having a car I've been able to pick up hitchhikers and meet people I would not otherwise have met. In Chile, this doesn't just mean backpackers – either Chilean or foreign – but also villagers, ranch workers and other people who have to hitch in areas where public transport is thin on the ground.

Car Rental
In Chile, you can either rent a car from one of the rental firms, or hire a taxi and driver for the day. Rates to hire a taxi are, of course, entirely negotiable. A number of international and local car rental firms operate in Chile. These include Hertz, Avis, National and Budget. The Automobile Club of Chile (Automóvil Club de Chile) also rents cars. Their addresses are listed throughout this book.

There is such a range of companies and rates that it's impossible to give an exact idea of how much you will have to pay for car hire. Hertz, for example, has small cars starting from US$15 per day, plus US$0.15 per km, plus insurance and 16% tax. A medium-size car costs from US$19 per day, plus US$0.20 per km, plus insurance and 16% tax. There are also weekend rates and discount rates if you hire for several days, a week or a month at a time. For example, the monthly rate for a medium car is about US$40 per day, plus insurance and 16% tax, but including 200 km free per day.

Budget has small cars from US$14 per day plus US$0.15 per km, plus insurance and 16% tax. Insurance rates are around US$8 per day, more with larger cars. If you rent a small car for one week you pay US$230 plus insurance and tax, but you get 1500 km free. There are, of course, other rates available depending on how long you rent for and the type of car you rent.

An example of how much you might pay: in the course of researching this book, I rented a medium-size Chevette from Budget in Calama. I drove from Calama to San Pedro, made several short side-trips, and then drove to Antofagasta via Calama. The total cost for four days was about US$250 plus petrol.

One-Way Rentals The larger companies like Hertz and the Automobile Club of Chile have offices in the major cities. Hertz, for example, can be found in all the major cities of the north, several cities in the Chilean heartland including Valparaíso and Santiago, and in Concepción, Temuco, Valdivia, Osorno, Puerto Montt and Punta Arenas in the south. The problem is that, except perhaps for the Automobile Club of Chile, the various offices of the car rental companies operate as independent franchises. This means that it is almost impossible to get a one-way rental. If you want to rent a car in Arica and drive it to Punta Arenas and leave it there, you will also have to pay for someone to drive the car back to Arica. Some offices will arrange this, but it makes the cost of renting cars shoot through the roof.

Petrol

Petrol is around US$0.35 per litre. There are two varieties: *93 octanos* is 'super', and *81 octanos* is 'regular'.

HITCHING

Both Chile and Argentina are pretty good for hitching – except south of Puerto Montt in Chilean and Argentine Patagonia where the distances are huge and the traffic is sparse. The time of the year is also an important consideration. You have more chance of getting a lift in the Lake District during the tourist season when there are more vehicles, but there is also more competition – young Chileans are really into hitching too! Bring some warm clothes with you; it can get *very* cold standing out on the roads in these places.

The usual warnings about hitching apply, of course, especially where women travellers are concerned.

The Atacama Desert

The Atacama is the most 'perfect' of deserts. There are areas where it has *never* been known to rain, and where no plant or animal life can be found or has ever been known to exist.

At higher altitudes, there are cacti which survive by drawing moisture from the thick fogs which occasionally descend on the desert. In some parts, the fog provides enough moisture for tiny oases called *lomas*, which attract birds and insects not commonly found in deserts. There is even one type of plant which grows underground, drawing enough light for photosynthesis through translucent sand.

Most of the water in the Atacama is provided by rivers which cut their way through the desert from the Andes, forming deep valleys along which agricultural settlements developed. For thousands of years the original Indian inhabitants fished along the coast or farmed along river valleys. Their most impressive creations were enormous murals (geoglyphs), made by grouping dark stones together on a light sand background, which decorate the barren mountain ridges. They include images of people, animals, geometric shapes and possibly even deities.

Northern Chile is part of South America's western coastal desert which extends northwards through Peru and into Ecuador. The southern boundary of the Atacama is the farming belt around Copiapó. Prior to the (ironically named) War of the Pacific in the 19th century, the desert to the north of Copiapó was Peruvian and Bolivian territory. Disputes over treaties, the presence of thousands of Chilean workers in the Bolivian mines, and attempts by Bolivia to increase taxation on mineral exports led to the War of the Pacific (1879 to 1883), in which Chile fought both Bolivia and Peru. In early 1880, after bloody fighting, the Chileans moved into Arica and Tacna. They went on to occupy Lima, which they held until 1883.

Chile gained the copper and nitrate-rich lands that are now the regions of Tarapacá (formerly Peruvian territory) and Antofagasta (formerly Bolivian territory). Tacna was eventually handed back to Peru. Arica has remained a Chilean port although Bolivia is permitted to export through it. Most of the large towns in the Atacama, such as Iquique and Antofagasta, owe their existence to the silver, gold, nitrates, copper and iron of this region. Mining towns like Humberstone, near Iquique, flourished during the nitrates boom, died when it ended, and are now ghost towns. Some of them are being repopulated as new extraction techniques make processing of low grade ore profitable.

One of the chief beneficiaries of the War of the Pacific was the British speculator, John Thomas North. In 1875, prior to the war, Peru expropriated nitrate holdings and issued bonds to their former owners. During the war, the value of these bonds plummeted and North, using capital obtained from the banks in Chile, bought as many as he could. After the war Chile decided to return ownership to the holders of the bonds, and John North found himself in a very healthy position. He then moved to gain control of all the other industries on which the nitrate industry depended. Before long he and his allies had turned Chile's new northern provinces into their private fiefdom.

The Chilean economy's dependence on nitrates and copper has meant that since the 19th century the Atacama has played an extraordinary role in determining the political fortunes of Chile. The wealth of the desert meant a steady flow of revenue into government coffers, which allowed

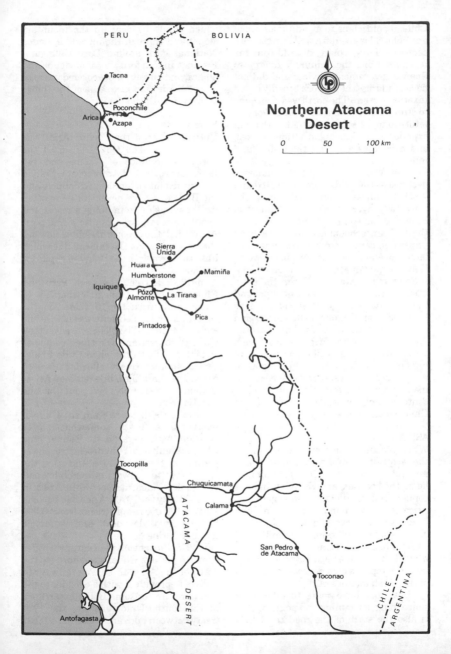

Northern Atacama Desert

Chilean politicians to avoid major social and political issues until well into the 20th century. They could depend on tax revenues from the mining industry to finance government services and did not have to address the idea of a broadly based taxation system. The north was also home to strong trade unions and when workers returned to the south they took with them experience of class organisation, strikes, and even massacres by the police and military.

After WW I, the nitrate industry declined as the fields were exhausted and synthetic nitrates (invented during the war) took over from natural nitrates. From then on copper became the basis of the Chilean economy, of which a large proportion came from the Atacama. The largest open-cut copper mine in the world is at Chuquicamata, near Calama.

South of the Atacama Desert there is a transition zone from desert to steppes and then to the fertile central valley. This transition zone was once called the 'region of 10,000 mines' and is also known as the 'little north' (norte chico). It was once a great silver mining region and is still an important copper and iron mining area. A number of rivers cross the region making agriculture possible, although it contains only a small percentage of Chile's total arable land.

ARICA

Where bloody battles were once fought for the acquisition of honour, desert and minerals, wealthy Bolivians now come to lie on the beaches, and Peruvian Indians come to sell handicrafts and vegetables. Arica is a year-round resort town, with beach weather every day of the year. There is never any rain. Despite its arid surroundings, Arica is an attractive place, nestled below a spectacular headland from the top of which are sweeping views of the ocean and desert.

Arica does have more to offer than sunbathing, swimming and politics. This is also the start of the road to Bolivia which winds its way up the mountain slopes and through the incredible Lauca National Park around Lago Chungará. Pre-Inca Indian forts, herds of vicuña and alpaca, and massive snow-covered volcanos on the border are just some of the things thrown in with the deal.

History

Until the War of the Pacific, Arica was part of Peru. The Chileans seized the Peruvian province of Tacna and the Bolivian province of Antofagasta. Bolivia was turned into a landlocked country and the Bolivians have never quite forgotten it! Today, aside from being a resort and peddler's town, Arica is also a free port. Almost half the exports of Bolivia flow out through Arica, via the railway line which links the town with the Bolivian capital of La Paz.

In 1883, a treaty between Peru and Chile recognised Chilean ownership of Tacna and Arica for 10 years, on the condition that a plebiscite was held at the end of that time. The plebiscite never took place of course, and the three countries squabbled until 1929 when Chile finally signed another treaty allowing Peru to recover Tacna while Chile retained Arica. Bolivia was simply left out of the negotiations.

Despite its distance from the Chilean heartland and its somewhat shaky position with regards to Bolivia, the Chileans built a large hydroelectric power station on the Río Lauca and used the electricity to power automobile and electronics industries set up in Arica in the 1960s. By the 1970s, Arica had become a city of 120,000 people (rising from 20,000 in just two decades) and a major manufacturing centre.

In 1975, Pinochet made a surprising offer to give a piece of Chilean territory (to the north of the Arica to La Paz railway) to Bolivia to provide it with a corridor to the sea, in return for some Bolivian territory to the south. Unfortunately, the 1929 treaty between Peru and Chile stated that neither country could cede any part of the Tacna region to Bolivia without the agreement of the other. Peru stopped the new scheme by proposing that a special zone (including Arica) be established and administered by all three countries. Chile backed off.

Information

Tourist Office The tourist office (tel 32101) is at Prat 375 (2nd floor) and is staffed by helpful people. They also have a useful map of the city. The office is open Monday to Friday from 8.30 am to 1 pm and 2.30 to 6.30 pm.

Post & Telecommunications The post office and TELEX Chile are in the same building at Prat 375. Long-distance phone calls can be made from ENTEL at Baquedano 388, near the corner with 21 de Mayo.

Banks Most of the moneychangers hang around the junction of 21 de Mayo and Colón. There are several permanent casas de cambio around the centre of town which will change US cash and travellers' cheques, as well as Peruvian, Bolivian and Argentine currency.

Consulates The Argentine Consulate is at Manuel Rodríguez 144, near the corner with Prat. The Peruvian Consulate is at Yungay 304, at the corner with Colón. The Bolivian Consulate is at 21 de Mayo 575, near the corner with Lagos.

Railway Memorabilia

There are a few reminders of earlier years around town, like the old German locomotive, vintage 1924, which used to pull trains on the Arica to La Paz line. It now stands in the Plazoleta Estación (also called the Parque Gral Baquedano) at the corner of 21 de Mayo and Pedro Montt. There is also a railway museum in the train station.

San Marcos de Arica Church

The Iglesia San Marcos de Arica was designed by Alejandro Gustavo Eiffel in 1875. This is the light-blue church which faces the Plaza Cristóbal Colón. Apart from his famous tower, Eiffel's achievements include the Estación Central in Santiago.

Museo Arqueológico San Miguel de Azapa

The Museo Arqueológico San Miguel de Azapa is in the Azapa Valley 12 km from the town. It has an excellent collection of exhibits which chronicle the various civilisations which have come and gone in the area, since the 7th century BC until the arrival of the Spanish.

The museum is open Monday to Friday from 9 am to 5 pm and on Saturday from 1 to 6 pm. To get there, take a taxi colectivo from the corner of Maipú and Patricia Lynch. Some of the local tour companies include the museum on their itineraries.

Beaches

Arica is one of the few places where you can catch some warm sea south of Ecuador. The best beaches are along the Avenida Costanera where there are a number of sheltered coves.

Places to Stay – bottom end

Many of Arica's bottom-end hotels are dirty and depressing. The cheapest place is the *Residencial Núñez* at Maipú 516, near the corner with Patricia Lynch. Rooms are US$2.50 per person. It's basic, has hot water, clean sheets but is otherwise glum.

The *Residencial Muñoz* at Patricia Lynch 565, near the corner with 18 de Septiembre, is ultra-basic and rundown. Ultra-shoestring travellers may find it tolerable at US$2.50 per person.

The *Residencial La Blanquita* (tel 32064) at Maipú 472 is clean and has hot water. It's good value at US$5 a single and US$10 a double. Of all the cheap places this is one which can be recommended.

Similar, and recommended by many travellers, is the *Residencial Madrid* (tel 31479) at Baquedano 685. It's also clean

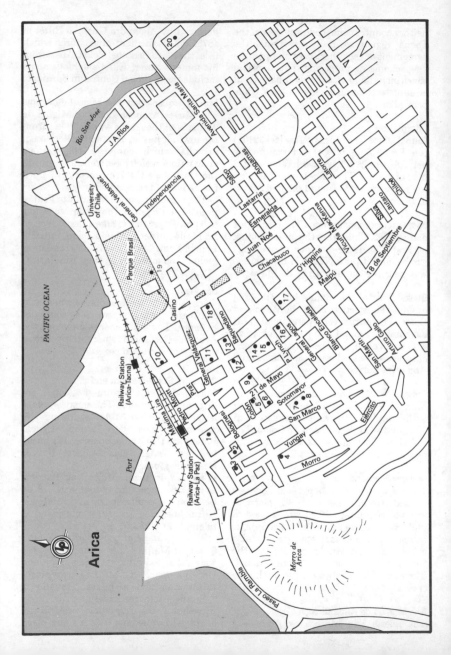

1	Tourist Office & Post Office
2	San Marcos Church
3	LAN-Chile
4	Peruvian Consulate
5	King Hotel
6	Hotel San Marcos
7	Residencial Sotomayor
8	Hotel Diego de Almagro
9	Ladeco
10	Argentine Consulate
11	Residencial Patricia
12	Hotel Aragon
13	Residencial Madrid
14	Residencial La Blanquita
15	Hotel Lynch
16	Residencial Núñez
17	Residencial El Cobre
18	Colectivos to Tacna
19	Hotel El Paso
20	Bus Terminal

and has hot water. Rooms are US$3 a single and US$6 a double.

Others which *may* be worth trying are the *Residencial Velásquez* at Velásquez 669, near the corner with Manuel Rodríguez; and the *Residencial Chillán* at Velásquez 719, also near Manuel Rodríguez.

Places to Stay – middle
One of the best places is the *Hotel Lynch* (tel 231581) at Patricia Lynch 589. Simple but clean rooms start from US$6.50/11 a single/double; US$20 with private bathrooms. It's a large place built around a central courtyard. Highly recommended.

Try the *Hotel Diego de Almagro* (tel 232927) on Sotomayor, just near the corner with Patricia Lynch. Bright, clean rooms with a private bathroom, TV, telephone and double beds are US$16/20 a single/double.

Similar to the Diego de Almagro, the *King Hotel* (tel 232094) is at Colón 376, near the corner with 21 de Mayo. Singles are US$14 and doubles are US$19. Another good place, used by foreign tour groups, is the *Hotel Savona* (tel 232319) at

Yungay 380. It has singles for US$13 and doubles for US$17.

The *Hotel Aragon* (tel 252088) is on Maipú, near the corner with Colón. It has bright motel-style rooms for US$16 a single and US$21 a double, all with private bathrooms. It can, however, be very noisy. Similar to the Aragon, but better situated, is the *Hotel San Marcos* at Sotomayor 367, near the corner with Baquedano.

Places to Stay – top end
At the top of the list is the *Hotel El Paso* (tel 31965) at Velásquez 1109, which is set in a pleasant garden. Rooms cost US$35 a single and US$39 a double.

Places to Eat
There are plenty of cafes along 21 de Mayo, 18 de Septiembre, Maipú, Bolognesi and Colón.

Typical of Arica's offerings is the cafe called *21* at 21 de Mayo 201, at the junction with Colón. It dishes up hamburgers, snacks, coffee and beer. There are other similar places along Bolognesi and Colón.

Arica, like other towns in northern Chile, has its share of Chinese restaurants. Try the *Chifa Chin Huang Tao* at Patricia Lynch 317. As far as Chinese restaurants go this place is fairly expensive but the food is good. Another Chinese place, with large servings, is the *Restaurant Shanghai* at Maipú 534, near the corner with Patricia Lynch.

For fish, there's the *El Rey del Marisco* in the Altos Mercado Colón. *Govinda's* at Bolognesi 367 is a vegetarian cafe.

Getting There & Away
From Arica you can head north to Tacna in Peru, south to Santiago or east to Bolivia.

Air Ladeco (tel 224412) is at 21 de Mayo 443. LAN-Chile (tel 231260) is at 7 de Junio 148, opposite the Plaza de Cristóbal Colón.

Ladeco has daily flights from Arica to Iquique, Antofagasta and Santiago. LAN-Chile has daily flights from Arica to Iquique and Santiago, and five days a week to Antofagasta.

The Santiago to Arica flight is one of the most spectacular in Chile, with awesome views of cliffs along the northern coastal desert.

Lloyd Aéreo Boliviano is at Patricia Lynch 298 at the corner with Sotomayor. They have three flights a week from Arica to La Paz.

Aero Perú has an agent in the basement at 7 de Junio 148, the same building housing the LAN-Chile office.

Bus & Colectivo - domestic The bus terminal is on Diego Portales at the junction with Santa María. It's quite a long way from the centre so take a taxi colectivo to get there.

Numerous companies operate buses out of Arica to destinations further south. There are day and night buses to Iquique (US$5, four hours), Antofagasta (US$13, 10 hours), Calama (US$9) and Santiago (US$32, 28 hours). Book a day or two in advance if possible, especially for the daytime buses.

Taxi colectivos to Iquique depart from the bus terminal. There are several companies and they each charge about US$8 per person.

Bus & Colectivo - international Two companies run buses to La Paz in Bolivia. These are Pullman Martínez at Pedro Montt 620, and Litoral at Chacabuco 454. Litoral has buses direct from Arica to La Paz twice a week. They take about 18 hours (possibly longer) and the fare is US$20 one way.

Several companies run taxi colectivos to Tacna. They leave throughout the day when full from Chacabuco, between Baquedano and Colón. The one-way fare to Tacna is about US$3.50 per person.

Fichtur has bus cama services from Arica (departing from the main bus terminal) to various Latin American destinations including Lima (US$30), Quito (US$68), Bogotá (US$114) and Caracas (US$158). They also have daily buses from Tacna to Lima for US$56.

Train From Arica there are regular trains to Tacna in Peru and to La Paz in Bolivia.

The railway station for trains to Tacna is at Máxima Lira 891. You need to turn up about half an hour before departure to give the officials time to get through exit formalities. There are departures twice daily for Tacna (usually around 12 noon and 6 pm) and the journey takes about 1½ hours. The fare is about US$2. You will generally find the colectivos much easier and more straightforward although the train could be interesting because of the many Peruvians who use it.

The railway station for trains to La Paz is in front of the Plazoleta Estación, at the corner of Pedro Montt and 21 de Mayo. The ferrobus service – a sort of bus on train bogeys – operates once a week. The trip takes about 11 hours and the fare is US$48.

The ordinary passenger train departs Arica for La Paz on the second and fourth Tuesday of each month. You must change trains at the border and this can take hours because there's a lot of smuggling going on and there are interminable bag searches. The changeover station is at about 4000 metres, so it can be snowing here even if it's baking in Arica. Don't use this route unless you have warm clothes! The fare from Arica to the border is around US$7. Generally, it's much better taking the buses on this route.

Getting Around
Local buses and taxi colectivos connect the town centre with the main bus terminal.

Cars can be rented from Hertz (tel 252373) in the Hotel El Paso at Velásquez 1109, American (tel 52234) at General

Lagos 559, and Viva (tel 251121) at 21 de Mayo 821.

Several tour companies operate in Arica. They have tours to the Lauca National Park, city tours of Arica, local archaeological sites, Tacna and Iquique. Several tour companies are listed in the section on the Lauca National Park.

LAUCA NATIONAL PARK

The Lauca National Park lies north-east of Arica beside the Bolivian border, at altitudes between 3000 and 6300 metres. It's a magnificent area, especially around Lago Chungará, which sits between two snow-capped volcanos and is supposedly the highest lake in the world. There's lots of wildlife in the park. Even on a short visit you'll see vicuña, alpaca, vizcacha, condor and waterfowl.

The Lluta Valley

The first place of interest en route to the park is the Lluta Valley just outside Arica

and on the road to Poconchile. On a mountain ridge on your right (as you head away from Arica) you can see a large mural of Indian geoglyphs – pictures made by grouping dark stones together against light-coloured sand. Images of alpaca, people and what appear to be birds (possibly condors) can be seen.

Poconchile

At the side of the road there is an adobe church, originally built in the 17th century, reconstructed in the 19th, and restored during this century. This is one of the oldest churches still standing in Chile. As the road climbs higher up the side of the desolate mountains you look down into the deep, narrow river valley of

Alpacas

Poconchile and its corridor of agricultural land. As you turn away from the river valley and start climbing into the mountains you can look down and see a strip of cleared land resembling an aircraft runway. It is not known who built it, or when, or why it was constructed.

The Old Road

For quite a distance the road follows a dry river bed that looks as if it hasn't seen water for centuries. About 50 years ago, a road was built in the river bed on the assumption that water would never again run in it – a freak flood washed the road away, although some pieces of it can still be seen.

Candle-Holder Cactus

Between 1300 and 1800 metres in altitude you'll see the appropriately named 'candle-holder' cactus (*cactus candelabros*). These cacti grow just five to seven *millimetres* a year and flower for 24 hours

Candle-holder cactus, Atacama Desert

just once a year. The cacti, and other plants, take their moisture from the fog which descends on the mountains and from humidity in the air. There is no ground water and no rain, although you will often see clouds.

Copaquilla

At Copaquilla there is a restored Indian fortress, which predates the Incas by 200 years, and was built to protect Indian farmlands in the valley below. Copaquilla is the name of the valley, and the fortress is set on a clifftop above it.

The Park

After Copaquilla, the road winds its way around the mountains until you gradually leave the desert. The candle-holder cacti disappear and at 2000 metres you enter the National Park. Although it's bone dry at low altitudes, at high altitudes it can snow during summer. Watch out for the llama, vicuña, alpaca, pink flamingo, and huemuelle herds. Alpaca are kept by the local Indians and their fleece is shorn and made into gloves, ponchos and hats, some of which are sold to tourists. The Indians at the village of Parincota sell beautiful ponchos and clothing made from alpaca wool.

Getting There & Away

The park is about 120 km from Arica and straddles the Arica to La Paz highway. The drive from Arica takes about four hours. The cheapest way of getting to the park is to take the Arica to La Paz bus and get off near Lago Chungará, where there is a refugio. Take food and warm clothing with you. The refugio may not be open in winter.

There are also day tours available from tourist agencies in Arica. Payachatas at Bolognesi 330, near the corner with Sotomayor, has day tours which leave Arica around 7.30 am and return around 8.30 pm. The cost is US$20 per person. Jurasi Tour at Bolognesi 370 organise the same trips.

Although a tour is one way of getting a glimpse of the park, you do tend to spend most of the time sitting on the bus. You 'see' the park, the animals and some small villages, but it's probably true to say that a day trip is not a very rewarding experience. If you are able to spend more time in the park you should be able to arrange for the tour company to drop you off at the refugio and take you back to Arica several days later.

You could also rent a car in Arica and drive to the park, but you'll be going higher than 4000 metres and you may feel the effects of altitude sickness. Although Lago Chungará is 4500 metres above sea level, you have to cross a 5000 metre high pass to get there. Take warm clothing! It can be blisteringly hot in Arica but snowing in the park.

IQUIQUE

During the 19th century, the products of the mining towns were shipped out through port towns like Antofagasta and Iquique, now large towns of well over 100,000 people each. It's hard to imagine that in the last century many of the port towns were not much more than a collection of tin shanties huddled at the base of barren cliffs, fed with minerals by railway lines stretching like umbilical cords into the interior.

At Iquique and Antofagasta, the wealthy built luxurious mansions (many can still be seen), water was piped in over long distances from the valleys, and topsoil was imported for the obligatory central plaza and private gardens. Eventually, these towns were as comfortable for the rich to live in as those further south. Iquique is a good example with its Plaza de Armas complete with a clock tower and a 19th-century theatre with corinthian columns, and many stately homes. Nearby ghost towns like Humberstone, and rusting nitrate-ore crushing plants are the last reminders of where the wealth came from.

Iquique is still one of the largest ports

Iquique's 19th century theatre

and towns of the north, but it has a very different feel to the other towns at this end of the country. It's ringed by packing-crate houses and its beaches are buffeted by powerful waves and awesome rips. During the day it's blisteringly hot and every night the town centre is as loud as New Year's Eve. Convoys of honking cars advertise marriages and strip joints, pick-up bars and other places of solace continue to ply their trade. Amidst the party the cheap hash-houses are filled with loners eating and drinking and whiling away the time watching TV.

On the roads heading northwards out of Iquique, you see innumerable crosses and roadside shrines plastered with the number plates of fallen highway heroes. It's all a bit inappropriate for a town whose name is said to be derived from an Indian word meaning 'rest and tranquillity'.

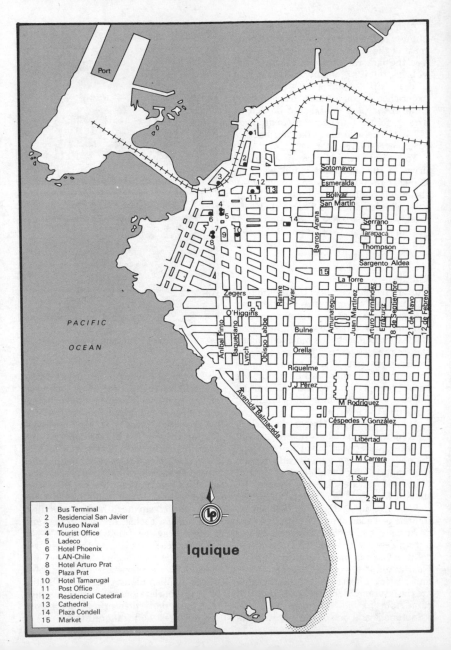

Iquique

1 Bus Terminal
2 Residencial San Javier
3 Museo Naval
4 Tourist Office
5 Ladeco
6 Hotel Phoenix
7 LAN-Chile
8 Hotel Arturo Prat
9 Plaza Prat
10 Hotel Tamarugal
11 Post Office
12 Residencial Catedral
13 Cathedral
14 Plaza Condell
15 Market

Information

Tourist Office The tourist office is at Pinto 436, next to the Ladeco office and opposite the Hotel Phoenix. They have a free leaflet which tells you what's on in Iquique including concerts, films, sports and other events.

Post & Telecommunications The post office is on Bolívar, between Labbe and Patricia Lynch. It's open Monday to Friday from 8.30 am to 12.30 pm and 3 to around 7 pm; Saturday from 9 am to 1 pm. The telephone office is at the corner of Tarapaca and Ramirez.

Bank The Banco de Chile is on Prat, facing the Plaza Prat, and will change foreign currency and travellers' cheques. It's open Monday to Friday from about 9 am to 2 pm.

Museo Naval

It's worth checking out the Navy Museum at the junction of Esmeralda and Pinto. It's open Tuesday to Saturday 9.30 am to 12.30 pm and 2.30 to 6 pm, and on Sunday and holidays from 10 am to 1 pm; entrance costs about US$0.20.

Regional Museum

The Regional Museum is at Sotomayor 706 and is interesting and well laid out. There's even a mock Indian village out the back with mud-brick houses and mannequins dressed in Indian costumes. There's a large collection of Indian relics including raft and canoe paddles, fishing hooks and sinkers, rope, fishing harpoons, arrows and arrow holders made of animal hide. There are also several disintegrating Indian mummies on display rather less intact than the ones you can see in the museum at San Pedro de Atacama. One of the bodies in the Iquique museum has a deliberately malformed, elongated skull. There's also an exhibition of Indian ceramics and weaving, and photos of the early days of Iquique. The museum is open Monday to Friday 9 am to 1 pm and 3 to 7 pm, and on Saturday from 10 am to 1 pm. Admission is about US$0.25.

Beaches

The Playa Bravo is a large beach, but it's far too rough for swimming, with big, dumping waves – bring your air-tanks and personal life-saving squad because this place really lives up to its name. It's a long stretch of greyish-white sand, not bad for sunbathing. The easiest way to get there is by taxi colectivo from the centre of town – US$0.40 per person. Further up and around a rocky headland is the Playa Cavancha, which is good for swimming, but rather crowded and not terribly attractive.

Places to Stay – bottom end

There's a cluster of residencials on Amunategui between Sargento Aldea and Thomson: the *Residencial Victoria* at 770 is US$2.50 per person; the *Residencial Viena* at 729 is US$2 and is not bad – spartan but clean, and the people are friendly; and the *Residencial Lucerna* at 723 is US$2 per person. There are one or two others but they're almost all permanently full with workers. If you're really on an ultra-low budget then give them a try – the Viena is definitely worth a look.

My pick of the residencials in Iquique is the *Residencial José Luis* at San Martín 601, at the corner with Ramírez. Singles are US$7 and doubles are US$10, with private bathrooms; it has cool, clean rooms, all with large double beds.

My next choice would be the *Residencial Catedral* on Labbe, opposite the large cathedral. Singles are US$7, doubles are US$10, and doubles with a private bathroom are US$15. There are two levels of rooms set around a pleasant courtyard and garden, and both the rooms and bathrooms are very clean.

Try the *Residencial Peterson* at Patricia Lynch 1257 which is US$5 a double, including bathrooms. The hotel is OK and the people are friendly; it may do for the night but I'm not overly keen on it.

The *Hotel España* at Tarapacá 465, near the Plaza Prat, can't really be recommended although you may be able to tolerate it for a night or two. You should think about taking a room with a bathroom, because the common bathrooms are fairly scungy. The hotel itself resembles a large warehouse divided into small boxes and you should bring a pair of earplugs to guard against the hordes of kiddies as well as the permanent residents' TVs punching through the thinly partitioned walls. Rooms without private bathrooms are US$3.50 a single and US$7 a double; rooms with private bathrooms are US$7 a single and US$12 a double.

Two cheap places near the bus station which may be worth trying are the *Residencial Esmeralda* at the corner of Esmeralda and Lynch, and the *Residencial Aluimar* at San Martín 486, between Lynch and Obispo Labbe.

Places to Stay - middle
One of the best places in Iquique is the *Hotel Phoenix* (tel 21315) at Aníbal Pinto 451. The simple rooms are clean and bright and the people are friendly. Singles are US$10, doubles are US$17, including a private bathroom and breakfast. There's a restaurant and pool hall on the ground floor.

Although it's a bit of a walk out of the centre, the *Hotel Barros Arana* (tel 24420) at Barros Arana 1330, near the corner with Orello, is well worth the effort. Singles with a bathroom are US$13, and doubles are US$20. They're clean, fresh-looking rooms all with TVs and private bathrooms. Highly recommended.

Places to Stay - top end
One of Iquique's top hotels is the *Hotel Arturo Prat* (tel 21414) on Pinto facing the Plaza Prat. Singles are US$37 and doubles are US$45.

The *Hotel Tamarugal* is at Tarapacá 639, just near the corner with Prat. Singles with private bathrooms and TVs are US$33 and doubles are US$40 - it's on a par with the *Barros Arana* which is half the price so the main advantage of staying at the Tamarugal is that you're in the centre of town.

At the Playa Cavancha is the *Hotel Cavancha* (tel 21158) on Los Rieles 250 which has rooms from US$37 a single and US$50 a double - or US$70 a single and US$85 a double for rooms facing the beach. The price includes breakfast. The beach is hardly scenic and I wouldn't troop down to Iquique just for a swim.

Places to Eat
Try the Chinese restaurants around town - there are lots of them. The *Chifa Chai-Wha* at Thomson 917 is very cheap and you can get a simple Chinese meal for around US$2.50 per person. Also very cheap and with generous helpings is the *Restaurant Chifa Can Loon* at Tarapacá 780. Others are the *Chifa Tung Fong* on Tarapacá between Barros Arana and Amunategui, and the *Chifa Ming Wang* at Barros Arana 668, near the corner with Thomson.

The city's trendiest snack bar is probably the *Restaurant Garbo* (an unfortunate coincidence, but *garbo* is actually a Spanish word meaning elegant) on Tarapacá between Barros Arana and Vivar. *La Merienda*, on Tarapacá between Barros Arana and Amunategui, has very filling humitas.

On the Plaza Prat at the corner of Prat and Tarapacá, the *Jugoslavenski Dom Club Social* is worth trying; its menu includes seafood. The place you should not miss is the illustrious *Club Español* two doors down on Prat; its incredibly ornate interior is painted in Moorish style and eating in the dining room is like eating inside an Arabian painting. A meal at the *Club Español* will set you back about US$9 to US$12 per person. If you can't afford the meal prices you should at least visit for a drink and gaze at the decor through an alcoholic haze.

The *Restaurant Circolo Italiano* at Tarapacá 477 serves pasta. Try the

Sociedad Protectora de Empleados de Tarapacá at Thomson 207, at the corner of Thomson and Pinto facing the Plaza Prat – it's open to foreign tourists.

Getting There & Away
Air Ladeco (tel 24794) is at the corner of Pinto and Serrano, facing Plaza Prat. LAN-Chile (tel 21479) is at the corner of Pinto and Tarapacá, facing Plaza Prat. Ladeco has flights from Iquique to Antofagasta (three days a week); Arica (daily); and Santiago (daily). LAN-Chile has flights from Iquique to Arica (daily); and Santiago (daily).

Bus There are numerous bus companies with offices at the bus terminal on Patricia Lynch. There are several bus companies which run day and night buses to Santiago and Arica. Most of these bus companies also have an office in town, so there's no need to walk all the way out to the bus station for tickets.

Typical fares from Iquique are: Antofagasta, US$11; La Serena, US$22; Valparaíso, Viña del Mar and Santiago, US$28; Arica, US$5.50; Calama, US$6.10.

For taxi colectivos to Arica, try Agencia Turistaxi at Barros Arana 897A, at the corner with Latorre; there are several vehicles per day in that direction. Bus companies, the addresses of their offices, and the destinations they service are:

Fénix Pullman Norte, Pinto 531 next to the Hotel Phoenix, and Barros Arana 881; to Santiago and Arica.
Buses Carmelita, Barros Arana 831; several departures daily to Arica and to Santiago.
Bus Julita St Rosa, Barros Arana 831; daily to Pica and, except on Sundays, to Mamiña.
Buses Ramos Cholele, Barros Arana 851; daily to Santiago.
Kenny Bus, Amunategui, near the corner with Sargento Aldea; to Calama, departing about 9 pm daily and arriving in Calama about 5 or 6 am.
Buses Cuevas & González, Sargento Aldea, between Amunategui and Barros Arana; several departures daily to Arica, daily to Calama and Chuqui.

Getting Around
For tours of the surrounding region try Iquitour at Tarapacá 465, next to the Hotel España. They have tours, every day except Sunday, departing about 9.30 am, which go to Pica, Humberstone, Santa Laura, Museo Pozo Almonte, La Tirana, Hayca, Canchane and Matilla. They cost US$15 and include lunch. They also have tours to the Termas de Mamiña, Santa Laura and Humberstone. Unfortunately – and inexplicably – there seem to be no tours which take in Sierra Unida.

It should be possible to arrange a one-day tour with a taxi driver for around US$42 to US$47 (perhaps rather less if you're a better bargainer) covering Sierra Unida, Pintados, Humberstone, La Tirana and Pica.

AROUND IQUIQUE
There are a number of geoglyphs near Iquique, including the mural sprawled across the side of the mountain ridge at Pintados, and the enormous image of a man, on the side of a hill known as Sierra Unida.

The Atacama is not the only place where giant images can be found. Huge men delineated by stones can be found near Blyth in California. They are almost impossible to detect from ground level and are clearly meant to be seen *from above*.

The desert between the Nazca and Ica valleys of Peru is criss-crossed by a vast picture book of lines, geometric figures and images, made by clearing away a layer of dark-brown stones to expose lighter-coloured soil beneath. Of all the known images designed on the ground these are the most extravagant. Some of the lines run for several km, unswervingly straight over plateaux and mountains, while others form giant enclosures (some say like runways). Like the Blyth figures, they seem to have been laid out to be viewed from above.

Nor are such images found only in the Americas. At least 50 giant figures are known in England. They were made by exposing the chalk which lies just beneath the turf, particularly in the West Country. In England, however, the designs were laid out on hillsides and can be clearly seen from ground level.

One theory explains the Nazca lines by proposing that the Indian designers could fly using hot air balloons made with rope and cloth. Others theories suggest that the designs represent an enormous observatory, with the lines aligned with the rising and setting of celestial bodies and the animal figures representing the constellations. But it seems only a small number of lines were aligned with stars and planets, allowing for the date the designs were laid out. The simplest theory is that the designs are meant to be seen by gods, not by people.

The Chilean geoglyphs, like the designs in England, are made on the sides of mountains rather than on flat desert plains, and can be viewed from the ground. It is not known how long ago the figures and designs were made or who or what they represent. One theory is that the Chilean geoglyphs were once signposts for Inca or pre-Inca traders. The giant figures may represent celestial beings or mythological figures, but it's always possible that they were produced without any religious or mystical motivation at all. They may simply be an artistic creation by a desert-dwelling people who used the materials which were available to them – dark stones on a canvas of light-coloured desert sand.

The Giant of the Atacama

The Giant of the Atacama, laid out on the slope of Sierra Unida, is the largest representation of a human figure in the world – a massive 120 metres long!

Twelve rays emanate from the human figure's head (which is square and supported by a thin neck), four from the top and four from each side, the eyes and mouth are square, the torso is long and narrow, the arms are bent (one hand

The Giant of the Atacama

appears to be an arrowhead), the size of the feet suggest the figure is wearing boots, and there are odd protrusions from the knees and thighs.

At its side is another odd creature sporting what appears to be a tail – perhaps a monkey, although others interpret it as a reptile of some sort. The two figures are set amidst a complex of lines and circles, and on one side of the hill (facing the Huara-Chuzmisa road, visible as you approach the hill) there are a number of enormous clearings resembling runways.

The Huara-Chuzmisa road is surfaced, as is the Arica-Iquique highway. Only the very short stretch (about a km) of road leading from the Huara-Chuzmisa road to the hill itself is across the desert. The only way to visit the site is to hire a car or taxi in Iquique (forget about hitching).

Strangely, very few Chileans seem to have an accurate idea of the location of the

Top: Landscape, near San Pedro de Atacama, Atacama Desert
Bottom: Road between Lago Chungara and Arica, 4000 metres above the
Atacama Desert

Top: Church at Parincote, Lago Chungara, Atacama Desert
Bottom: Valley of the Moon, near San Pedro de Atacama, Atacama Desert

Giant of the Atacama. When I was trying to find it I was given vague estimates of its location which ranged between Arica and Antofagasta, until the tourist office in Iquique finally came good. For some reason, the ordinarily reliable *Gran Mapa Caminero de Chile*, which shows innumerable geoglyph sites, makes no mention of either the Sierra Unida or Pintados sites.

The best views of the giant would be from the air but the whole figure – including the head – can be clearly made out if you stand several hundred metres back from the base of the hill. Avoid climbing the hill since doing so damages the pictures. The hill itself is completely alone on an immense desert plain.

Pintados

This is one of the biggest outdoor murals in the world – the whole side of a mountain ridge is adorned with some 390 individual geoglyphs grouped in 60 panels. From close up it is almost impossible to discern what most of the figures represent, but from a distance you can make out images of people, llamas, circles, squares, chequerboard patterns and even a gigantic arrow. Try to refrain from climbing up the mountain ridge and over the geoglyphs as this will inevitably damage them.

Pintados lies some distance off the Iquique-Antofagasta highway. It's actually a derelict railway yard with a number of ruined buildings and rusting rolling stock still on the dilapidated rails. The mountain ridge forms a huge barrier behind this old settlement, running roughly parallel with the highway. The only way to visit this site is by car, taxi or tour from Iquique.

Humberstone

A former nitrate-mining town and now an eerie ghost town, Humberstone is on the Iquique-Arica highway about 47 km due east of Iquique. It's now totally deserted apart from curious tourists and some scrap metal merchants. Walk around and you'll find the main plaza flanked by a large theatre, a church and a market. Almost all the original buildings are still

A rusting steam locomotive, Humberstone

standing, although they're crumbling into dust.

At one end of the town, the electrical generating plant still stands and you can see the remains of the train line running across the desert to the Oficina Salitera Santa Laura (the ore crushing plant) in the distance just to the side of the road to Iquique. A rusting steam locomotive, railway cranes, shovels, wheelbarrows – many things have been left as if everyone deserted the town simultaneously. With a bit of imagination you can almost see the ghosts.

Humberstone is not the only ghost town in the Atacama Desert. Some are now being repopulated as modern processing techniques make excavation of low grade ores profitable.

CALAMA

Calama sits on the high plain in the middle of the Atacama Desert. This is the commercial centre for the nearby open-cut copper mines of Chuquicamata, the largest in the world. Coming up from Antofagasta you can see the smoke pouring out of the stacks at Chuquicamata for miles before you arrive. Calama is the jumping-off point for visits to the mine and to the oasis villages of San Pedro de Atacama and Toconao. It's also the terminus of the Calama to La Paz railway, used by many people on their way to and from Bolivia.

Information

Tourist Office The tourist office is at Latorre 1689, near the corner with Vicuña MacKenna. It's open Monday to Friday from 9 am to 1 pm and 2.30 to 7 pm, and Saturday 10 am to 1 pm.

Post & Telecommunications The post office is on the Plaza Héroes de la Concepción.

Banks You *cannot* change travellers' cheques in Calama or Chuqui in the banks, hotels or restaurants; you can only change US cash. To do this go to the Banco

de Chile on Vivar, just near the corner with Vargas, or to the Banco de Credito.

Places to Stay – bottom end

The *Residencial Toño* at Vivar 1968 has been popular with foreign visitors for years. It has clean sheets and provides lots of blankets. Rooms are US$3 per person. It's clean and fairly quiet, though a bit dingy. Don't expect too much.

The *Residencial Capri* (tel 212870) at Vivar 1639 is tolerable by low-budget standards. Rooms are US$3.20 a single and US$6.40 a double, and the rooms are generally clean but rather dingy. Reactions to this place are mixed; it satisfies some visitors but is definitely substandard for others.

The *Residencial Splendid* (tel 212141) at Ramírez 1960 is clean, homely and secure. It's popular with travelling salesmen and the like. Rooms are US$6 a single and US$11 a double. More expensive rooms have private bathrooms.

Another place I'd recommend is the *Residencial El Tatio* (tel 212284) at Gallo 1987, which has rooms at US$4 per person. It has hot water and the people are friendly.

One place recommended by several people is the *Residencial Internacional* on General Velásquez, near Vargas. It's clean, cheap and comfortable.

Places to Stay – middle

The *Hotel Atenas* is at Ramírez 1961. It has small, clean, neat rooms at US$7 a single and US$10 a double, although this does not include private bathroom.

A brighter place is the *Hostal El Sol* at Sotomayor 2064, with rooms for US$14 a single and US$19 a double.

Also worth trying is the *Hotel Casablanca* (tel 211722), opposite the main plaza, which has bright, neat double rooms for US$26.

Places to Stay – top end

At the top of the range is the *Hostería Calama* (tel 211511) at Latorre 1521. It

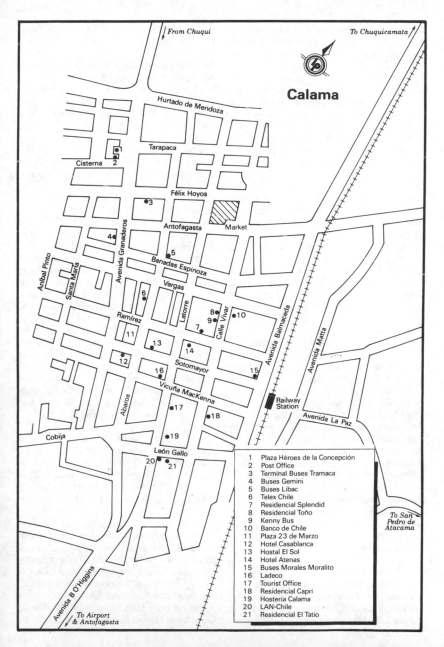

Calama

1   Plaza Héroes de la Concepción
2   Post Office
3   Terminal Buses Tramaca
4   Buses Gemini
5   Buses Libac
6   Telex Chile
7   Residencial Splendid
8   Residencial Toño
9   Kenny Bus
10 Banco de Chile
11 Plaza 23 de Marzo
12 Hotel Casablanca
13 Hostal El Sol
14 Hotel Atenas
15 Buses Morales Moralito
16 Ladeco
17 Tourist Office
18 Residencial Capri
19 Hostería Calama
20 LAN-Chile
21 Residencial El Tatio

has rooms for US$33 a single and US$41 a double, which includes a private bathroom and breakfast. It's a very pleasant place.

Places to Eat

There are dozens of bars, restaurants and holes-in-the-wall around the main plaza and streets in the centre of town. Sotomayor and Ramírez are two good streets for hunting down restaurants.

One of the more interesting places for food is the local market, with its entrance on Antofagasta near the corner with Latorre. Look for a peculiar Chilean cheese known as *quesillo*, and an apple-like fruit called *membilla*. Thick, fresh fruit juices are sold here. If you're hoping to lose weight you might check out the so-called 'dieting tea' – the illustrations on the plastic packets tell all!

The *Hotel Restaurant Victoria*, at Vargas 2102 on the corner of Abaroa, is an average price cheapie with meals for a few dollars. Similar is the *Restaurant Osorno*, upstairs at Granaderos 2013B, near the corner with Espinoza.

For Chinese food try the *Restaurant Tong Fong* on Ramírez between Granaderos and Santa María, and the *Restaurant Chi Kang* at Vivar 2037, near the corner with Espinoza.

The *Club Yugoslavia* on Abaroa, facing the Plaza de 23 Marzo, is a slightly more up-market place. Around the corner from the plaza is the *Bavaria Restaurant*, at the corner of Sotomayor and Abaroa. Although Bavarian in name only, it's a pleasant enough place to laze around.

Getting There & Away

From Calama you can head north to Iquique and Arica, south to Antofagasta, east by train to Bolivia, or by bus to Salta in Argentina.

Air Ladeco (tel 211355), at Vicuña MacKenna 2016, has daily flights from Calama to Antofagasta, Iquique and Santiago. LAN-Chile (tel 211394), at the corner of Latorre and Gallo, has flights six days a week from Calama to Antofagasta and Santiago.

Bus The various bus companies have their offices scattered around Calama.

Typical fares from Calama are: Arica US$9, Iquique US$7, Santiago US$24, Calama US$7, Antofagasta US$4, San Pedro de Atacama US$2.50 and Toconao US$4.

Tramaca is on Felix Hoyes, near the corner with Granaderos. They have numerous buses daily to Antofagasta. They also have several buses daily to Santiago, Arica and Iquique, and twice daily to San Pedro de Atacama.

Flecha Norte is at the corner of Ramírez and Balmaceda. They have daily buses to Santiago via Antofagasta and Copiapó.

Buses Gemini is on Granaderos near the corner with Espinoza. They have daily buses to Santiago, Antofagasta, Arica and Iquique. Every Wednesday they have a bus from Calama to Salta in Argentina. The one-way fare to Salta is US$33. They have buses to San Pedro de Atacama on Sundays only. Buses Libac is at the corner of Espinoza and Abaroa. They have daily buses to Santiago and Antofagasta.

Buses Morales Moralito is at the corner of Balmaceda and Sotomayor in Calama. They have buses to San Pedro and Toconao three days a week.

Train There is normally a ferrobus and an ordinary train service from Calama to La Paz in Bolivia. Tickets can be bought from either the Buses Tramaca terminal or from the train station, which in Calama is on Balmaceda, at the top end of Sotomayor.

At the time of writing both services had been suspended. Normally, the ferrobus departs Calama for La Paz every Friday; the one-way fare is US$64. The ordinary train normally departs Calama for La Paz on Wednesday afternoons and the journey takes about 36 hours. If the trains are running, take your passport when buying tickets and make sure you have a Bolivian visa if you need one. At the time of writing it appears the Bolivian Consulate in Calama had closed, so you may have to go to the Bolivian Consulate in Antofagasta. Temperatures can drop way below freezing so don't take this train unless you have warm clothing.

Getting Around
There are a number of car rental companies in Calama. Possibly the best is Budget (tel 211076) at Punta de Diamante. Hertz (tel 211380) is at Latorre 1510.

THE CHUQUICAMATA COPPER MINE
Chile is the biggest copper producer in the world and production has been steadily increasing all through this century. Copper mining in Chile during the 20th century has relied on the bulk mining of relatively low grade ore using foreign capital, and techniques originally developed in the copper mines of the western USA.

In 1911, the huge Chuquicamata deposit was discovered. The original owners sold it to the US Anaconda Company and in 1916 excavations began. Today, it is the largest open-cut copper mine, and the largest single supplier of copper in the world. The pit is 350 to 400 metres deep and is responsible for half of Chile's total copper output and at least 25% of Chile's total annual export income.

The scale of the Chilean copper industry has given it remarkable importance in the politics of the country. By the 1960s, the three largest mines accounted for over 80% of Chile's copper production, over 60% of the total value of exports and 80% of government revenue from taxes. With the Chilean economy so tightly wrapped up with the production of copper, the idea of nationalising the copper industries inevitably developed. Leftists in the National Congress – including Allende – introduced nationalisation bills in the early 1950s, but support for nationalisation also grew amongst the Christian Democrats and other non-leftist parties. In the late 1960s, during the Christian Democrat government of President Frei, Chile

The Chuquicamata copper mine

gained a majority shareholding in the Chilean assets of the Anaconda and Kennecott companies.

In 1971 the Congress, including the members of the right-wing National Party, voted unanimously in favour of nationalising the copper industries. After the overthrow of Allende in 1973, agreement was reached between the US companies and the new military government about compensation for the loss of their mines. The US companies have since returned, though the large mines are still run by the state Corporación del Cobre de Chile (CODELCO) company.

Copper-Processing

Chuquicamata mines low grade copper ore and it is only because such large quantities of material are processed that production is economical.

The ore is quarried by blasting and power shovel work. At the mining stage, material is classified as ore or waste depending on the copper content. The material with sufficiently high metal content is dumped into a crusher, beginning a treatment process which reduces it to fine particles. The metal is then separated from the rock by a flotation process.

The flotation process separates and concentrates the copper. This is done using chemically induced differences in surface tension to carry it to the surface of pools of water. The large pools of blue solution at the processing works are the concentrators where this process is taking place. The copper concentrate is turned into a thick slurry from which the copper is finally extracted by heating it in the smelters.

Tours

The mine and smelter plant can be visited on three-hour guided tours on Monday, Wednesday and Friday. These leave at 1 pm from the Public Relations Office (Relaciones Públicas) in Chuquicamata. Bring your passport for identification.

Children under the age of 12 are not permitted on the tour. You have to wear proper shoes, long pants and a long-sleeved jacket if you want to go inside the smelter building. They generally provide the jackets, as well as helmets and protective glasses.

Getting There & Away

The Public Relations office is at Puerto Uno. To get there from Calama take a taxi colectivo from the corner of Abaroa and Ramírez at the Plaza de 23 Marzo. These take you to the central bus terminal in Chuqui, from where you have to get a local taxi colectivo the last two km to the Public Relations office. There are public buses from Calama to Chuqui, leaving Calama from the corner of Granaderos and Ramírez. They only go as far as the Chuqui bus terminal where you have to catch a taxi colectivo to the mine. All the long-distance bus companies have offices and terminals in Chuqui. You could tour the mine and get a bus straight back to Antofagasta if you don't want to hang around Calama. Check departure times and allow for the tour to run longer than expected.

SAN PEDRO DE ATACAMA

San Pedro de Atacama is an oasis village at the edge of the Salar de Atacama, a completely flat and almost dry salt lake. On the eastern side of the Salar rise enormous volcanos, some snow capped and smoking. From San Pedro you can see one of the highest extinct volcanos in the Andes, Licancábur, which rises some 5900 metres. Close to San Pedro is one of the weirdest places in the Atacama – the famous Valley of the Moon.

San Pedro is just one of the oasis villages in the region, but it is the most important. It's about 120 km south-east of Calama and lies about 2400 metres above sea level and has a population of about 1600. Almost all the dwellings are stone and mud brick. Many of them are enclosed in

San Pedro de Atacama

separate compounds by mud brick walls and others are built in long rows.

The villagers' income seems to come from a number of sources. Some work in the local sulphur mine, others are farmers. There are three or four hotels which cater to the tourist trade. Handicrafts, including wood carvings and woollen ponchos, are sold to tourists. It appears to be, to a large extent, a subsistence economy.

The Museum
The area around the village has been inhabited since prehistoric times. In 1955 the former village priest, Father Le Paige, with the help of villagers and the University of the North (in Antofagasta), began to put together one of the most remarkable and interesting museums in South America.

The museum gives an overview of the history and archaeology of the whole area, and an extraordinary range of Indian artefacts and remains are on display. Some of the most interesting are the mummies of Indian children and adults,

including a child buried in a pottery urn, and skulls which show deliberate malformation. All the bodies are in a good state of preservation because they were buried in arid, salty soil. There are also fragments of ancient woven fabrics, pottery, tools, jewellery, and even a collection of paraphernalia for preparing, ingesting and smoking psychedelic plants and mushrooms. It's exceptionally well organised and cared for.

The museum is just near the main plaza. Admission is US$0.40.

Around the Plaza
Almost 450 years ago Chile's first unwanted European tourist, Pedro de Valdivia, came this way with his band of warriors. They brought everything they needed for the colonisation of a new country, including wheat, pigs and chickens, and agricultural tools. Valdivia set out from Cuzco in Peru with only 14 or 15 men, but others joined him along the way to make up a total of 150 Spanish soldiers. Peruvian Indians carried the supplies. Women and children also went

with the expedition, although there was only one Spanish woman among them, Inés Suárez, Valdivia's mistress.

On one side of San Pedro de Atacama's main plaza stands a restored adobe house, typical of the early colonial period, which was originally constructed in 1540, apparently for Valdivia. On the other side stands the local church. Originally built in the 16th century, it is one of the oldest churches in Chile. The present building makes use of local cactus wood, thatching, clay and large straps of leather instead of nails.

Places to Stay & Eat

For very cheap accommodation there are a couple of possibilities. The *Residencial La Florida*, just down from the plaza, is spartan but generally clean with sheets and blankets provided. It's run by a friendly family. They were once assisted by a bombastic parrot but he seems to have flown the coop. Rooms are about US$2 per person and good, cheap meals are available. My one criticism is that the bathrooms (cold showers only) and toilets need cleaning. The similar *Residencial El Pukara* is next door, with rooms for about US$2 per person.

As you come in to San Pedro, on the main road from Calama, you pass very near the *Residencial Chiloé*. It's similar to the Florida but the bathrooms are much cleaner. It costs US$4 per person and there's a restaurant attached.

In the centre of the settlement is the *Residencial Porvenir*, which has double rooms for US$10 with private bathroom. It's very basic, but clean and very agreeable. Across the road is another hotel worth trying, the *Hostal Takha Takha*. Both the Takha Takha and the Porvenir have restaurants.

The *Hostería San Pedro* has the best accommodation in the oasis. Rooms are a relatively modest US$20 a single and US$24 a double, which includes private bathroom. The hotel is run by an Australian woman and her Chilean husband. Together they've set up one of the best hotels in Chile. There's a swimming pool, restaurant and solar-heated hot water showers. It's popular with all kinds of visitors to San Pedro, including backpackers, tour groups and

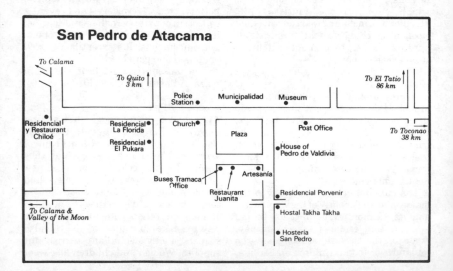

Valley of the Moon, near San Pedro de Atacama

even foreign film crews who find the nearby Valley of the Moon a captivating backdrop.

Other than the restaurants in the hotels, there is the *Restaurant Juanita* on the plaza. There are also a number of small shops in the village where you can buy bread, cheese, fruit, vegetables, wine, beer and canned food.

Things to Buy
There is a good craft shop on the plaza where you can find carved cactus wood and ponchos made from llama and alpaca wool. Crafts are also sold at the Hostería San Pedro and at Toconao village.

Getting There & Away
Buses Tramaca has a daily bus from Calama to San Pedro (US$3). The journey takes about 1½ hours along a surfaced road and offers spectacular vistas of snow-covered mountains and volcanos. The Tramaca office in San Pedro is by the main plaza. Buses Gemini has buses from Calama to San Pedro on Sundays only. Buses Morales Moralito has buses from Calama to San Pedro and Toconao three days a week.

Getting Around
Hector Ochoa Olivares, at Brasilia 1102 in San Pedro, runs tours in his Range Rover to places of interest around the oasis. Also enquire at the Hostería San Pedro.

AROUND SAN PEDRO DE ATACAMA
Valley of the Moon
On the other side of the Salar is the famous Valley of the Moon, so-called because its strange rock formations, sculptured by wind and water, make it look like a lunar landscape. The edge of the valley is about 10 km from the oasis. The best time to see the valley is during the full moon when the moonlight gives the reddish earth a strange glow and reflects off the salt crystals in the rocks and mounds. There is a road running straight through the valley. This starts from the main Calama to San Pedro road, cuts through the valley and carries on to San Pedro. It's motorable in an ordinary vehicle but if you come to stretches where

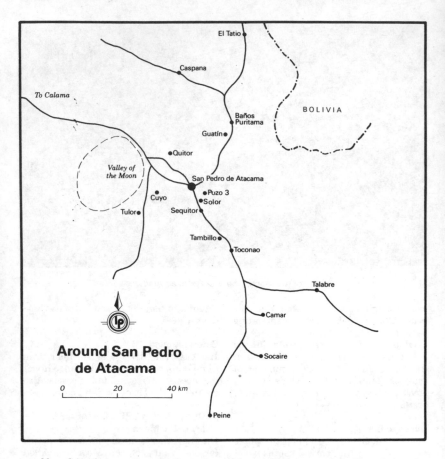

Around San Pedro de Atacama

0   20   40 km

sand has drifted across the road then turn back otherwise you *will* get bogged.

Quitor Ruins

Just three km north-west of San Pedro, bordering the river of the same name, is the ruin of an Indian fortress built over 700 years ago. From the top of the fortress you can see the whole of the oasis. The turret of this fortress was the residence of the last Indian chief of the area, and the fortress was also the last bastion against Pedro de Valdivia and the Spanish. Archaeologists have rebuilt parts of the ruined walls and

it's possible to gauge some idea of what the place once looked like.

Termas de Puritama

About 30 km from the village, en route to El Tatío, there are some hot springs, the Termas de Puritama.

There are no buses to the springs so, unless you have your own transport, you have to arrange transport with the drivers of the sulphur mine trucks. The sulphur mines are past the hot springs and the trucks leave San Pedro every day in the morning. You ride in the back of the truck and the journey takes about an hour (it's a rough ride). They'll let you off at a sign for the springs, on the left-hand side of the road. Pay the driver; don't use the trucks as a free taxi service.

From where you are put down, it's a 20-minute walk along an obvious gravel track down into a small canyon. If you drive your own car then park on the main road and walk down the track to the springs – don't take the car. The temperature of the springs is about 33°C and there are a number of waterfalls and pools. Bring food and water with you.

You can stay all night if you like but there's not much fuel for a fire – and it gets very cold! There are a number of ruined stone buildings for shelter. If you don't want to stay, then get back to the main road by 1 pm and flag down the first truck which comes by. On the return journey you may be dropped off several km short of San Pedro, at the mine's crushing plant, so you'll have to walk the rest of the way.

Walking along the dusty roads of the Atacama is hot, hard work! If you really want to go to the springs you are much better off taking a tour or hiring a car. Even then the road to the springs can be difficult for an ordinary vehicle, with lots of rocks and stretches of thick sand and gravel.

Toconao

The village of Toconao is about 40 km south of San Pedro. Most of the buildings in Toconao are built with volcanic rock. The church in the plaza, with its two-storey bell tower, dates back to the early 1600s. Toconao is a major fruit-growing oasis, noted for its grapes, pomegranates, apples and even herbs. The women of the village make and sell very fine llama wool ponchos, pullovers, gloves and socks. There are buses from Calama to Toconao, via San Pedro, although they arrive in Toconao late at night.

ANTOFAGASTA

With a population of 250,000, Antofagasta is the largest port and city on the coast of northern Chile. The port handles most of the nitrates and copper mined in the Atacama Desert, in particular, the copper from the mine at Chuqui.

The city is also an important import/export centre for Bolivia. Until the War of the Pacific it was actually a part of Bolivia; after the annexation by Chile, Bolivia was given duty free facilities for the export of its goods.

On a warm evening the centre of the city has a certain understated charm, but there's not much to see or do. For most visitors this city is just a jumping-off point for visits to the Atacama Desert or Bolivia.

Information

Tourist Office There is a tourist kiosk on Balmaceda at the junction with Prat. It's open Monday to Saturday from 9.30 am to 1.30 pm and 4.30 to 7.30 pm, and Sunday from 10.30 am to 2 pm.

Post & Telecommunications The post office and TELEX Chile are in the same building on Washington, between Prat and Sucre, opposite the main plaza. ENTEL is on Prat, near the corner with Matta.

Banks You may find some street money-changers on Prat but don't count on it. The Banco Estado de Chile on the corner of San Martín and Prat seems to be the only bank which will change US dollar travellers' cheques and cash.

Consulates The Argentine Consulate is at Manuel Verbal 1632. Manuel Verbal branches off Grecia, which runs along the beach front. The Bolivian Consulate is in Office 23, Grecia 563.

Places to Stay – bottom end

The *Residencial Paola* (tel 222208) at Prat 766 has rooms for US$3 per person. It's very clean, well kept and relaxing with rooms arranged around a central lounge.

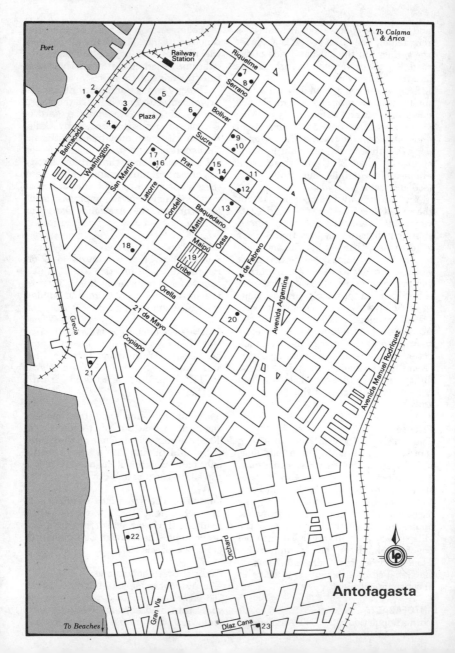

Antofagasta

1	Hotel Antofagasta
2	Tourist Office
3	Post Office & Telex Chile
4	Ladeco
5	LAN-Chile
6	Flecha Dorada
7	Hotel San Marcos
8	Residencial Astor
9	Buses Flota Barrios & Hotel Imperio
10	Residencial O'Higgins
11	Hotel Rawaya
12	Residencial El Cobre
13	Residencial Paola
14	ENTEL
15	Hotel Diego de Almagro
16	Hotel Plaza
17	Banco Estado de Chile
18	Hotel San Antonio
19	Main Market
20	Buses Tramaca
21	Bolivian Consulate
22	Argentinian Consulate
23	Bus Terminal

There's hot water all day and the people are very friendly. There is a similar place at Prat 776 with rooms for the same price

although it's not as well kept as the Paola.

The *Hotel Rawaya* (tel 225399) at Sucre 762 is friendly, clean and excellent value at US$3 a single and US$5 a double. There's hot water all day in the common bathrooms.

The *Residencial El Cobre* (tel 225162) on Prat, opposite the Residencial Paola, has clean but very small, dark rooms for US$4 a single and US$6 a double. It's a big place so you'll always find a room, but its only real attraction is the price. It's a bit squalid.

The *Residencial Astor* at Condell 2995 is worth trying. It's quite a decent place with a pleasant courtyard garden. Doubles are US$8, breakfast is available and there're hot showers in the common bathrooms.

Places to Stay – middle
The *Hotel San Marcos* (tel 22412) at Latorre 2946 has rooms for US$15 a single and US$20 a double with private bathroom. It's clean, has hot water and its own restaurant.

Antofogasta

The *Hotel Plaza* (tel 222058) is at Baquedano 461. Rooms start from US$15 a single and US$24 a double, with private bathroom and TV. The hotel has its own restaurant and bar and is a fairly quiet place.

Places to Stay - top end
The *Hotel Antofagasta* (tel 224710) on Balmaceda, at the junction with Prat, is the city's largest hotel and has rooms from around US$25 a single and US$28 a double.

Also worth trying is the *Hotel Diego de Almagro* (tel 222519) at the corner of Prat and Condell. Rooms are US$22 a single and US$30 a double.

Places to Eat
By far the best place to eat in Antofagasta is the *Sociedad Protectora de Empleados* at San Martín 2544, just off the main plaza. It's very popular with local people at lunch time because of the *enormous* meals. The service is great and the place is spotlessly clean.

The popular *Apoquindo* at Prat 616 is rather like the Dino's chain you see in southern Chile and serves a good range of drinks, milkshakes, sweets and snacks. Another good place for cakes and snacks is *Cari* on Matta, between Baquedano and Prat.

For cheap Chinese food try the *Restaurant Chifa Lung Fung* at Sucre 721, and the *Bar Restaurant Los Reyes* at Condell 2540.

The *Café Oriente* at Baquedano 634 has a mixture of European and Latin American food.

Getting There & Away
Air LAN-Chile (tel 222526), at Sucre 375 facing the main plaza, has daily flights to Santiago and Iquique, six days a week to Calama and five days a week to Arica. Ladeco (tel 222942) is at Washington 2589, near the corner with Prat, and has daily flights to Arica, Iquique, Calama and Santiago.

Bus Most bus companies operate out of their own terminals in the centre of town. Many of these have buses to Santiago, Arica and intermediate stops.

Typical fares from Antofagasta are: Arica US$13, Iquique US$10, Calama US$4 and Santiago US$24. A bus cama to Santiago is US$46.

Buses Tramaca are on Uribe, near the corner with 4 de Febrero. They have numerous buses daily to Calama. They also have daily buses to Arica, Iquique and Santiago, and a weekly bus from Antofagasta to Salta in Argentina, via Calama. The fare from Antofagasta to Salta is US$33.

Flota Barrios is on Condell, between Bolívar and Sucre. They have daily buses to Santiago, Valparaíso and Arica. Buses Flecha Dorada is on San Martín, near the corner with Bolívar. They have daily buses to Calama, Santiago and Arica.

A number of other bus companies, with buses to various destinations, have their offices in a large terminal at the corner of Latorre and Riquelme.

Getting Around
Cars can be rented from: Avis (tel 221668), at Prat 272; Budget (tel 251745), at Prat 206; National (tel 223433), at Latorre 2702; and Hertz (tel 223549) at Balmaceda 2566.

The Central Valley

The central valley, the fertile region also known as the Chilean heartland, begins at the southern boundary of San Felipe de Aconcagua Province. At its widest, the central valley measures only about 70 km between the Andes and the coastal mountains and the sea; and only at the southern boundary does the flat valley floor extend all the way to the Pacific.

It contains about 70% of the country's total population and provides most of its industrial jobs. Endowed with rich soil and a pleasant Mediterranean climate, the central valley is Chile's chief farming region, ideal for cereal farming, fruit production, vineyards and livestock grazing. There are also copper mines in the provinces of Santiago, Valparaíso and O'Higgins.

For much of Chilean history, the central valley has been dominated by a relatively small number of large estates, only a minority of which had taken up modern agricultural practices by the mid-1960s. After 1964, large scale agrarian reform programmes expropriated the estates from their owners and created co-operatives. After the military coup of 1973, many of the large farms were handed back to their former owners and efforts were made to break up the remaining co-operatives into individual family farms.

Here, you find the capital of Chile – Santiago – with almost a third of the country's population, as well as Valparaíso, which is Chile's major port.

This chapter also discusses one of

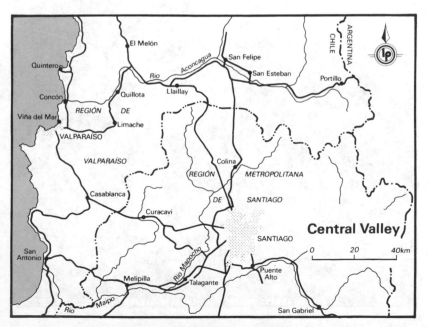

Chile's two Pacific outposts, the Juan Fernández Islands, which were the temporary home for the Scotsman Alexander Selkirk, on whose experiences Daniel Defoe based the novel *Robinson Crusoe*.

Santiago

History

Looking down on Santiago from the rocky crag of Cerro Santa Lucía it's hard to imagine that just six months after the city was founded (by Pedro de Valdivia in 1541) it was almost obliterated by the Mapuche Indians. Several Spanish settlers were killed and legend has it that all their supplies were destroyed bar three hogs, two chickens and two handfuls of corn. The faith of Valdivia was not blunted, however. The Spanish troops were gathered on the summit of Cerro Santa Lucía and plans were made for the rebuilding of the settlement while they were still surrounded and outnumbered by the marauding Indians.

For two years, Cerro Santa Lucía was the capital of a tiny fortified country the size of a postage stamp. Its houses were built of adobe to guard against fire, its inhabitants were on the brink of starvation

The founding of Santiago, from an old banknote

and under repeated attack from the Indians. Not until 1543 did any help arrive from Peru. Valdivia attempted to expand his colony but the new force was still inadequate, and he returned to Peru to seek new troops and supplies. These enabled him to push southwards; Concepción was founded by him in 1550 and Valdivia in 1552.

The new settlements were no more than fortified villages. In Santiago, many of the houses were built around central courtyards, often planted with gardens or fruit trees, although open sewers ran down the middle of the streets. As the settlements gradually became more secure, soldiers formed households with Indian women, and tradespeople (such as shoemakers, blacksmiths, armourers and tanners) moved in to supply the settlers. In their early years, the towns served as administrative centres for the new colony and base camps for further bloody forays into Mapuche territory. The majority of the colony's population, however, did not live in the towns but in the countryside, on the encomiendas or at the mines.

By the end of the 16th century, Santiago was a settlement of just 200 houses, inhabited by 500 to 700 Spaniards and mestizos and several thousand Indian labourers and servants. It was occasionally flooded by the Río Mapocho and lacked a safe water supply. Communications with, and travel into, the countryside was difficult. Despite their precarious position, the wealthy colonists sought to emulate the lifestyle of European nobility, accumulating servants and importing luxury goods from Europe and China. The colony was short on ammunition, weapons and horses, and it had just lost all its territory south of the Río Bío Bío to Indian counterattacks, but in wealthy houses you could find velvet, silk and other luxuries.

Chile remained a backwater of the Spanish Empire for the next three centuries, an appendage of the Viceroyalty of Peru, yielding few minerals or metals of any value. As the colonial period drew to a close at the end of the 18th century, Chile's population – including the 100,000 or so independent Indians south of the Río Bío Bío – was maybe 500,000, of which 90% lived in the countryside. Santiago was a backwater town of 30,000 people whose nearest competitors were overgrown villages. The city streets were still unpaved and the country roads were still potholed trails. There were few schools and public libraries. The University of San Felipe, founded in 1758 chiefly as a law school, provided a few intellectuals, but cultural and intellectual life was weak.

It was not until the last quarter of the 18th century that Santiago began to be shaped into a city, with new dykes to restrain the Río Mapocho, improved roads between Santiago and Valparaíso to handle increased commerce, and various beautification projects. The city became the home for the colonial aristocracy. By the 19th century, a railway and telegraph line linked Santiago, now a large town of over 100,000 people, and Valparaíso, a bustling port and commercial centre of over 60,000 people.

Sumptuous houses were built, and adorned with imported luxuries; prestigious social clubs and societies were established; and the very wealthy maintained haciendas as holiday retreats. Social life for the rich revolved around the clubs, the racing season, the opera, or outings to the exclusive Parque Cousiño. Chile was governed by men who thought themselves gentlemen, people who valued civilised customs, tradition and good breeding and who sent their children to be educated in Europe.

From its humble and bloody beginnings, Santiago has grown to be one of the largest cities in South America. Ask a Chilean where they live and there's a one-in-three chance it will be Santiago. The metropolitan area and surrounding districts contain something like 4,300,000 people. The growth of the city from its original boundaries to the sprawling mass of the present day is well documented in the Museo de Santiago, which is in the Casa Colorado off Santiago's Plaza de Armas.

The growth of Santiago, and other Chilean cities, is very much a product of the oppression in the countryside. Poverty, lack of opportunity and the stifling haciendas drove rural workers north to the mines and into the cities in search of work. Between 1865 and 1875, Santiago's population increased from 115,000 to more than 150,000. The increase was mainly due to domestic migration. The trend continued in the 20th century and by the 1970s over 70% of all Chileans lived in cities, most of them in the central valley.

After WW II, rapid industrialisation offered jobs in the cities but there were never enough to satisfy demand. Continued dissatisfaction in the countryside led to further emigration to the cities during the 1960s and this resulted in the growth of squatter settlements (the *callampas* or 'mushroom' settlements) and shanties which ringed the major cities of the central valley. Planned decentralisation has managed to ease some of the pressure on Santiago, and housing projects have managed to eliminate many callampas. In stark contrast to the economic depression of the poor and lower income districts are the fine houses and suburbs for the rich: El Golf, Vitacura, La Reina, Las Condes and Lo Curro.

As for *el presidente*, work started on his new residence at Lo Curro in 1979 and is estimated to have cost between US$13 million and US$18 million. In 1984, opposition leaders laid charges of corruption against Pinochet in the Supreme Court, claiming that the land had been obtained for an artificially low price after it had been bought with public money. The government reacted by threatening to sue the litigants for 'injury' to the president, and the judge ruled that he did not have the constitutional power to try the president. A few days later, the litigants appealed and also brought a second case which claimed that Pinochet had defrauded the state of US$30,000 in the purchase of land adjoining his residence at Melocoton on the outskirts of Santiago.

Orientation

Although Santiago covers an immense area, the central core of the city is a relatively small, roughly triangular-shaped region bounded in the north by the Río Mapocho, in the west by the Vía Norte Sur and in the south by the Avenida del Libertador General Bernardo O'Higgins. The apex of the triangle is the Plaza Baquedano, where O'Higgins forms a junction with two of Santiago's other main thoroughfares, Avenida Providencia and Avenida Vicuña MacKenna.

The centre of this triangle is the Plaza de Armas, the chief plaza of Santiago, bounded on its northern side by the main post office and on the western side by the cathedral. The streets between the Plaza de Armas and O'Higgins are wall-to-wall shops, restaurants, snack and fast-food bars, cinemas, expensive hotels and office blocks. The Presidential Palace, 'La Moneda', is on Avenida Moneda, facing the Plaza de la Constitución. Near the Plaza de Armas is the National Congress building.

One of Santiago's main parks, Cerro Santa Lucía, is in the triangle facing O'Higgins. The other main park is Cerro San Cristóbal, a mountain which rises dramatically from the plain, to the north of Avenida Providencia. Between this avenue and the mountain, on either side of the Avenida Pío Nono, is Santiago's 'Paris quarter'.

You can still find some of the landmarks which Valdivia used to lay out the boundaries of the original city: to the east is the Huelén, today called Cerro Santa Lucía; to the north is the Río Mapocho; to the south is what used to be the San Lazaro Causeway and is now the city's main thoroughfare, O'Higgins.

The centre of the city is set out in monotonous, right-angled blocks, too narrow for the impatient peak-hour traffic. Seen from the vantage points of Cerro Santa Lucía or Cerro San Cristóbal, the centre juts out of an immense sea of low, flat roofs, overhung by a thick pall of smog. The central triangle of the city is the home to government and public buildings and some very fine colonial architecture – La Moneda, San Francisco and Santo Domingo cathedrals, and the Casa Colorado, amongst others. There are many beautifully landscaped parks and gardens, artists' colonies, and impressive views over the city to the snow-capped peaks of the Andes – when the weather and smog permit.

Information

Tourist Office The tourist office is at Monjitas (tel 6960474), opposite the National Congress. It's open Monday to Friday from 9 am to 5 pm and, in summer, on Saturday from 9 am to 1 pm. The staff are friendly and helpful, and they have a good range of maps and other information including lists of restaurants and bars, transport out of Santiago, hotels, museums, art galleries, and leaflets on other parts of the country. There is also a tourist information office inside the international terminal at Pudahuel Airport. English is spoken at both offices.

Post & Telecommunications The GPO is on the Plaza de Armas in the centre of the city. The post restante is also here and is well organised. The post office is open Monday to Friday from 8 am to 10 pm, Saturday from 8 am to 6 pm and Sunday from 9 am to 1 pm.

Long-distance overseas phone calls can be made from ENTEL at Huérfanos 1133. It's open Monday to Friday from 8.30 am to 10 pm, and Saturday and Sunday from 9 am to 2 pm.

Telegrams and telexes can be sent from TELEX Chile on Morande, facing the Plaza de la Constitución. It's open Monday to Friday from 8.30 am to 8.30 pm,

Saturday from 9 am to 2 pm, and Sunday from 9.30 am to 1.30 pm.

Banks There are a number of casas de cambio on Agustinas, between Bandera and Ahumada, which will change travellers' cheques and foreign cash. There is a bank at the airport, by the tourist office as you exit from Customs.

The easiest way to change money, if you have US cash, is to walk down Agustinas or Huérfanos in the city centre. There are numerous moneychangers along these two streets. They usually accept travellers' cheques but sometimes the rate isn't so good. It's best to change cheques to US cash at a bank and then change the cash with the moneychangers.

Take American Express cheques to the American Express office at Agustinas 1360. They will change them for US cash. Thomas Cook is at Agustinas 1058 but it only deals with replacing lost and stolen cheques. The Casa de Cambio Andes Ltda at Agustinas 1036 changes Thomas Cook travellers' cheques for US cash.

Embassies & Consulates A number of countries have consulates in several Chilean cities. Peru, Bolivia and Argentina are particularly well represented. Many other countries have a consulate or embassy in Santiago:

Argentina
    Vicuña MacKenna 41 (tel 22288977)
Australia
    Gertrudis Echeñique 420 (tel 2285065)
Austria
    3rd floor, Barros Errázuriz 1968 (tel 2234774)
Belgium
    Providencia 2653 (tel 2321071)
Bolivia
    Avenida de Santa María 2796 (tel 2328180)
Brazil
    15th floor, MacIver 225 (tel 398867)
Canada
    10th floor, Ahumada 11 (tel 6962256)
France
    Condell 65 (tel 2251030)

1   Terminal de Buses Norte
2   Airport Buses
3   Terminal de Buses Sur
4   Central Railway Station
5   Mapocho Railway Station
6   Mercado Central
7   Tourist Office
8   National Congress
9   Ladeco
10 ENTEL Chile (Overseas Service)
11 Plaza de la Constitutión
12 LAN-Chile
13 Palacio de la Moneda
14 Telex Chile (Telegraph & Telex)
15 Cathedral
16 Main Post Office
17 Plaza de Armas
18 Casa Colorado Museum
19 Universidad de Chile
20 Opera House
21 Iglesia San Francisco
22 Biblioteca Nacional
23 Sociedad de Arte
    Precolombiano Nacional
24 Edificio Diego Portales
25 Universidad Católica
26 Holiday Inn Crowne Plaza
    Low Budget Hotel Area (Hotels
    Souvenir, Caribe, Indiana etc)
    Metro Station

Santiago

0   250   500 m

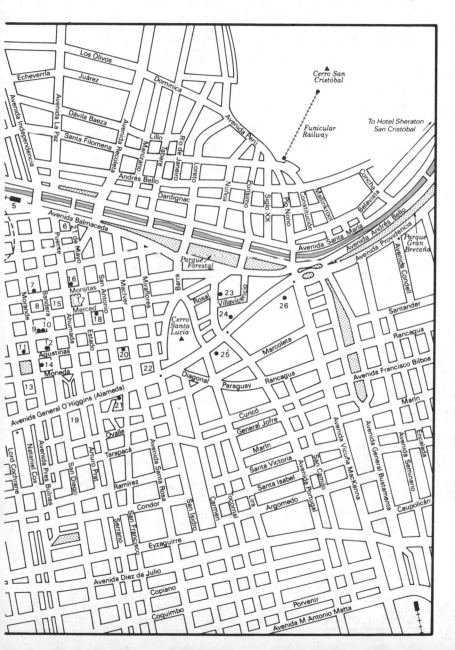

Holland
　　Las Violetas 2368 (tel 2236826)
Israel
　　5th floor, San Sebastián 2812 (tel 2461570)
Japan
　　Avenida Providencia 2653 (tel 2321807)
New Zealand
　　Isidora Goyenechea 3516 (tel 2314204)
Paraguay
　　Apartment 514, Huérfanos 886 (tel 394640)
Peru
　　Avenida Providencia 2653 (tel 2326275)
Switzerland
　　Office 1602, Avenida Providencia 2653
　　(tel 2322693)
Uruguay
　　Pedro de Valdivia 711 (tel 2238398)
UK
　　4th floor, La Concepción 177 (tel 2239166)
USA
　　embassy: Agustinas 1343
　　consulate (visas): Merced 230 (tel 710133)
West Germany
　　7th floor, Agustinas 785 (tel 335031)

Airlines There are a large number of
airlines with offices in Santiago:

Aerolíneas Argentinas
　　Moneda 756 (tel 393922)
Aero Perú
　　Teatinos 335 (tel 715035)
Air France
　　Agustinas 1136 (tel 6982421)
Alitalia
　　O'Higgins 949 (tel 6983336)
Avianca
　　Moneda 1118 (tel 714105)
British Airways
　　Ahumada 370 (tel 726339)
Canadian Pacific
　　Huérfanos 669 (tel 393058)
Eastern Airlines
　　Huérfanos 1199 (tel 713004)
Ecuatoriana
　　Bernardo O'Higgins (tel 6964251)
Iberia
　　Agustinas 1115 (tel 714510)
KLM
　　Agustinas 802 (tel 398001)
Ladeco
　　Huérfanos 1157 (tel 712960)
LAN-Chile
　　Agustinas 1197 (tel 723523)

Líneas Aéreas Paraguayas
　　2nd floor, Agustinas 1141 (tel 721142)
Lufthansa
　　Moneda 970 (tel 722686)
Lloyd Aéreo Boliviano
　　Moneda 1170 (tel 712334)
Pan American
　　23rd floor, Bernardo O'Higgins 949 (tel
　　6990055)
SAS
　　15th floor, Miraflores 178 (tel 391105)
Swissair
　　Agustinas 1046 (tel 6981848)
Varig
　　Miraflores 156 (tel 395976)
Viasa
　　Agustinas 1141 (tel 6982401)

Maps The *Plano del Centro de Santiago* is
available free from the tourist information
office. It covers the central core and inner
suburbs of the city and also includes a
map of the metro system. It's detailed and
easy to use.

Trekking For trekking and mountaineering
information, go to CONAF (Corporación
Nacional Forestal) at General Bulnes 285.

Cerro Santa Lucía
Cerro Santa Lucía is a hill in the city
centre, honeycombed with gardens,
footpaths and fountains, and crowned by
the remains of a fortress. Local people will
advise you not to walk here after dark as
muggings are not unknown, but it's
perfectly safe during the day. At the foot
of the hill, on the Alameda, a large stone is
engraved with the text of a letter that was
sent to the king of Spain by Pedro de
Valdivia extolling the beauty of the newly
conquered territories. Take the metro to
Santa Lucía station.

Cerro San Cristóbal
Cerro San Cristóbal is a peak which
sprouts from the plain on the other side of
the Río Mapocho. It's much higher than
Santa Lucía and is crowned by a white
statue of the Virgin Mary. There is a
funicular railway, built in 1925, which

Monument on Cerro Santa Lucía

takes you to the 485-metre summit. The one-way fare is about US$1. It operates daily from about 10 am to 8.30 pm, with slightly longer hours on Saturday, Sunday and holidays. You board the railway at Plaza Caupolicán at the top of Pío Nono.

There is also a minibus from the plaza to Tupahue, about three-quarters of the way up the mountain. There's a large swimming pool at Tupahue, and from there you can continue walking up the road to the peak.

There's also a cable car service to the summit from the Estación Oasis Teleférico on Avenida Pedro de Valdivia Norte (metro station Pedro de Valdivia) which operates the same hours as the funicular railway.

Museums

There are at least two museums worth seeing to get some feel for the history of this place. The first is the Museo Precolombiano, Bandera 361, which catalogues 4500 years of South American civilisation before the arrival of the Spanish. It's open Tuesday to Saturday from 10 am to 6 pm, and Sunday from 10 am to 1 pm.

The second is the Museo de Santiago housed in the Casa Colorado, a fine colonial building. The growth of the city from its original boundaries to the sprawling mass of the present day is documented in this museum. It's at Merced 860 opposite the Plaza de Armas and is open Tuesday to Saturday from 10 am to 6 pm, and Sunday from 10 am to 2 pm.

Other museums are listed in a leaflet called *Galerías de Arte y Museo*, available from the tourist office. This also lists opening times and transport. Most museums are closed on Monday.

The Tourist Hike

The tourist circuit starts at the northern side of the central triangle with several interesting colonial buildings. Starting at the Mercado Central, head down 21 de Mayo to the Posada de Corregidor, the houses of Velasco and Bernardo O'Higgins and the Iglesia de San Domingo.

The Posada de Corregidor is an 18th-century colonial building at Esmeralda 732, with a whitewashed front and an attractive wooden balcony. It was built in 1780 and is open to the public.

Turn the corner at Enrique MacIver and head down San Domingo. Just around the corner is the Casa Velasco which is similar to the Posada de Corregidor. Nearby is the Casa O'Higgins, home of the first Chilean president. Or head along San Domingo to the Iglesia de Santo Domingo, a massive stone church originally built in 1808.

Next is the Plaza de Armas, which is the centre of the city, flanked by the Correo Central (GPO), the Museo Histórico Nacional and the massive Catedral. The

Congreso Nacional

Museo Catedral is on Bandera and houses collections of colonial religious ornaments.

Between Bandera and Morande stands the Congreso Nacional. At the corner of Morande and Catedral is the Palacio Edwards which is now used for government administration offices. Immediately behind the Congreso Nacional is the Tribunales de Justicia (Law Courts) on Compañía.

A short walk westwards along Compañía brings you to a Moorish-style building called the Palacio de la Ahlambra at Compañía 1340, now used as an art gallery. Or head east to the Museo Precolombiano.

Leading south from one corner of the plaza is the Paseo de Ahumada, which is the main mall of Santiago. It's a street market with dozens of pavement hawkers flogging everything from plywood models of clipper ships to pan pipes and seat belts. Buskers congregate in the evening and you can hear anything from solo bagpipers to gypsy opera ensembles and Chilean folk groups.

The chief government building is the Palacio de la Moneda, a hornet's nest of police and military, set behind the Plaza de la Constitución. It was badly damaged during the coup when it was bombed by air force jets, but it has since been restored. Turning east up O'Higgins takes you to the Universidad de Chile. Next up is the unmistakable Iglesia de San Francisco and, inside, the Museo del Arte Colonial; the latter houses colonial art and paintings depicting the curing of lepers and bloody representations of the crucifixion. The exhibits include a wall-size painting, attributed to an 18th-century artist, showing the genealogy of the Franciscan order and the various alumni of the Catholic church who patronised the order. There are also several rooms exhibiting over 50 paintings from the 18th century depicting the life of St Francis of Assisi – tasteless in their execution but extraordinary in their conception!

The scene outside the cathedral is one unchanged for centuries, with crippled beggars and fat women armed with tiny babes in swaddling clothes huddled around the entrance begging for alms. The church is one of Santiago's oldest buildings. It was originally built in the second half of the 16th century and was later enlarged to its present size. The museum is open daily, except Monday, from 10 am to 1 pm and from 3 to 6 pm.

Further up O'Higgins is the monolithic Biblioteca Nacional at the corner with McIver. Another building of interest is the impressive Opera House, at the corner of Agustinas and San Antonio, with its entrance on Agustinas.

Parque Quinta Normal

I don't normally rate parks a mention but the Parque Quinta Normal at the western edge of the central triangle is an interesting one. Take the metro to Estación Central and then catch a bus up Matucana.

On the southern boundary of the park at Avenida Portales 3530 is the Museo Aeronáutica (Aeronautical Museum), which is housed in a bizarre building built for the Paris Exhibition of 1900, and later installed opposite the Quinta Normal. Even if you're not the least bit interested in aircraft it's worth seeing the building itself – it looks rather like a cross between a Greek temple, the Albert Hall, the Taj Mahal and a beehive.

In the park is the Museo Nacional de Historia Natural. Exhibits include the body of a 12-year-old child who was sacrificed at least 500 years ago and whose body was preserved in ice at the summit of El Plomo, a 5000-metre peak near Santiago. The body was recovered in 1954 by a team from Chile University. Bone fragments from a milodon (giant sloth) found in a cave near Puerto Natales in southern Chile are also on display.

Near the entrance to the park, opposite the Museo Aeronáutica, there's a collection of steam locomotives.

Places to Stay - bottom end

How much you like a place often depends on where you stay, and Santiago is no exception. This city is liked by some and hated by others, and the chances are that if you hang out in the dank hotels near the northern bus terminal you'll belong to the latter group.

The main low-budget hotel area is around the Terminal de Buses Norte, on the corner of General MacKenna and Amunátegui. Most of the hotels are on General MacKenna, Amunátegui, San Pablo and San Martín. They're mostly gloomy hovels. Locks are flimsy, but luckily this is not Lima or Bogotá so baggage is relatively safe. The area has something of a reputation for being a rough neighbourhood. Lone women should be wary about walking around these streets late at night.

Probably, the best place in this area is the *Hotel Caribe* at San Martín 851. It's clean and, by Santiago standards, good

value at around US$3 per person. The common bathrooms have hot showers. Rooms are bare little boxes with windows that face onto a passageway. The manager is friendly and speaks some English. I find this place rather dingy and depressing but many travellers think it's good value. There are token locks on the doors but you can leave valuables in the safe.

Besides the Hotel Caribe, nothing in this northern region can seriously be recommended. There's the *Hotel Indiana* at Rosas 1334, which is a dilapidated old mansion. Rooms are US$4 a single and US$6 a double. Hot water is available.

The *Hotel Souvenir*, at Amunátegui 856, caters to people with a fascination for antediluvian plumbing fixtures, 25-watt light bulbs and undulating wooden stairs and corridors. It has clean sheets, hot water and is generally dark and depressing. Rooms are US$3 a single and US$6 a double.

There are a number of other hotels in this area with rooms resembling prison cells. These include the *Hotel Retiro* at MacKenna 1266 with singles for US$4 and doubles for US$7. It's a reasonably clean place (there's not much to get dirty) and if you're stuck this will probably do.

Rubbing shoulders with the Retiro are a number of similar places including the *Hotel Colonial* at MacKenna 1262, and the *Hotel Florida* at MacKenna 1250. Both have rooms for around US$2.50. The best of the bad bunch is probably the *San Felipe* at MacKenna 1248, where half an attempt has been made to make the cells look half tolerable. Whatever you do, avoid the front rooms of all these hotels; MacKenna is a main street and buses storm down it day and night. Better still, stay somewhere else.

Outside this area there is one place which can be wholeheartedly recommended and is very popular with visitors. This is the *Residencial Londres* at Londres 54, very close to the Iglesia de San Francisco on O'Higgins. (Calle Londres runs down the side of the church.) It's great value with rooms for US$5 a single and US$10 a double. There's hot water, the rooms are secure and clean, and the staff are pleasant and helpful. Get there as early as possible, as it's popular with local people too and fills up quickly. This is the best hotel in Santiago for the price.

Conveniently located is the *Hotel España* at Morande 510. It's a bit of a rabbit warren and can be quite noisy. The rooms are clean, stark and bare. Don't expect too much. Rooms start from US$10 a single and US$13 a double. Slightly more expensive rooms have private bathrooms.

Places to Stay – middle

Santiago hotels don't really come into their own until you get into the mid-range hotels. Many of these have agreeable little rooms with their own bathrooms and toilets, and as you move up a few dollars more there is usually a telephone, TV and sometimes a refrigerator. Places like the *Gran Palace Hotel* at Huérfanos 1178 and the *Hotel Santa Lucía* at Huérfanos 779 are typical. Mid-range and up-market hotels are listed in a free pamphlet from the tourist office called *Alojamiento – Región Metropolitana*.

One place I unconditionally recommend is the *Hotel Metropoli* (tel 723987) on Dr Satero del Río 465. This is a small street which runs off Catedral between Teatinos and Morande, just a few blocks from the Plaza de Armas. You can't get much more central. Rooms are US$27 a single and US$34 a double. The rooms are clean and comfortable and have private bathrooms.

Another reasonably cheap hotel in the middle of the city is the *Hotel Sao Paulo* (tel 398031) at San Antonio 357 near the corner with Merced. The hotel has singles from US$13 and doubles from US$15. Rooms with private bathroom cost only a dollar or two more. It's a bit dingy but is extremely well located.

The *Hotel Cervantes* (tel 6965318) at Morande 631, near the corner with Santo Domingo, is a good place. Rooms with private bathroom are US$14 a single and US$25 a double. There are slightly cheaper doubles without private bathroom. There's hot water all day and the hotel has its own restaurant. Some of the rooms are small and dingy but others are spacious and bright.

One of the best hotels in this price range is the *Hotel Monte Carlo* at Victoria Subercaseaux 209, opposite Cerro Santa Lucía. The rooms are small but have private bathrooms. The hotel is bright and the staff are friendly. However, if noise disturbs you then it may be best to go elsewhere as this is a busy street.

The *Hotel Santa Lucía* (tel 398201), 3rd floor, Huérfanos 779, is good value at around US$36 a single and US$43 a double. Rooms are attractive with TV, telephone, refrigerator and private bathroom.

There are a number of other decent hotels, all with rooms for around US$28 a single and US$35 a double. These are: the *Hotel Gran Palace* (tel 712551), at Huérfanos 1178; the *City Hotel* (tel 724526), at Compañia 1063; the *Hotel El Libertador* (tel 3942112), at O'Higgins 853; the *Hotel Ritz* (tel 393401), at Estado 248; and the *Hotel Panamericano* (tel 723060), at Teatinos 320.

Places to Stay – top end

Santiago has a large number of international-class hotels, including most of the well-known chains, equipped with restaurants, cafes and bars. A number of top-class hotels also have moneychanging services for their customers.

The *Hotel Tupahue* (tel 383810) is at San Antonio 477, near the corner with Monjitas. Singles are US$64 and doubles are US$76, which includes continental breakfast.

The *Hotel Conquistador* (tel 6965599) is at Miguel Cruchaga 920, which is a small street which runs off Estado near the junction with O'Higgins. The hotel is on the corner of Cruchaga and Estado. Singles with breakfast start from US$64 and doubles from US$76.

The *Hostal del Parque* (tel 392694) is at Merced 294, at the junction with Lastarria, and in front of the Sociedad de Arte Precolombiano Nacional. Rooms are US$69 a single and US$80 a double.

The *Hotel Carrera* (tel 6982011), at Teatinos 180, is one of a matching pair of monoliths which overlook La Moneda and the Plaza de la Constitución. Rooms start from US$104 a single and US$116 a double.

If external appearances are anything to go by then try the glittering *Hotel Galerías* (tel 384011) at San Antonio 65, a block or two up from the junction with O'Higgins. Singles are US$80 and doubles are US$90. It also has a swimming pool.

The *Holiday Inn Crowne Plaza* (tel 381042) O'Higgins 136, near the junction with Vicuña MacKenna, has singles from US$106 and doubles from US$112. The hotel has offices, shops, rental car service and a post office.

The *Sheraton San Cristóbal* (tel 2745000) at Santa María 1742, at the junction with Calle El Cerro at the foot of Cerro San Cristóbal, has rooms for about US$143 a single and US$156 a double.

Places to Eat

There is a phenomenal number of places to eat in Santiago, especially around the bus stations, the pedestrian streets of Huérfanos and Ahumada, the Plaza de Armas and along O'Higgins. You can find Italian pasta, Indian curries, stuffed vine leaves and Chilean parrilladas. The tourist office has a pamphlet listing many of these restaurants, which will give you an idea of the formidable range.

For cheap eats, snacks, drinks and cakes there's a whole string of places shoulder to shoulder in the arcade on Plaza de Armas. Try the *Pollo Montserrat* for cheap fried chicken. The *Chez Henri* in the Plaza de Armas gets rave reviews from visitors. It's renowned for its large meals, and also has a takeaway section at the front with cheap dishes like lasagna,

empanadas and tortillas. It's also very good for seafood meals.

Many people have recommended the *Bar Central* at San Pablo 1063. It's popular with local people and has good seafood in generous portions.

The best self-serve place in town is the *Sylvestre*, at Huérfanos 956. You can eat enough to last you all day for a few dollars. They dish up ravioli, rice, mixed vegetables, tortillas, fried chicken, deserts and drinks and much more. Self-service is only at lunch; in the evenings it's an ordinary restaurant.

Greasy imitations of McDonalds and Kentucky Fried Chicken are well represented in Santiago – such as the *Burger Inn* chain recognisable by its hamburger logo sporting two cow's heads. The quality of the food varies, and you can't really call them *fast* food.

There are many cheap seafood restaurants at the Mercado Central (Central Market) on San Pablo, east of the old Mapocho Railway Station. Every conceivable form of marine life is served up by dozens of tiny restaurants. Dishes are usually already made up and displayed in windows and prices are usually shown. You have to be quick to escape the restaurant touts and their machine-gun Spanish. The food is usually served raw, covered in salt and vinegar, and if you're not used to it you could be touring Chilean toilets for the next week. If you haven't got a blast furnace digestive system then give this place a wide berth!

A happy hunting ground for restaurants is Santiago's 'Paris quarter'. Its main street is Pío Nono, which runs north from the junction of O'Higgins and Vicuña MacKenna to Cerro San Cristóbal. Restaurants in this area include the Italian pizza joint *La Zingarella* at 185 Pío Nono, *La Venezia* at 200 Pío Nono, and the *Restaurant Arabe Karim*, which is very congenial and has cheapish kebabs and other Arabic dishes.

It's worth checking out the *Pérgola de la*

Plaza bar and restaurant, which is in the artist's colony on Victorino Lastarria 305-321, at the back of the Hostal del Parque. It's very popular with the locals for wine and pastries. The surrounding houses have all been renovated and are used as artists' studios. This is also the location of the Sociedad de Arte Precolombiano Nacional. The complex is largely a collection of art and handicraft shops, with a museum taking up a small part of it.

Vegetarians can eat at *El Naturalista* at Moneda 846, and *El Vegetariano* at Huérfanos 827. Both are moderately priced.

Santiago is a gastronomic potpourri. For spicy food, try the *Lung Fung* at Agustinas 715; for a wide selection of pasta dishes there's *De Carla* at McIver 577; for German food and live piano there's *Der Münchner* at Diego de Velásquez 2105; for French scallops and onion soup try *Les Assassins* at Merced 297; and for drinks, snacks and top-40 music in the company of Santiago's English speakers, try the *Red Pub* at Suecia 29. One of the most congenial Italian restaurants is *San Marco* at Huérfanos 618.

Getting There & Away

As the capital of such a long, skinny country, you can't really detour around Santiago. Santiago is either your introduction to Chile or a place you have to pass through.

Air Ladeco (tel 712960) is at Huérfanos 1157. LAN-Chile (tel 723523) is at Agustinas 1197.

Ladeco has daily flights from Santiago to Antofagasta, Calama, Iquique, Arica, Puerto Montt and Punta Arenas. They also have flights several days a week to Temuco, Valdivia and Osorno.

LAN-Chile has daily flights from Santiago to Antofagasta, Iquique, Arica, Puerto Montt and Punta Arenas. They have flights about six days a week to

Calama, and two or three days a week to Easter Island.

There are many international flights out of Santiago, particularly to other South American destinations. For fares and details of international services, see the Getting There chapter.

Bus - domestic There are two bus terminals in Santiago - the Terminal de Buses Norte and the Terminal de Buses Sur.

The Terminal de Buses Norte, at the corner of General MacKenna and Amunátegui, is for buses heading north and to Mendoza in Argentina. There is no metro access to this station, although the Cal y Canto station is close by.

Buses to the south leave from the Terminal de Buses Sur at O'Higgins 3800. The easiest way to get there is to take the metro to the Universidad de Chile station. The Terminal de Buses Sur actually consists of two terminals on adjacent blocks - the main terminal and a smaller one known as Alameda. A subway and steps lead direct from the metro platform to the Alameda terminal. The main terminal is a short walk away, one block to the west.

The Alameda terminal only handles two companies, the main one being Tur-Bus, which is a luxury bus company with frequent buses all day to Valparaíso and Viña del Mar. Tur-Bus also serves various destinations in the Lake District such as Temuco, Valdivia, Osorno, Villarrica and Puerto Montt.

Sometimes the same bus company will have north and southbound buses, and you can usually buy tickets at either bus terminal - including tickets to other South American countries - but you will have to catch northbound buses from the Terminal de Buses Norte and southbound buses from the Terminal de Buses Sur.

Fares vary from company to company and often special discounts may be offered. Some approximate fares (in US dollars) and journey times from Santiago are:

Antofagasta	$23	18 hours
Arica	$36	28 hours
Iquique	$30	25 hours
La Serena	$10	
Osorno	$13	14 hours
Puerto Montt	$15	16 hours
Puerto Varas	$15	
Punta Arenas	$80	60 hours
Temuco	$10	11 hours
Valdivia	$14	13 hours
Valparaíso	$ 2	
Villarrica	$14	
Viña del Mar	$ 2	

For long trips, consider taking a bus cama. These are buses with seats equipped with footrests, calf-rests and extra legroom. The seats recline right back to make a sleeperette. A bus cama ticket from Santiago to Arica costs around US$52.

Companies which cover northern destinations include Flota Barrios, Tramaca, Fenix Pullman Norte, Chile Bus, Flecha Norte, Buses Carmelita and Tarapacá.

Companies which cover southern destinations include Buses Norte, Tas Choapa, Tur-Bus, Cruz del Sur, ETC, Transbus, Igi Llama, Turibús, Pullman Lit, Vía Tur and Nuevo Longitudinal Sur.

Bus - international There are direct buses from Santiago to many other South American countries, including Brazil, Paraguay, Argentina, Peru and Ecuador.

Chile Bus has buses from Santiago to Río de Janeiro via Mendoza, Rosario, Santa Fe, Paraná, Paso de Los Libres, Uruguaiana, Porto Alegre, Florianopolis, Curitisa and São Paulo. The fare to Río is about US$92 and the trip takes about three days. There are departures several days a week.

A number of companies, such as Fenix Pullman Internacional, run buses to Argentina. Typical fares from Santiago are: Buenos Aires US$48, Bariloche US$40 and Mendoza US$16. Between the various companies you can usually get a bus to Argentina any day of the week.

Several companies, such as Buses

Norte Lagos del Sur, have buses from Santiago to the southern Chilean city of Punta Arenas, via Osorno and Argentine Patagonia.

Coitram has taxi colectivos from Santiago to Mendoza, with connections to Buenos Aires. They leave from the Terminal de Buses Sur.

Typical bus fares from Santiago to other international destinations include: Caracas (Venezuela) US$192, Lima (Peru) US$66, Quito (Ecuador) US$104, Bogotá (Colombia) US$150, La Paz (Bolivia) US$66 and Montevideo (Uruguay) US$72.

Train Trains south to Concepción, Temuco, Valdivia, Osorno and Puerto Montt leave from Estación Central on O'Higgins. Take the metro to Estación Central.

There used to be trains west to Valparaíso leaving from the Estación Mapocho, at the junction of Balmaceda and Morande, but at the time of writing, this service appears to have been discontinued. The only public transport from Santiago to Valparaíso and Viña del Mar is bus or taxi colectivo.

For trains going south you don't need to go to Estación Central to book tickets. You can get them at Venta de Pasajes e Informaciones in the Galería Libertador at O'Higgins 851. It's open Monday to Friday from 9 am to 6 pm, and Saturday from 9 am to 1 pm. This office is at the end of an arcade which runs off the street – look for the yellow sign.

For details of fares and timetables, see the Getting Around chapter.

Getting Around
Airport Transport Arturo Merino Bénitez International Airport is at Pudahuel, 26 km from the city centre. The best way to get between the two is to take the Tour Express bus from the downtown terminal at Moneda 1523 just near the junction with San Martín. There are about 30 departures per day from the city terminal between 6.30 am and 9 pm, and from the airport from 7 am to 9.15 pm. At other

times of the day they meet incoming flights when they arrive. The fare is US$0.90 and the journey takes about 30 minutes. Buses from the airport leave from in front of the airport terminal. They will drop you off at the city terminal or just about anywhere en route to it.

There is a taxi rank outside the airport terminal. A taxi to the city centre costs about US$6.

Metro Santiago has an excellent metro system with two lines presently in operation. It's the most convenient system of public transport and you should use it whenever possible. For example, the Terminal de Buses Sur, Estación Central and the foreign embassies (most of which are in Providencia or Las Condes) can all easily be reached on the metro.

The most recent addition to the metro is the extension from Los Héroes to Puente Cal y Canto, the entrance of which is at the junction of Bandera and General MacKenna.

Signs on the station platforms indicate the direction in which the trains are heading. 'Direcion Las Condes' refers to the line heading towards Escuela Militar station. 'Direcion Pudahuel' refers to the line heading towards San Pablo station. 'Direcion Centro' refers to the new line heading towards Puente Cal y Canto station. 'Direcion La Cisterna' refers to the line heading towards Lo Ovalle.

The metro operates Monday to Saturday from 6.30 am to 10.30 pm and on Sunday and public holidays from 8 am to 10.30 pm. There are trains every few minutes.

The two lines are known as Centro and Pudahuel. Fares on the Centro line are a flat US$0.10; fares on the Pudahuel line are a flat US$0.20. Carnets (booklets of ten tickets) are also available on both lines. While the saving is absolutely minimal for a foreign tourist it is

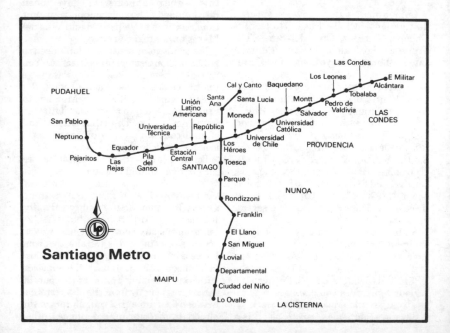

Santiago Metro

convenient to buy a number of tickets beforehand.

You buy your ticket from the ticket offices at each station. The tickets have a metallic strip on the back and you slip the ticket into a slot in the turnstile. The turnstile keeps your ticket and does not return it to you; when you get off at your stop you walk straight through the exit gates.

Bus There is said to be a system to Santiago's buses but the sheer number of buses – all of which appear to be independently operated – means that outsiders have a hard time breaking the code. Santiago's buses are really only useful if you already know which one to catch. There are no route maps. All have signs in their front windows displaying their destinations. Fares are usually a flat rate of around US$0.25 per trip.

Taxi Santiago has abundant metered taxis – all black with yellow roofs.

Car Rental For full details of car rental rates see the Getting Around chapter.

Budget, Hertz, Western, National, Avis, Galerías and American all have offices at the airport in front of the airport terminal building.

City offices are:

Hertz
    Costanera 1469 (tel 2259328)
Galerías
    San Antonio 65, in the Hotel Galerías (tel 3884011)
Budget
    Hotel Carrera, diagonally opposite La Moneda (tel 6982011)
Avis
    Hotel Sheraton, Santa María 1742 (tel 747621)
National
    La Concepción 212 (tel 2232416)
Bond
    Vitacura 2737 (tel 2325824)
American
    Las Condes 9225 (tel 2202354)

Also, try the Automobile Club of Chile (Automóvil Club de Chile) (tel 2744167) at Marchant Pereira 122 in the Providencia district.

Tours If your time is limited then consider taking a tour of Santiago and the surrounding region. For example, Tour Service in the Hotel Carrera, diagonally opposite La Moneda, has city tours for US$14, a Viña del Mar and Valparaíso day tour for US$28, and a trip to the Portillo ski resort for around US$96. Other companies worth trying are Rahue Tours in the Holiday Inn Crowne Plaza, and Gray Line at the corner of Agustinas and Morande.

A Santiago city tour takes in places like the Iglesia de San Francisco, Cerro Santa Lucía and Cerro San Cristóbal. There are also half-day tours to Santiago's major museums including the Museo Precolombiano, the National Museum of Natural History and the Museum of Colonial Art at the Iglesia de San Francisco. Day tours to Valparaíso and Viña del Mar take in the dock and wharf area, the Naval Academy, Santa María University, the Baburizza Museum of Paintings and the Viña del Mar Casino.

Valparaíso

A more unlikely place for the country's principal port and second largest city is hard to imagine. The commercial and industrial sector is crammed into a narrow strip of land along the seafront with steep mountains rising abruptly behind it.

However steep they might be, they're all covered with suburbs and shantytowns connected by tortuous roads, incredibly long flights of steps and *ascensores* (funicular railways) similar to the ones in Salvador (Brazil). The shanty dwellers are very poor and local people will warn you against displaying any conspicuous

19th century Valparaíso architecture

wealth in these areas. The commercial centre is quite safe and has a sort of cluttered charm with its narrow, winding, cobbled streets, attractive buildings and many sailors' bars and clubs.

Information

Tourist information (maps of the city but not much else) is available from the municipal building, Condell 1490, or from the kiosk on the quay next to the Customs House.

Things to See

Apart from strolling around the city there's not a great deal to do in Valparaíso – mainly because those with money to spend on pleasure and luxuries go to Viña del Mar. The contrast between the poverty of Valparaíso and the conspicuous wealth of Viña del Mar is like the difference between chalk and cheese. But since Valparaíso is also a naval base you could take a look at

the Museo del Mar, Calle Merlet, which was formerly Lord Cochrane's house. It overlooks the harbour.

Places to Stay

The cheapest place is the *Youth Hostel* at Cuarto Norte 636 which costs about US$3 per person, but travellers who have stayed there have called it a dump.

There are very few hotels around the bus terminal itself; most of the cheap hotels are along Serrano, Cochrane and Blanco, close to the Plaza Sotomayor. Try the *Residencial Lily*, Blanco Encalada 866 next to the Bar Ingle's or the *Hotel Reina Victoria*, Plaza Sotomayor 190. The latter has singles for around US$4.50 to US$5.50, and doubles are from US$5.50 to US$6.50 including breakfast; it's an old building in a fine location and there's hot water.

Similarly priced, the *Garden Hotel* at Serrano 501 is opposite one of the funicular railways and just off the Plaza Sotomayor. It has large, clean rooms with good showers and toilets and a restaurant.

Getting There & Away

From Santiago, the most convenient bus company for Valparaíso and Viña del Mar is Tur-Bus. The buses leave from Santiago's Terminal de Buses Sur. There are frequent departures every day from Santiago around 6.30 am to 10 pm and from 6 am to 9 pm from Valparaíso and Viña del Mar. Some of the buses to Viña del Mar go via Valparaíso but others go direct.

Valparaíso and Viña del Mar are only a few km apart and in any case it's easy to take a local bus between the two. From Santiago to Valparaíso, it takes about 1¾ hours and to Viña del Mar about two hours. The fare is the same at around US$2.30 one-way and US$3.80 return.

The bus terminal in Valparaíso, Terminal Rodoviario, is at the junction of Pedro Montt at Rawson. If you're arriving in Valparaíso on a bus which is going to Viña del Mar, then you may be dropped

Top: The Cathedral, Santiago
Left: Old building, Santiago
Right: Iglesia San Francisco, Santiago

Top: One of the oldest churches in Chile, San Pedro de Atacama
Left: Church, Chol Chol, near Temuco
Right: Iglesia de San Francisco, Castro

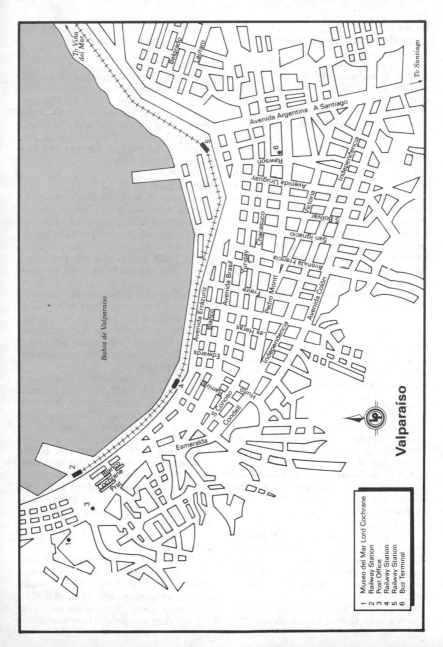

Valparaíso

1 Museo del Mar Lord Cochrane
2 Railway Station
3 Post Office
4 Railway Station
5 Railway Station
6 Bus Terminal

on Avenida Argentina at the junction with Pedro Montt, which is only one block from the bus terminal.

Alternatively, take the train between Valparaíso and Santiago; it runs along the seafront and through Viña del Mar before climbing inland into the hills. There are three or four trains a day between the two cities; they take about three hours and cost US$2.

VIÑA DEL MAR

About nine km round the headland from Valparaíso, Viña del Mar is Chile's premier beach resort, a sort of Latin American version of Surfer's Paradise or Waikiki Beach. All Chileans with money, and many other wealthy Latin Americans, own houses here. There is (or was) a Haitian Consulate here! Naturally with that sort of clientele, you would expect things to be expensive – and they are. The only cheap thing about Viña del Mar is getting there.

Information

The regional tourist office (tel 882285) is at Avenida Valparaíso 507. There is also a municipal tourist office near the junction of Quillota and Arlegui.

Museums

The Museo Naval, in the castle on the seafront on the Valparaíso side of the Marga Marga estuary, is definitely worth a visit, not only for the exhibits (the history of the Chilean navy and especially the War of the Pacific) but also for the building itself. It's open daily from 10 am to 12.30 pm and 3 to 6 pm. Entry is only about US$0.30.

The Palacio Vergara and the Museo de Bellas Artes in the beautifully landscaped Parque Vergara are worth a visit; concerts are performed here in the summer months and this is where the Song Festival is held.

And if you don't have the money to go to Easter Island, there's a moai on a traffic island between the Museo Naval and the Hotel Miramar at Caleta Abarca.

Song Festival

Apart from beach-bumming, Viña del Mar's much-touted attraction is the yearly Song Festival. It's a bit like the Eurovision Song Contest only this one has to be endured for a whole week. The Song Festival is held in the Parque Vergara, also the site of the Palacio Vergara and the Museo de Bellas Artes.

Places to Stay

Unless you're lucky enough to meet someone who offers you hospitality at their summer home, then the cheapest place to stay in Viña del Mar is the *Youth Hostel* at the Sausalito Stadium. It costs around US$2 per person but you must have a YH membership card to stay there.

Anywhere else is outside the scope of low-budget travellers. There are quite a few residencials on Calle von Schroeder, and in the town centre near the bus station on Calle Quillota. Off-season prices for most of these residencials are around US$5 per person.

One place in Viña del Mar that's been recommended is the *Residencial Oxaron* on Villanello, a quiet street between Arlegui and Valparaíso. It has very clean rooms, hot water and serves breakfast.

Viña del Mar is an almost entirely modern town with very high real estate values so there are no old centres where you might find budget hotels. If you're determined to spend time in Viña del Mar, it's much cheaper to stay in Valparaíso and come in daily on the train or bus.

Getting There & Away

The bus terminal is between Valparaíso and Arlegui, which is one block from Quillota. There are frequent local buses between Valparaíso and Viña del Mar which take about 10 minutes and cost US$0.30. You can catch them anywhere along Arlegui. They're marked 'Puerto' or 'Advana' – very few are marked 'Valparaíso'.

Juan Fernández Islands

In search of the real Robinson Crusoe

Robinson Crusoe's name has come to be fairly firmly connected with thoughts of tropical palms, buccaneers, cannibals – and the test of survival. The Crusoe legend has an extraordinary capacity to mirror the reader's ideals – to Rousseau, he was an admirable model for man-in-nature; to Joyce, an English Ulysses; to Karl Marx, by contrast, he was a capitalist. Tour companies use his name to promote island holidays (Man Friday undergoing a subtle change, serving cocktails to a suntanned couple). And to the people of the tiny Juan Fernández Archipelago, Crusoe is a cottage industry. He's right there on your ticket from Santiago – goatskins, parrot and all.

It was on these islands, 670 km off the Chilean coast, that the real Crusoe – a Scottish mariner named Alexander Selkirk – was marooned in 1704. The fact that Daniel Defoe set his novel about 5000 km away in the Brazils – leading to counterclaims by Caribbean islands – did not deter the inhabitants of Juan Fernández from happily renaming their island after Crusoe 15 years ago.

Selkirk had himself put ashore from an English frigate after quarrelling with his captain. He took along a few supplies, and when these were used up, he made the best of the island's resources. Four years later, when Captain Woodes Rogers chanced across the Scotsman, he was clad in goatskins and could scarcely speak English.

Rogers remarked that Selkirk was in superb physical condition and, having devoted much of his time to Bible-reading, 'he was a better Christian while in this solitude'. It remained for Defoe to explore the philosophical dimensions Rogers had touched upon. Drawing on contemporary accounts of castaways, Defoe spiced his version with a shipwreck, thoughtfully provided an arsenal of ammunition to cover Crusoe's stay of 28 years and, finally, relocated the island to accommodate an Amerindian.

Crusoe's prototype was apparently something of a statistician. He counted the days he'd been kept marooned, and 'he kept an Account of the 500 [goats] that he kill'd while there, and caught as many more which he marked on the ear and let go'. It seems he was involved in an ecological experiment of sorts. Juan Fernández, the Spanish navigator who discovered the islands in 1574, had stocked them with goats for future settlement but, as Rogers explains, other animals ran amok from visiting ships:

'The rats gnaw'd [Selkirk's] Feet and Clothes while asleep which oblig'd him to cherish the Cats with Goats-Flesh; by which many of them became so tame that they would lie about him in hundreds and soon deliver'd him from the Rats.'

Defoe chose to ignore these surreal cat banquets, in keeping with the sober nature of his tale. The Chilean Tourist Board, stretching fact and fiction a little further, offers the following information: 'Visitors to the island today may enjoy many of the sporting activities which allowed the legendary beachcomber to survive.' This refers, of course, to skin-diving; Selkirk's manner of diversion was actually a little more bizarre.

Because he couldn't stomach the seafood without salt, the mariner's staple was goat flesh. His gunpowder spent, he simply outran the beasts, and discovered the joys of goat-tagging. It could be a dangerous sport: once he stumbled over a precipice clutching the

quadruped he had tackled (the goat, luckily, cushioned his fall). The wild sailor demonstrated his great agility by supplying goats for Rogers' crew while they harboured there. He outdistanced Rogers' dogs with ease. Should any one doubt that Selkirk had the makings of a truly immortal quarterback, there are still enough feral goats on the islands to test your legs against.

There was another sport the hermit indulged in – bull-fighting. In his day, the islands were thickly populated with sea lions; Rogers sighted one monstrous mammal 20 feet in length and weighing at least a ton. A bull sea lion like this would charge any intruder interfering with his harem, and could snap a man's leg with his powerful jaw or tail. Selkirk noticed that while these sea monsters were agile enough on land, they had trouble turning around; if he got towards the middle of one, he could despatch it with a matadorial flourish of his hatchet.

Hunting was also a favourite pastime of the buccaneers who put in at the islands; they boiled down the sea lions' blubber for oil. Between 1797 and 1804, it is estimated that commercial sealers took three million skins, driving the amphibians to the verge of extinction. In Selkirk's time, however, the howling of the sea lions in breeding season could be heard a mile offshore. Rather than the walls of silence that one imagines for a castaway's island, the air must have been filled with a cacophony of barking sea lions, bleating goats and wailing cats. Solitude? With the armies of tamed cats and goats around his hut, and the seal-carpeted foreshores, Selkirk cannot have felt *too* lonely.

In fact he came to enjoy his status as absolute monarch. All the same he felt it his duty to get himself returned to civilisation, and regularly hiked up to a lookout point to tend his signal fire – with a singular lack of success. The hardy Scotsman lived roughly where S Juan Bautista is now located; his original cave is close by, and the visitor can retrace his steps to the lookout. Since it first appeared on the map, Robinson Crusoe Island gained a reputation as a health resort for scurvy-wracked crews. Its lush vegetation, temperate climate, abundant wildlife and fresh water attracted Dutch and English pirates. This forced the Spanish to claim the hideaway; the forts they set up have been excavated, along with rusty cannons dating back to 1750. A more recent piece of salvage is the wreck of the German cruiser *Dresden*. The vessel retired to the islands for repairs; when the British bore down on it in 1915, the captain blew up his own magazine.

But, you ask, whatever became of seadog Selkirk? Well, after getting used to shoes, liquor and English voices again, he was given command of a captured galleon. En route to England, Selkirk learned that Captain Stradling, the man who'd let him off at Juan Fernández, had passed four miserable years in a Lima jail after the Spaniards came across his foundered vessel – so Selkirk's fate had not been so bad at all. Back in London, Selkirk was an overnight celebrity – and a rich man with his share of plundered Spanish gold. But, as he confided in an interview, 'I shall never be so happy as when I was not worth a Farthing.' After an abortive attempt to construct a cave behind his father's house in his native Scotland, Selkirk set sail again in 1717 and died aboard ship from a fever in 1723, at the age of 47. He was never to know that his story would live on for centuries. In his birthplace in Lower Lago, Fife, Scotland, there stands a bronze statue of a mariner with his goatskins and flintlock, hopefully scanning the horizon for a distant ship.

Daniel Defoe, the veteran journalist who so successfully passed off the mariner's story as his own, kept his creditors at bay with his sensational novel. Defoe was a formidable writing machine: in 1719, the year the bestseller appeared, he penned seven other works and contributed to four newspapers. The classic he knocked out in a matter of months has kept critics, artists, editors, scholars and translators busy for the last two centuries. Not to mention hotel owners, advertising people, film directors, souvenir vendors. . .and the present writer.

Michael Buckley

The Lake District

There are few areas in the world which can match the Lake District for scenic grandeur. South of the Río Toltén and sprawled across the provinces of Valdivia, Osorno and Llanquihue, you'll find everything from snow-capped mountains to deep-blue lakes, smoking volcanos, forests and glaciers.

Outside noisy cities, such as Puerto Montt, the loudest sound you're likely to hear is the roar of waterfalls streaming down cliff faces into crystal-clear pools. Yet, had you come this way in the early 17th century you would have found a far less peaceful scene. The Spanish settlements south of the Río Bío Bío were being reduced to piles of ash by Indian counterattacks.

The most important urban centres in this region are Valdivia, Osorno and Puerto Montt, although, about half the population still lives in the country. Tourism plays an important part in the local economy, but lumbering, cereal and dairy farming and livestock rearing are also important. Local industries, such as sawmills and leather works, tend to be based largely on rural production.

Temuco, which is in the Región de la Araucanía, is the jumping-off point for the Lake District. From Temuco, you can head to Villarrica on the shores of Lago Villarrica. From there, you can wind your way south to Licán Ray and Coñaripe on Lago Calafquén, Panguipulli and Choshuenco on Lago Panguipulli and Futrono on Lago Ranco. You can visit Puerto Varas and Ensenada on Lago Llanquihue, then head east to Lago Todos los Santos, the most beautiful of all the lakes, crossing it by ferry from Petrohué to Puella.

History

Around Concepción, and to the south, the Spanish conquistadors found gold mines, good agricultural land and a large potential workforce of Indians. The lands were so tempting that some conquistadors gave up their encomiendas in the central valley for grants of land south of the Río Bío Bío. Despite their optimism, this area was a dangerous frontier for the entire colonial period, its settlements constantly under threat of Indian attack or some other calamity.

Concepción, for example, was founded in 1550, destroyed in 1554, refounded the following year and then abandoned, re-established in 1558 and destroyed by an earthquake and tidal wave in 1570. Until the end of the 16th century, it was nothing more than a military camp. It was only after 1603, when a large permanent garrison was stationed there, that it took on the appearance of a permanent town.

Places south of the Río Bío Bío such as Osorno, Valdivia and Imperial were constantly threatened by the Mapuche Indians. In the early 17th century, they rose in revolt against the Spanish and destroyed these settlements. Attempts by the Spanish to regain control over them failed dismally.

By the mid-17th century, the Spanish gave up hope of colonising the area south of the Río Bío Bío and Concepción became the southern outpost of the Spanish Empire in Chile.

The one exception to this ignominious retreat was the resettlement and fortification of Valdivia in 1645 and 1646. It was a century before the Spanish once again built permanent settlements south of the Río Bío Bío.

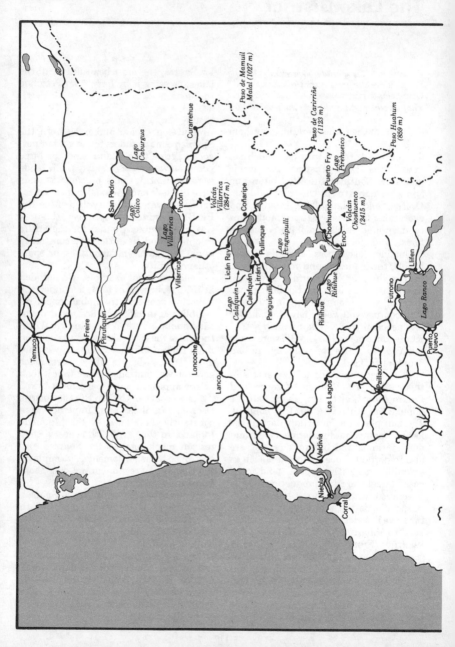

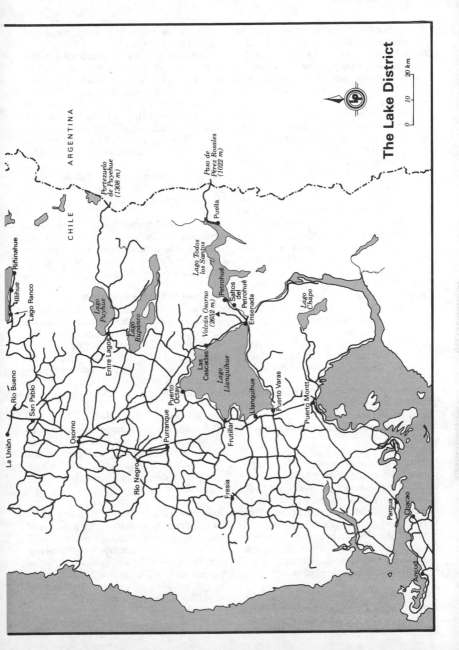

The Lake District

It was not until the 1880s, however, that the Mapuche Indians were finally subjugated and the region was made safe for European settlement. The Indians were pushed further south, their land was divided into large rural estates and the hacienda system was introduced.

Today, the provinces between the Río Bío Bío and the Río Toltén are still home for the several hundred thousand remaining Mapuche Indians. Deprived of much of their land by Spanish conquerors and later by Chilean capitalists and politicians, the Mapuche now make a precarious living from agriculture and crafts. From 1965 to 1973, land reform programmes improved their lot but since the military coup (in 1973), the land that was occupied (or 'recuperated') has once again been taken from them. The repression of organised rural militancy, including the murder of Mapuche leaders and farmers, restored 'peace' to the area.

Many local industries were started by German immigrants who settled in the Lake District in the 19th century. Breweries, tanneries, brick factories, bakeries, machine shops, furniture factories and mills were all established before the end of the 19th century. The German influence is still evident in places such as Valdivia where there are many people of German descent and where many central European-style buildings can be seen.

TEMUCO

This city, of a quarter of a million people, arose in 1881 out of the dust of Chile's own version of the American wild west. In the 19th century, this was the wild south, the Chilean frontier and the home of the Mapuche Indians. The frontier region is mainly a rural area, though there is a wide range of industrial activity including steel and textile production, coal mining and the processing of rural products.

Information

Tourist Office The tourist office (tel 34293) is at the corner of Bulnes and Claro Solar, opposite the plaza. It has city maps and many free leaflets.

Temuco has few attractions for the visitor and is mainly a starting point to visit the Lake District or Mapuche Indian settlements in the surrounding region. It's also a market town for the Mapuche and the best place to buy their fine handmade woollen ponchos, pullovers and blankets. You will see many Indians coming into town with fruit, vegetables and handicrafts.

Post & Telecommunications The post office and TELEX Chile are at the corner of Diego Portales and Prat.

Banks Cash and travellers' cheques can be changed at Turismo Money Exchange, Galería Centenario, Prat 656, and the Banco del Estado de Chile, at the corner of Bulnes and Claro Solar.

Regional de la Araucanía Museum

Housed in an attractive colonial building at Alemania 84, this museum has an interesting exhibition recounting the story of the Mapuche Indians before, during, and after the Spanish invasion. It's open from Tuesday to Saturday, 9 am to 1 pm and from 3 to 7 pm, and Sunday and holidays from 10 am to 1 pm.

City Market

The main market runs for several blocks along Pinto – from the railway station to the provincial bus station. Many of the vendors are Mapuche Indians, whom you'll see entering the town in horse carts and bullock drays.

Galería Artesanal

The Galería Artesanal, at the junction of Balmaceda and Bulnes, mainly sells Indian-made woollen blankets, ponchos and pullovers. Most goods are price tagged, so it might be worth coming here to get an idea of prices before buying anything at the markets.

Places to Stay - bottom end

Temuco doesn't have much bottom-end accommodation. The only particularly cheap place is the rambling *Hotel Terraz* which has singles/doubles from US$5/9. Many of its rooms have no windows other than those opening out into passageways, so you may find it worthwhile to pay more and take a room facing the street. There's a fairly cheap restaurant downstairs.

The *Hotel Turismo* (tel 232348) at Claro Solar 636 has singles/doubles from US$7/13. Rooms with a private bathroom are twice the price.

Places to Stay - middle

The *Hotel Emperador* (tel 237124) at Bulnes 853 has pleasant singles/doubles for US$15/25, with private bathrooms. The people are friendly and the place is good value for the price.

Another recommendation is the *Hotel Continental* (tel 231166) at Varas 708. A great, rambling wooden building, it's very clean and the people are friendly. Doubles cost US$16.

The *Hotel Espellate* (tel 234255) at Claro Solar 492 is also good. It has singles/doubles from US$12/21, with private bathrooms.

The pick of the hotels is the *Hotel Nicolás* (tel 235547) at General MacKenna 420. It has smallish rooms, but these are bright and clean and have a bathroom and TV. Singles/doubles cost US$23/34.

The *Hoteles de la Frontera* (tel 236190) at Bulnes 733 has singles/doubles from US$20/28.

Although not very impressive from the outside, the *Hotel Aitue* (tel 234933) at General Cruz 40 is a pretty good place and offers reasonable value with singles/doubles at US$17/25.

Places to Stay - top end

Across the road from Hoteles de la Frontera, the *Nuevo Hotel de la Frontera* (tel 236190) at Bulnes 726 is the biggest, most expensive hotel in town. Singles/doubles cost US$52/64.

Places to Eat

Cheap meals are available in many of the small restaurants and from the snack places around the Bus Terminal Rurales. The best value is the *Nueva Hostería Allen Clei* at Manuel Bulnes 902, where a full meal with generous servings costs only a few US dollars. Also, try the spiffy *Pizzaria Dino* at Bulnes 368 and the more up-market *Julio's Pizza* at Bulnes 478. Check out the *Centro Español* at Bulnes 883 - if the food's no good you can go bowling in the basement.

Things to Buy

The handicrafts market, the Mercado Municipal, is at the corner of Diego Portales and Aldunte. Although it has an immense amount of junk and mass-produced souvenirs, this is a good place to buy Indian woollen ponchos, blankets and pullovers. Many Indian women also hawk these goods on the streets. Look for jewellery, pottery, polished stone mortars and musical instruments such as pan pipes and drums.

Getting There & Away

Air Ladeco (tel 36414) is at Prat 535, near the plaza, and LAN-Chile (tel 34977) is at Bulnes 667, near the corner with Varas. Only Ladeco flies from Temuco. It has flights several days a week to Santiago and Puerto Montt.

Bus From Temuco, you can head north to Santiago, south to Valdivia, Osorno and Puerto Montt, or to nearby towns such as Villarrica, Licán Ray and Curarrehue in the Lake District.

There are international buses to Zapala, Neuquén, Mendoza, Bariloche and Buenos Aires in Argentina.

The main bus companies have terminals around the town centre. Typical fares from Temuco are: Santiago US$10; Valdivia US$2.50; Osorno US$4; Puerto Montt US$6; Villarrica US$1.50; Coñaripe US$2.50; and Licán Ray US$2. Typical

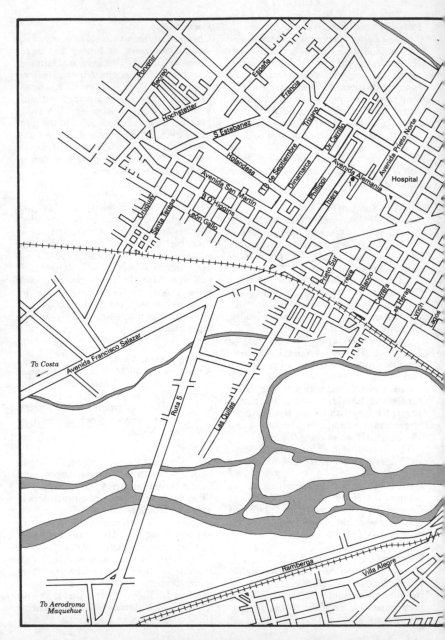

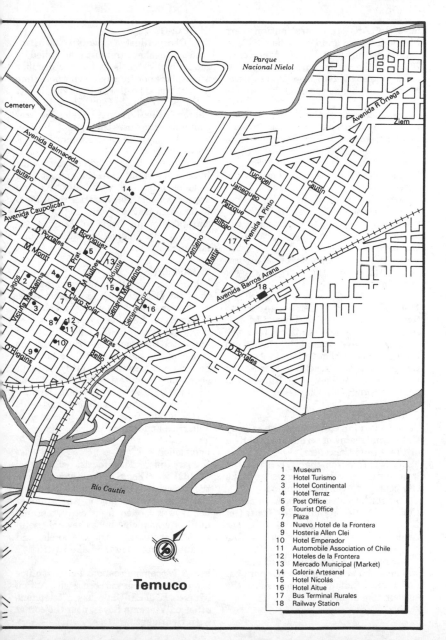

Temuco

1 Museum
2 Hotel Turismo
3 Hotel Continental
4 Hotel Terraz
5 Post Office
6 Tourist Office
7 Plaza
8 Nuevo Hotel de la Frontera
9 Hosteria Allen Clei
10 Hotel Emperador
11 Automobile Association of Chile
12 Hoteles de la Frontera
13 Mercado Municipal (Market)
14 Galoria Artesanal
15 Hotel Nicolás
16 Hotel Aitue
17 Bus Terminal Rurales
18 Railway Station

fares to Argentine destinations are Mendoza US$28 and Bariloche US$25.

Cruz del Sur is at Vicuña MacKenna 761, near the corner with Varas. It has daily buses to Santiago and Puerto Montt, stopping at various towns on the way.

Tas Choapa is at the corner of Pedro Lagos and Claro Solar and has daily buses to Santiago and Puerto Montt and to Mendoza and Bariloche via Osorno.

Buses García is at the Bus Station Rurales on Balmaceda. It has several buses daily to Villarrica and Licán Ray.

Buses Jac is on Vicuña MacKenna, near the corner with Varas. It has about two dozen buses daily to Villarrica as well as daily buses to Santiago, Licán Ray, Coñaripe and Curarrehue.

The time and frequency of departures change throughout the year, with fewer buses in winter.

Train Daily trains from Temuco go north to Santiago and south to Puerto Montt, stopping at various stations (see the Getting Around chapter). Buy train tickets either at the station on Avenida Barros Arana or at the Ferrocarriles del Estado Venta de Pasajes at Bulnes 582, near the corner with Claro Solar.

Getting Around
Temuco is a large town and the railway station and main bus terminal are quite a distance from the centre.

Bus No 1 runs from the city centre to the train station and Bus No 9 runs from the city centre to Avenida Alemania.

Cars can be rented from the Automobile Club (tel 238400) at Bulnes 763, Hertz (tel 236190) at Bulnes 726, Avis (tel 231914) at Arturo Prat 800 and National at the airport.

Car rental is worth considering since it will give you easy access to the national parks and Indian settlements in the surrounding area.

CHOL CHOL
Chol Chol is a dusty village of wooden, tin-roofed bungalows and dirt roads plied by Indian bullock carts. It has the peculiar atmosphere of a frontier town where time has either stood still or, at least, run slowly.

Buses to Chol Chol depart from Temuco's Bus Terminal Rurales. Several companies run buses throughout the day. The trip takes about 1½ hours along a gravel road.

The bus is likely to be crammed with Indians returning from the market with bags of fruit and vegetables. As you approach Chol Chol, you'll see traditional Indian *ruca* houses. From Chol Chol, you can take a bus back to Temuco via Imperial, an interesting ride through farming country.

VILLARRICA
Villarrica is one of the chief resort towns of the Lake District, with impressive views of the smoking, snow-covered Volcán Villarrica on the other side of the lake. At night you can sit by the edge of the lake and watch the flames flickering above the throat of the mountain. White-hot lava pouring out over snow, a fairly frequent occurrence, is quite a sight. The last time this mountain blew its top was in the early 1980s. You can buy photos and postcards of the event from the shopkeepers in Villarrica and Pucón.

Information
Tourist Office The tourist office (tel 411162) is on Pedro de Valdivia, close to the junction with Acevedo. It's often closed in winter, but in the summer holidays it's open from early morning until late at night. It has several useful leaflets including lists of hotels and camping grounds in the Lake District.

Post & Telecommunications The post office is on Urrutia, near the corner with Anfion Muñoz. ENTEL Chile has a telephone office on Vincente Reyes, near the corner with Henríquez.

Volcán Villarrica

Ruca

Although the scenery is the main reason to visit Villarrica, it does have other attractions. At the corner of General Körner and Pedro de Valdivia, there is a reconstruction of a ruca, a traditional Mapuche Indian house. It's roughly oblong-shaped with thatch walls and roof. Two wooden burial figures stand outside.

Museum

Nearby is an interesting museum with an exhibition of Mapuche Indian artefacts, including jewellery, musical instruments and several peculiar roughly hewn wooden masks – powerful carvings despite their simplicity.

Places to Stay – bottom end

One of the cheapest places in Villarrica is the *Hotel Fuentes* at Vincente Reyes 665. It's very popular with travellers and

hikers, and rooms cost about US$5 per person. Although the rooms are just basic, they are pleasant and comfortable. Downstairs there is a bar and cheap restaurant where there's usually an open log fire during winter. The staff are very friendly.

There are several cheap hospedajes around town and you can identify most of them by the handwritten signs in the windows. They are usually ordinary family homes and they charge a few US dollars per person. One that seems to operate on a permanent basis is upstairs at Letelier 702. It's run by a local family, is very clean, has hot showers and bright, comfortable rooms. Also, try the hospedaje at the corner of Urrutia and General Körner. There are similar places along Körner.

Other recommended cheap places include the *Residencial Victoria* at Anfion Muñoz 530, which at US$4 per

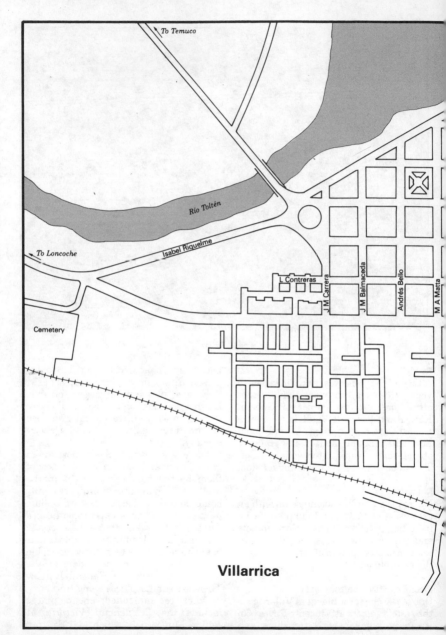

To Temuco

Río Toltén

To Loncoche

Isabel Riquelme

L Contreras

J M Carrera

J M Balmaceda

Andrés Bello

M A Matta

Cemetery

Villarrica

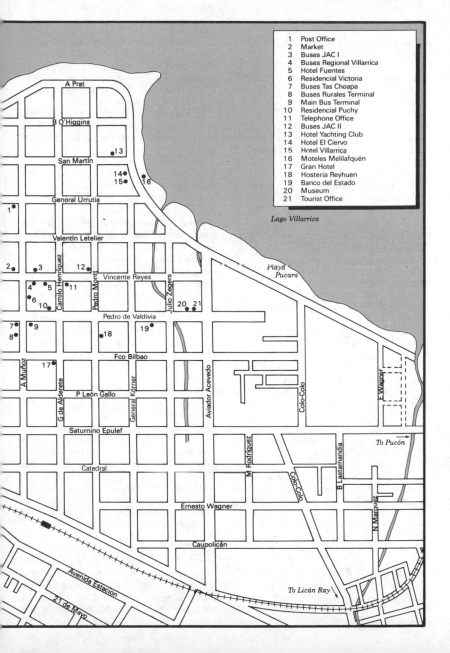

1   Post Office
2   Market
3   Buses JAC I
4   Buses Regional Villarrica
5   Hotel Fuentes
6   Residencial Victoria
7   Buses Tas Choapa
8   Buses Rurales Terminal
9   Main Bus Terminal
10 Residencial Puchy
11 Telephone Office
12 Buses JAC II
13 Hotel Yachting Club
14 Hotel El Ciervo
15 Hotel Villarrica
16 Moteles Melilafquén
17 Gran Hotel
18 Hostería Reyhuen
19 Banco del Estado
20 Museum
21 Tourist Office

Lago Villarrica

Playa Pucara

A Prat
B O'Higgins
San Martín
General Urrutia
Valentín Letelier
Camilo Henriquez
Vincente Reyes
Pedro Montt
Julio Zegers
Pedro de Valdivia
Fco Bilbao
A Muñoz
G de Alderete
P León Gallo
General Kórner
Aviador Acevedo
Saturnino Epulef
Catedral
M Rodríguez
Colo-Colo
B Laatamandia
F. Wagner
N Marquez
Ernesto Wagner
Caupolicán
Avenida Estacion
21 de Mayo

To Pucón
To Licán Ray

person is not bad. There's a good, cheap restaurant on the ground floor. Also, try the *Residencial Puchy* at Valdivia 678.

There are lots of campsites around the lake, some of them free. A list of sites and prices is available from the tourist office.

Places to Stay – middle

The *Gran Hotel*, at the corner of Alderete and Bilbao, is a large, highly recommended hotel in a quiet part of town. Singles/ doubles cost US$16/28.

The *Hostería Reyhuen* at Pedro Montt 668 is a beautiful place with hot showers, room heating and a restaurant. Singles/ doubles with breakfast cost US$13/22. It's run by Gualberto Lopez, who is very friendly and speaks English. This is my pick of the hotels in Villarrica.

Places to Stay – top end

The *Hotel El Ciervo* is at General Körner 241. It's one of several good hotels at the lakeside-end of General Körner. Singles/ doubles with breakfast start at US$38/46. The *Hotel Villarrica*, on the same street, has double cabins from US$48.

The *Hotel Yachting Club* at San Martín 802, overlooking the lake, has rooms for US$31, which includes breakfast. It also has a restaurant and swimming pool.

Places to Eat

There are many restaurants along Henríquez, Valdivia and Alderete.

The *Club Social Bar-Restaurant* at Valdivia 640 has good, cheap meals. The *Scorpio Café Bar*, at the corner of Valdivia and Pedro Montt, is typical of Villarrica's tourist cafes.

The *Peña La Tranquera* at Acevedo 761, between Bilbao and Gallo, is a bar and folk club with live music.

Getting There & Away

Bus The main bus terminal is on Pedro de Valdivia at the junction with Anfion Muñoz. From Villarrica, there are daily buses to Santiago, Puerto Montt and other places in the Lake District. There are frequent buses to Mendoza, Zapala, Neuquén, San Martín de los Andes and Bariloche in Argentina. Fares are similar to those from Temuco.

Tur-Bus is at the main bus terminal and has daily buses to Santiago.

Igi Llaima is at the main bus terminal and has buses three days a week to San Martín de los Andes and Neuquén in Argentina.

Tas Choapa is at the corner of Pedro de Valdivia and Anfion Muñoz. It has buses three days a week to Bariloche, via Temuco and Osorno. It also has buses to Santiago and Puerto Montt.

Buses Regional Villarrica is on Vincente Reyes, next to the Hotel Fuentes, and has daily buses to Pucón, Curarrehue and Puerto Basa.

Buses Jac has two terminals. There are several departures daily to Licán Ray and Coñaripe from the terminal on Vincente Reyes, near the corner with Anfion Muñoz. There are frequent buses to Temuco and Pucón from the terminal at the corner of Vincente Reyes and Pedro Montt. It also has daily buses to Santiago and Valdivia.

Getting Around

Villarrica is really a starting point for visiting the surrounding area and not so much a destination in its own right. To get to some of the beautiful waterfalls and thermal springs in the nearby hills you need a car, which can be rented from Hertz in the Hotel Yachting Club, at the corner of San Martín and Pedro Montt. You can also ask at the tourist office about local people who take tourists on day trips through the surrounding area.

PUCÓN

Apart from windsurfing and building sandcastles on a mediocre beach, there's not much to do in Pucón. The town is purely a resort and is of no interest to foreigners and, if the bored faces of the inmates are any indication, it's of no

Top: The Lake District
Left: Volcán Osorno, Lake District
Right: Volcán Villarrica, Lake District

Top: Shop, Futrono, Lake District
Left: Riverfront, Valdivia, Lake District
Right: Street scene, Valdivia, Lake District

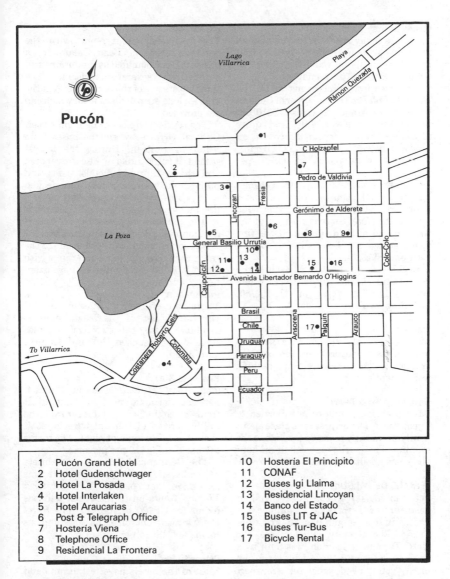

Pucón

1   Pucón Grand Hotel
2   Hotel Gudenschwager
3   Hotel La Posada
4   Hotel Interlaken
5   Hotel Araucarias
6   Post & Telegraph Office
7   Hostería Viena
8   Telephone Office
9   Residencial La Frontera

10   Hostería El Principito
11   CONAF
12   Buses Igi Llaima
13   Residencial Lincoyan
14   Banco del Estado
15   Buses LIT & JAC
16   Buses Tur-Bus
17   Bicycle Rental

interest to the Chileans either. It may serve as a useful base to explore the surrounding area, but I'd opt for Villarrica which is sometimes a lively place.

Information

The staff at the tourist office (tel 125) on Brasil, near the junction with Caupolicán, can tell you about tours of the area.

Places to Stay

There are many hotels in Pucón, though none are particularly cheap. You can find them very easily by walking around the streets – Pucón is only small.

The cheapest hotel seems to be the *Hostería Don Pepé* at the corner of General Urrutia and Arauco. It costs US$10 per person and is clean, tidy and quite pleasant. The *Residencial Lincoyán*, on Lincoyán between Urrutia and O'Higgins, is similar with rooms at US$7 per person.

One of the obvious signs of the German influence in the south is the fine chalet hotels in the Lake District. One such place is the *Hotel Gudenschwager*, at the western end of Valdivia, which has fine views across the lake. Singles/doubles start at US$13/24.

Backing on to the tacky beach is the very grand *Pucón Grand Hotel* where singles/doubles start at US$52/80, including meals.

Places to Eat

Most of the hotels in Pucón have their own restaurants. There are many places to eat around the town centre, but nothing worth mentioning.

Getting There & Away

Bus Buses Jac handles the Villarrica to Pucón route. Departures take place about hourly, from early morning through to the evening. The journey takes half an hour and costs about US$0.50.

TERMAS DE PALGUIN

You can forsake Pucón altogether and head for the Termas de Palguin, a hot spring in the mountains 30 km from Pucón. The attractive chalet here, the Hotel Termas de Palguin, was built by a German in the mid-1940s. Unless you can hitch, you'll need your own transport here. Ask at the Pucón tourist office about day tours.

LICÁN RAY

This is a lively popular resort town on the northern shore of Lago Calafquén, a beautiful lake bounded by mountains and studded with several small islands. The town boasts one of the best beaches in the area – a long strip of black sand which can get crowded.

The tourist strip is on the main street, General Urrutia, where the buses from Villarrica pull in. During the tourist season, it turns into a night carnival area and the restaurants, hotels, cafes and billiard sheds are bustling and packed with people. At other times, this place is like an overgrown village with dirt roads and a curious appearance of under-development, despite the tourist trade.

As soon as you hit the other side of the river, cars give way to local farmers with heavy wooden carts drawn by huge oxen.

Information

There's a useful tourist office on General Urrutia. A list of the local hotels is available. Also, the staff can organise tours to places such as Termas de Liquiñe and Inquine.

Places to Stay

The *Hotel Bellavista* is on Punulef, between Cariman and Marlchanguln. It fronts on to the beach and is far from the milling crowd of General Urrutia, so it should be fairly quiet at night. The rooms are basic at US$10 per person.

The *Residencial Temuco* on Gabriela Mistral is simple and homely with rooms for US$4 per person. The *Hostería Victor's* fronts on to the beach and has rooms for US$20 per person. The *Hotel Refugio* also fronts on to the beach and has rooms for US$14 per person.

Places to Eat

Most of the hotels have restaurants and there are half a dozen cafes, restaurants and bars along General Urrutia and several fronting the Playa Grande.

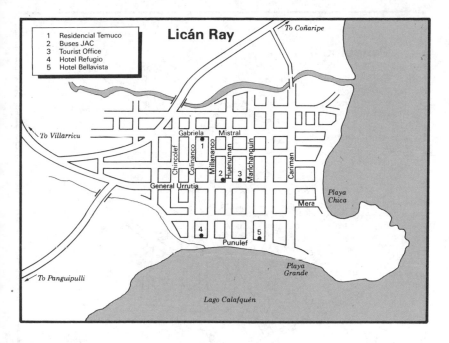

Licán Ray

1 Residencial Temuco
2 Buses JAC
3 Tourist Office
4 Hotel Refugio
5 Hotel Bellavista

To Coñaripe

To Villarrica

Gabriela   Mistral

Chincolef
Colinanco
Millanenco
Huenuman
Marichanquin
Cariman

General Urrutia

Playa
Chica

Mera

Punulef

Playa
Grande

To Panguipulli

Lago Calafquén

Getting There & Away

Bus You can easily make a day trip to Licán Ray from Villarrica. Buses Jac has several buses daily. The trip takes about 45 minutes and there are good views of Volcán Villarrica on the way.

In Licán Ray, the bus office is at the corner of General Urrutia and Huenuman. Every morning, a local bus goes from Licán Ray to Panguipulli. This takes about two hours, as it travels the back roads picking up passengers, most of whom are Mapuche Indians.

COÑARIPE

About 45 minutes drive from Licán Ray is Coñaripe, a one-horse lakeside town. Less developed than Licán Ray, its black-sand beaches sprout multi-coloured tents during the summer holidays. If you don't want to camp, stay at the pleasant though very basic *Hotel Antulafquen* on the main street, where rooms cost US$4 per person.

Buses Jac has several buses daily from Villarrica to Coñaripe via Licán Ray. The fare is about US$0.60.

PANGUIPULLI

This quiet little town nestled on the slopes bordering the northern edge of Lago Panguipulli, a beautiful lake, has marvellous views of Volcán Choshuenco. The town is quieter, slower-paced and less touristy than some of the other towns in the Lake District. Just outside the town is a small, uncrowded black-sand beach.

Information

The tourist office is at the main plaza. Pick up the leaflet *Panguipulli – capital de las rosas*, which has a very useful map of the Lago Calafquén, Panguipulli, Riñihue and Pirehueico region.

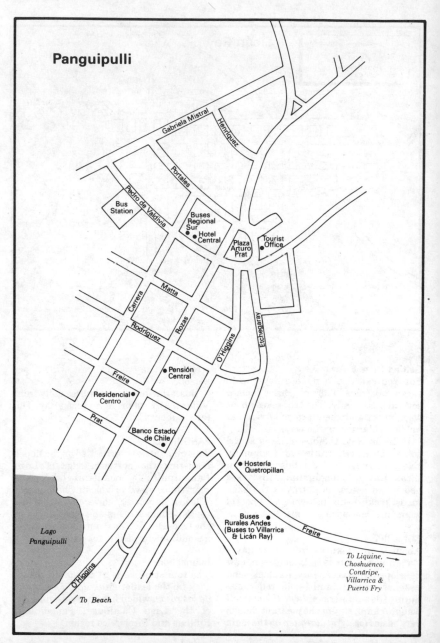

Panguipulli

Places to Stay – bottom end

There are several hotels and residencials to choose from in Panguipulli but the *Residencial Centro* on the corner of Rozas and Freire, is friendly, pleasant and good value at US$4 per person. It has hot showers.

The *Hotel Central* is on Pedro de Valdivia between Carrera and Rozas. Rooms are US$7 per person. It's a decent place with airy rooms and clean bathrooms (even bathtubs) and a very friendly and helpful manager. Take an upstairs room, not a matchbox-size downstairs room. It has hot showers.

Places to Stay – top end

Try the *Hostería Quetropillan* at Etchegaray 381, on the corner with Freire. Doubles cost US$18, with a private bathroom and hot water. It's a quiet location and the staff are friendly.

Places to Eat

There are a couple of bars and restaurants along Rozas, though nothing particularly worth noting. Try the *Restaurant Chapulin* at Rozas 639, which has meat and seafood dishes.

Getting There & Away

Bus There are two bus stations in Panguipulli. The one on Pedro de Valdivia has buses to Temuco, Valdivia, Santiago and down the lake to Choshuenco, Neltume and Puerto Fry.

Buses Pirehueico, Valdivia and Chile Nuevo each have daily buses to Valdivia, which take about 2½ hours. Buses Regional Sur has daily buses to Temuco. Buses Transpacar has several buses daily to Choshuenco, Neltume and Puerto Fry. Buses Urrutia has daily buses to Licán Ray and Calafquén.

The smaller of the two bus stations is on Freire and is used by Buses Rurales Andes for its daily service to Coñaripe, Licán Ray and Villarrica.

CHOSHUENCO

Choshuenco is barely more than two streets hemmed in by Lago Panguipulli, some farms and a rocky cliff. It's a tiny settlement relying for its survival on what it can grow, a local sawmill and a few stray banknotes from the tourists who find their way to its attractive black-sand beach. It's even quieter and more relaxed than Panguipulli. There are many fine walks in the surrounding countryside along dirt tracks through the vegetable fields and the grazing land.

Places to Stay & Eat

One of my favourite places in Chile is the *Hotel Rucapillan* next to the beach. It's very clean, with room heating, a good restaurant on the ground floor, hot showers and friendly staff. Rooms are US$6 per person. It has boats for hire.

Another decent little place is the *Claris Hotel*. It's basic but agreeable, with rooms

for US$3 per person. Similar to this is the *Hotel Choshuenco*, with rooms for US$4 per person. It also has a restaurant.

The *Hostería Pulmahue* is a beautiful place, just a short walk out of town on the road leading to Enco, set amidst a garden overlooking the lake. The dining room is filled with a collection of polished tree roots. Pleasant rooms with private bathrooms cost US$30 per person, which includes all meals. It's a great place to stay.

There are a couple of small shops along San Martín where you can buy fresh fruit and vegetables, as well as some groceries.

Getting There & Away

Bus Panguipulli is the starting point for Choshuenco. Buses going from Panguipulli to Choshuenco continue on to Puerto Fry where they stop overnight and depart early the next morning for the return trip to Panguipulli. The one-way trip takes about two hours.

VALDIVIA
History
Valdivia was one of the very first Spanish settlements in Chile. It was rebuilt as a military outpost after the original settlement was reduced to rubble early in the 17th century. The remains of fortifications can still be seen. There are large Spanish forts at the mouth of the Río Calle Calle at Corral, Niebla and Isla Mancera.

In 1820, during the war of independence, a single ship of the Chilean navy under the command of a mad Scotsman, Lord Thomas Cochrane, launched an apparently suicidal but ultimately successful attack on the forts at Corral. The story goes that after seizing a Spanish ship he had found in the harbour, Lord Cochrane landed 300 musketeers and took the fort in a surprise assault – no mean feat since it was supposed to be defended by more than 700 soldiers and 100 cannons.

Lord Cochrane had apparently led an equally stormy career in the British navy.

He was convicted of fraud and jailed before becoming one of the world's highest-ranking mercenaries, serving such diverse countries as Chile, Brazil and Greece. Perhaps his exploits redeemed him because in 1842 he was restored to his rank in the British navy and in 1854 was made an admiral.

Much of Valdivia's present character, however, is the result of German immigration in the mid-19th century. Until recently, most people likened arrival in Valdivia to stepping back in time to the Germany of pre-WW I.

The comparison seems rather forced now, although the German influence remains in the European architecture and the hotels with German names such as Schuster and Germania. Also, there are still many German-speaking people and people of German descent.

Many of the older buildings, however, were destroyed in the earthquake of 1960 and modern concrete constructions are now the going concern, though off the main streets it's still a town of weatherboard houses with corrugated iron roofs. There are still many older European-style buildings and fine mansions along Gralle Lagos near the waterfront.

Information
Tourist Office The tourist office (tel 213596) is on Avenida Costanera A Prat (otherwise known as Avenida Prat) on the waterfront between Libertad and Maipú.

Post & Telecommunications The post office is on O'Higgins opposite the Plaza de la República. The telephone office is at the corner of Yungay and Santa Carlos.

Bank You can change money and travellers' cheques at the Banco Concepción on Avenida Rámon Picarte, near the Plaza de la República.

Torreón del Barro
The Torreón del Barro is the turret of a Spanish fort built in 1774. It stands to the

River front, Valdivia

east of Valdivia's bus terminal. A second turret, built in the 17th century, stands at the corner of Yerbas Buenas and Yungay, facing the Río Valdivia.

The Corral Forts

Outside Valdivia, where the Río Valdivia and the Río Tornagaleones join the Pacific Ocean, there are 17th-century Spanish forts at Puerto Corral, Niebla and on the island of Mancera. The most interesting are the forts at Corral.

The Fuerte de Corral, near the jetty, is the largest and most impressive. It was first built in 1645 and restored and added to in the middle of the 18th century. Its battlements and cannon can still be seen. The second is the Fuerte Castillo de Armagos, a half-hour walk from Corral, set on a crag above a small fishing village.

Corral and Armagos can only be reached by boat, and the third fort, at Niebla, can be reached by bus and boat from Valdivia. The best way to get to any

of them is by one of the regular ferries which leave from the docks in front of the Valdivia tourist office. Buy your ticket from the kiosks on the riverfront. Departure times vary according to the day and season. The trip takes about 2½ hours from Valdivia to Corral via Mancera Island, Niebla and Armagos.

In Corral, there are a few places to eat on the waterfront, some of which serve enormous mixed plates of mussels, sausages, potato and chicken.

The Museum of History & Archaeology

This is one of the most beautiful museums in Chile, housed in a fine timber mansion near the riverfront on Teja Island. It has a large collection of Mapuche artefacts and household items from the early days of German settlement. To get there, walk across the bridge over the Río Valdivia, turn left at the first street and it's about 200 metres along on the left.

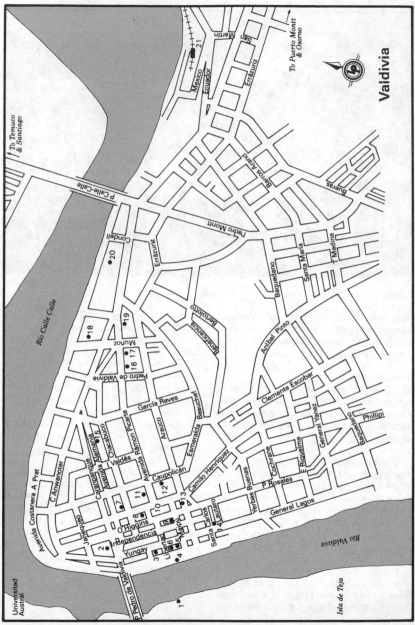

Valdivia

1	Archaeology Museum
2	Hotel Pedro de Valdivia
3	Market
4	Tourist Office
5	Hotel Schuster
6	Hotel Unión
7	Hotel Palace
8	Banco de Chile
9	Post Office
10	Plaza de la República
11	Banco Concepcíon
12	Ladeco
13	Restaurant Palacio & Train Booking Office
14	Telephone Office
15	Hotel Melillanca
16	Hotel Montserrat
17	Residencial Ainlebu & Residencial Germania
18	Bus Terminal
19	Hotel Regional
20	Torreón del Barro
21	Railway Station

Places to Stay – bottom end

Valdivia isn't a particularly cheap town in which to stay. Most of the private houses which offer rooms are full of students from Valdivia University, so there's no point trying to find a room in one of them.

There are a couple of decent places opposite the bus terminal. Try the *Hotel Regional* at Rámon Picarte 1005, where rooms cost US$6 per person. It's a fairly basic place but it's clean, has hot water and the people are friendly. There's a small restaurant attached.

If the Regional is full, try the *Residencial Picarte* next door. It can't be recommended, but it's there and costs about US$3 per person.

The *Residencial Ainlebu* is at Avenida Rámon Picarte. It's more basic than Residencial Picarte, though rooms are the same price and some can be very noisy. Otherwise, it's an agreeable place, with hot showers, decent meals and terrible beds.

If you'd like to stay on the riverfront, try the old *Hotel Unión* at Prat 514, opposite the tourist office. Rooms are US$6 per person. It's overpriced but clean and there's a bar downstairs.

Places to Stay – middle

The *Residencial Germania* (tel 212405) at Avenida Rámon Picarte 873 is next door to Residencial Ainlebu. It is a very decent place with singles/doubles for US$8/16, which includes breakfast. It has hot showers, room heating and a restaurant. The owners are friendly and speak German.

One hotel I would highly recommend is the *Hotel Montserrat* (tel 212032) at Rámon Picarte 849, a few doors from the Residencial Germania. The rooms are small, but clean and bright. Singles/doubles cost US$23/28, which includes breakfast.

For some old-world charm try the *Hotel Schuster* (tel 213272) at Maipú 60. It's a rambling old timber hotel with very clean, spacious rooms. It's been closed for renovations, but it should be an ideal place to stay.

The *Hotel Palace* (tel 213319) at Chacabuco 308 has singles/doubles with private bathroom for US$16/20. The rooms are small but it's a good hotel in an ideal location.

Places to Stay – top end

The *Hotel Pedro de Valdivia* (tel 212931) at Caranpangue 190 is surprisingly cheap with singles/doubles at US$34/44, including breakfast. It's a fine hotel with pleasant gardens.

Places to Eat

There are some good restaurants on Arauco between Caupolicán and García Reves, near the river. They're popular with the local people and the food is very good. The large market facing the river has many cheap restaurants.

For coffee and snacks, check out the *Restaurant Palacio* on the corner of O'Higgins and Arauco. It's popular with young people, especially on Saturday mornings.

The *Restaurant El Conquistador* on O'Higgins, facing the Plaza de la República, has a simple cafe downstairs (good for morning empanadas) and a restaurant upstairs with tablecloths and candles and a balcony overlooking the street and plaza.

For the best cakes and pastries in town, try the *Establecimientos Delicias* at Camilo Henríquez 372. You could eat elsewhere and then come here for drinks and dessert.

Also, try the *Centro Español* on Henríquez, near the Plaza de la República, and the *Bomba Bar & Restaurant* at the corner of Arauco and Caupolicán.

Getting There & Away
Air Ladeco is on Caupolicán, near the corner with Arauco. It has flights several days a week to Santiago and Puerto Montt.

Bus The bus terminal is on the corner of Anwanoter and Muñoz.

There are frequent buses to large towns and cities such as Santiago, Temuco, Osorno and Puerto Montt. These are served by companies such as Tas Choapa, Buses Norte and Cruz del Sur. Typical fares from Valdivia are: Santiago US$12; Temuco US$3; and Puerto Montt US$4.

Companies such as Turibús and Buses Norte have buses to Bariloche and Neuquén in Argentina. You should be able to get a bus any day of the week. Fares from Valdivia to Bariloche are US$22 and to Neuquén US$18.

There are daily buses to Punta Arenas in southern Chile, via Osorno and Argentine Patagonia. Enquire at companies such as Buses Norte. The fare to Punta Arenas is US$56. A bus cama is US$68.

Several companies have buses to destinations in the Lake District. Buses Línea Verde, Pirehueico, Valdivia and Chile Nuevo have buses to Panguipulli. Buses Línea Verde has daily buses to Futrono. Buses Jac has daily buses to Villarrica and Temuco. Fares to Panguipulli and Villarrica are around US$2.

Train Valdivia lies on the Santiago to Puerto Montt line. The train station is quite a long way from the town centre on Ecuador, a street which branches off Rámon Picarte. Tickets can also be bought from the booking office at the corner of O'Higgins and Arauco in the town centre. For schedules and fares, see the Getting Around chapter.

Getting Around
From the bus station or the train station, any bus marked 'Plaza' will take you to the Plaza de la República. From the plaza to the bus station, the buses go down Arauco before turning down Rámon Picarte. There are taxis too.

Cars can be rented from Hertz (tel 215252) at Picarte 624, Power at Cotapes 690 and the Automobile Club (tel 212376) at Caupolicán 475.

FUTRONO
Futrono is a dusty little town set on the slopes overlooking Lago Ranco. There's nothing much to the town, but the lake with its gently sloping hills flanking either side is a pretty sight. At the edge of the town, a track leads down to a black-sand beach, where you can swim in the calm, clear water. Although it's a tourist resort, relatively few people go there, so you'll find Futrono peaceful and very underrated.

Places to Stay & Eat
People often camp by the lake alongside the beach, a lovely spot, if you've got your own tent.

Otherwise, stay at the *Hostería El Ricán Arabe*, just off the main street on the edge of town as you arrive from Valdivia. It's on a hill overlooking the lake and has a swimming pool and restaurant.

The exuberant proprietor is Yelila Osman, daughter of a Palestinian couple who emigrated to Chile in the 1940s. She dishes up some extraordinary Arabic

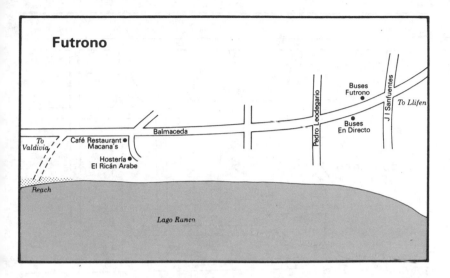

meals, including rack of lamb, stuffed vine leaves and cucumbers, accompanied by wine and Arabic songs. Rooms are about US$10 per person, which includes breakfast.

Apart from the hostería, there are several small restaurants and grocery stores on the main street.

Getting There & Away
The two bus companies operating from Futrono have offices on the main street. Buses Futrono and Buses En Directo each run several buses daily to Valdivia (US$2) via Paillaco.

LAGO RANCO
Lago Ranco, on the southern shore of the lake of the same name, is a remarkably ugly town, although the trip over the hills from Río Bueno is pretty, going through cattle-grazing country.

Information
The tourist office is on the main road as you arrive from Río Bueno. It has free maps of the town and leaflets on the Lake District. A small museum in the middle of town has mainly exhibits of Mapuche pottery.

Places to Stay & Eat
The *Hotel Casona Italiana*, on the lake front at Viña del Mar 145, is a clean, bright place with moderately priced rooms. Slightly cheaper is the *Hostería Phoenix*, a door or two away. The *Pensión Osorno* at Temuco 103 is a neat, spartan little hotel with cheap rooms. Apart from the hotels, you can eat at one or two small restaurants in town.

Getting There & Away
There are daily buses from Lago Ranco to Osorno. Otherwise, take a bus or taxi colectivo to Río Bueno. From there, you can easily get buses to Osorno, Valdivia or any number of other towns.

OSORNO
Osorno is one of the largest towns in southern Chile. It has a population of more than 110,000 and is a main transport centre for buses and trains to the Lake

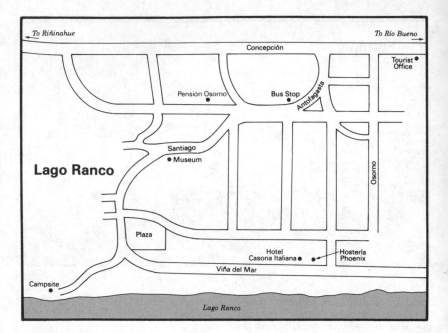

To Riñinahue

To Río Bueno

Concepción

Tourist Office

Pensión Osorno

Bus Stop

Antofagasta

Santiago
Museum

Lago Ranco

Osorno

Plaza

Hotel
Casona Italiana

Hostería
Phoenix

Viña del Mar

Campsite

Lago Ranco

District, especially to Lagos Puyehue and Rupanco and to the Parque Nacional Puyehue. Like Valdivia, there are many people of German descent.

Information

Tourist Office The tourist office (tel 232522) is in the Centro Cultural at Matta 556.

Bank Change money at Turismo Frontera Ltda at Galería Catedral, Ramírez 949.

Catholic Cemetery

Osorno is really just a transit stop on the way to somewhere else, but if you've got a few hours to spare this is an interesting place to wander around. The Catholic cemetery is on Rodríguez at the corner of Eduvijes. Its massive, ornate family crypts, far surpass others in Chile.

Old District

The most interesting part of the town is the old district between the Plaza de Armas and the railway station. There is a profusion of buildings left over from the early part of this century, including old factories and numerous weatherboard houses.

Fuerte Reina Luisa

Like Valdivia, Osorno also has its Spanish fort, the Fuerte Reina Luisa, built in 1793 on the orders of the Governor of Chile, Don Ambrosio O'Higgins, father of Bernardo O'Higgins. The restored fort guards the river entry to Osorno and stands to the west of the railway station.

Places to Stay – bottom end

One reasonably good cheap hotel is the *Residencial Ortega* at Colón 602, near the corner with Errázuriz. Rooms are US$3 per person, which includes breakfast. While it has hot showers, it's a bit rundown and in need of renovation.

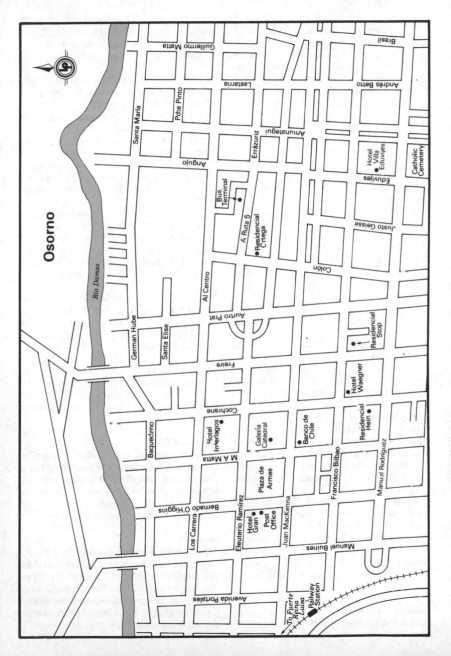

The *Residencial Hein* (tel 234116) on Cochrane, between Bilbao and Rodríguez, is much better. Although the rooms are small, they're much better maintained than the Ortega. The owner, who's part-German and part-Mapuche Indian, will keep you entertained with hearty tales of love and lust in the Indian rucas. Rooms cost US$8 per person.

Places to Stay – middle

The highly recommended *Villa Eduvijes Hotel* (tel 235023) is at Eduvijes 856, a few minutes walk from the bus terminal. It's good value, friendly and clean. Rooms cost US$11 and include hot water.

Places to Stay – top end

The pick at the top is the *Hotel Gran* (tel 232171), facing the Plaza de Armas. Simple, clean and neat singles/doubles with a phone and private bathroom cost US$21/35.

The *Hotel Waegnar* (tel 233721) is a large, highly respectable establishment at the corner of Cochrane and Bilbao. Singles/doubles cost US$30/40. It also has a restaurant.

Also, try the *Hotel Interlagos* (tel 234695) at Cochrane 551, which has singles/doubles for US$24/36.

Places to Eat

The *Club Social Ramírez* on Eduvijes, almost next door to the Villa Eduvijes Hotel, has good cheap food and generous portions. There are a couple of small snack bars along this street, serving good empanadas.

Fresh fruit and vegetables are available from the market at the corner of Errázuriz and Angujo. In town there's a *Dino's* at the corner of Matta and Eleuterio Ramírez, facing the plaza – good for drinks, snacks, grills and ice cream. *Luca's Pizzas* at Cochrane 559 is bright and popular.

Getting There & Away

Air LAN-Chile (tel 236688) is at Bilbao 777 and Ladeco (tel 234355) is at MacKenna 975. Ladeco has flights several days a week to Puerto Montt and Santiago.

Bus From the Osorno bus terminal, there are buses to most towns in the Lake District. Buses frequently go north to Santiago and south to Puerto Montt and Chiloé.

Schedules and fares to all the main towns, such as Santiago, Temuco and Puerto Montt as well as to destinations in Argentina, are the same as those for Valdivia (see the Valdivia section in this chapter).

There are several smaller places in the Lake District which can be more conveniently reached from Osorno. For example, Buses Via Octay have several buses daily from Osorno to Puerto Octay on the shores of Lago Llanquihue.

Train Osorno is on the Santiago to Puerto Montt train line. The railway station is on Portales, at the western end of town. For schedules and fares, see the Getting Around chapter.

Getting Around

Cars can be rented from Hertz (tel 5401) at Bilbao 857, the Automobile Club (tel 2269) at Bulnes 463 and Budget (tel 6688) at Bilbao 777.

PUERTO OCTAY

Puerto Octay is a peaceful, attractive little town on the low hills bordering Lago Llanquihue. One of my favourite towns in the Lake District, Puerto Octay is reminiscent of a European village, as it has many people of German descent.

Museum

The museum is on Independencía. It seems as though the whole town contributed to the displays by digging up their old farm machinery and rifling through attics and cellars for old porcelain, rusting irons, forgotten gramophone records and steam-driven telephones.

Places to Stay

Near the lake and next to the large church is a hospedaje upstairs at Wulf 712. Rooms are US$5 per person, including breakfast. Though basic, it's clean, the people are friendly and there are hot showers. The same people run the Restaurant Cabaña across the road.

The *Hotel Haase* at Pedro Montt 344 is an amazing place run by an elderly German lady who will probably give you a guided tour of the whole establishment. It's a rambling building with spacious interiors, high ceilings and no less than three dining rooms. This place is unique! Singles/doubles without a private bathroom cost US$14/22. Doubles with a private bathroom are US$25.

Just before you get to the Hotel Centinela on the Centinela Peninsula there's the Playa La Baja and the *Hostería La Baja*. It's a basic but an agreeable place with rooms for US$6 per person, which includes breakfast. There are also two campsites for which it costs US$5 to pitch a tent.

Further on is the *Hotel Centinela* at the end of Andrés Schmoelz, the road which runs from the town along the Centinela Peninsula. It's a massive timber chalet with simple but spacious rooms and a fine view across the lake. Singles/doubles cost US$16/28. It has a large restaurant.

Places to Eat

Apart from the hotels, the *Café Kali* opposite the plaza is a good place for breakfast, drinks and cakes. For morning empanadas, try the *Restaurant Naranja* on Independencia.

Getting There & Away

Bus There are several buses daily from Puerto Octay to Osorno. There is one bus in the late afternoon, Monday to Friday, from Puerto Octay south to Las Cascadas.

LAS CASCADAS

Las Cascadas is a tiny settlement so named because of the nearby waterfalls. The bus ride from Puerto Octay provides a grand view of Volcán Osorno and takes you through dairy country with many small farms and tiny, shingle-walled churches – all painted yellow with red corrugated iron roofs. Las Cascadas fronts

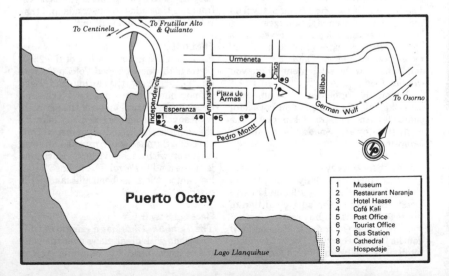

Puerto Octay

Lago Llanquihue

1	Museum
2	Restaurant Naranja
3	Hotel Haase
4	Café Kali
5	Post Office
6	Tourist Office
7	Bus Station
8	Cathedral
9	Hospedaje

Cafe Kali, Puerto Octay

on to a black-sand beach on the shores of the lake.

Places to Stay & Eat

The *Hostería Irma*, one km out of town on the road to Ensenada, charges about US$8 per person. It has a bar, serves meals and is a very agreeable and highly recommended place. There are several small shops in the settlement where you can buy food.

Diagonally opposite the hostería, alongside the lake, is a quiet and peaceful campsite. Another three km down the road towards Ensenada is a second campsite.

Getting There & Away

Bus One bus goes daily, Monday to Friday, between Las Cascadas and Puerto Octay. Because of the poor condition of the road, there is no bus service further south from Las Cascadas to Ensenada. If you don't have a car you'll have to walk or hitch. The bus from Puerto Octay gets

into Las Cascadas in the early evening, so unless you can hitch you'll have to stay the night in Las Cascadas. Despite what people and tourist leaflets say, it is 20 km from Las Cascadas to Ensenada and that is four hours of solid walking.

ENSENADA

Ensenada lies in the shadow of the 2660-metre high, snow-capped Volcán Osorno, on the shore of the biting-cold Lago Llanquihue. There's a good black-sand beach and beautiful views of the perfectly conical volcano across the misty lake. To the south is the jagged, demolished cone of Volcán Calbuco which must have blown its top off with a massive burp. Ensenada is on the road to Petrohué and Lago Todos los Santos, the most beautiful lake in the district.

Places to Stay & Eat

The *Teski Ski Club* has a refugio outside Ensenada with great views over the lake. It's a good base for climbing Volcán

Osorno and it's worth making the effort to get there.

Take the Ensenada to Puerto Octay road and turn off at the signpost about three km from the town and continue nine km up the side of the mountain. The refugio is below the snow line. It's open all year and has a warden who looks after the place. Getting there does entail a long, hard uphill trek, particularly if your pack is heavy!

The *Hostería Ruedas Viejas* has rooms for US$6 per person. You stay in cosy cabins with double beds, a private bathroom and a small wood burner for heating. The restaurant is cheap and the helpings are considerable.

On the main street, a few minutes walk from the hostería is an unsignposted hospedaje. It's a two-storey, wooden house with very clean, tidy rooms for US$5 per person, which includes breakfast.

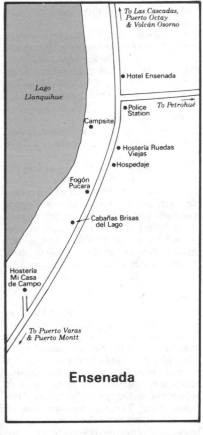

Ensenada

Volcán Osorno

Up the road the *Fogón Pucara* has rooms for US$12, with a private bathroom. The main attraction is the restaurant with its barbecue and very fine seafood dishes, featuring big fish.

At the top of the list is the *Hotel Ensenada*, the first large building you pass as you arrive from Las Cascadas. It's a fine place, similar to the Centinela in Puerto Octay, and has a large restaurant decorated with odd bits of ironwork and machinery. Lurking amongst the scrap metal is a raging fireplace. Rooms are

US$45, which includes breakfast and dinner.

A bit of a hike out of town on the way to Puerto Varas are the *Hostería Mi Casa de Campo* and the *Cabañas Brisas del Lago*. Both places have cabin accommodation at about US$50 per cabin. The cabins can accommodate five or six people.

Getting There & Away
There is no bus between Ensenada and Las Cascadas, so you must either walk or hitch.

From Las Cascadas, there is a daily bus to Puerto Octay. There is also a daily bus from Ensenada to Petrohué which comes through Puerto Varas and passes through Ensenada late in the morning. It then goes on to Petrohué then turns around and heads back to Puerto Varas. It does not arrive in Petrohué in time for you to catch the ferries to Puella, so you must spend a night at Petrohué.

PETROHUÉ
Petrohué is not much more than a hotel and CONAF (*Corporación Nacional Forestal* or National Parks) base, but it's one of the biggest tourist destinations at this end of the Lake District.

Lago Todos los Santos, its skyline completely overwhelmed by the perfect cone of Volcán Osorno, is the climax of the Lake District. The most dramatic views of the volcano are from the lake, a narrow body of water hemmed in on every side by high, forested hills. Peeking over the hills is Volcán Puntigudo.

Of course, the main reason to come to Petrohué is to leave it – by ferry to Puella across the striking blue waters of Lago Todos los Santos, with the awesome sight of Volcán Osorno providing a backdrop for almost the whole trip. Ferries leave Petrohué in the morning and return in the afternoon, after lunch at Puella.

Information
Post There is a small post office at Petrohué by the jetty.

CONAF CONAF has built an exhibition hall in front of the Hotel Petrohué, with exhibits on the Vicente Pérez Rosales National Park. The park includes Volcán Osorno and Lago Todos los Santos. The exhibition includes descriptions of the park's fauna and flora, geography, geology and the formation of the volcanos, glaciers and lakes.

Playa Larga
From the Hotel Petrohué, you can walk along a dirt track to the Playa Larga, a large black-sand beach which is much better than the one near the hotel. Follow the road through the CONAF campsite and then look for the sign which points to the beach. It's a half-hour walk from the hotel.

Isla Margarita
A tourist boat goes daily from Petrohué to Isla Margarita. It leaves in the afternoon during summer only. Margarita is a beautiful island with one small farm. The round trip lasts about two hours.

Places to Stay & Eat
Apart from camping by the beach, there are only two places to stay at Petrohué. A cheap place is the Küscher family's house. They're on the other side of the river, so you'll have to hire a rowboat to get there. You can camp in their grounds, otherwise, rooms cost about US$4 per person. It makes an interesting change from ordinary accommodation and they're friendly people.

There is a campsite on the beach on the shore of the lake a few minutes walk from the Hotel Petrohué. The charge is US$5 per tent.

A small shop at Petrohué sells a few provisions, but it may be better to stock up in Puerto Varas.

The large *Hotel Petrohué* is the only hotel. It's very comfortable and has a restaurant. Singles/doubles cost US$18/25, all with private bathrooms.

Getting There & Away

Bus There is a daily bus from Puerto Varas to Petrohué via Ensenada, departing Puerto Varas in the late morning. The bus gets to Petrohué after the ferries to Puella have left, so you have to stay overnight at Petrohué. There may be additional buses operating during the summer holidays. Hitching can be difficult due to lots of competition from other hitchhikers.

Boat Andina del Sur and Transporte Lago del Sur have daily ferries departing Petrohué early in the morning for Puella. Tickets can be bought at the kiosks near the jetty. The return fare is US$7 and the one-way trip takes about three hours. Both ferries connect with buses which are on the first leg of the journey from Puella to Bariloche in Argentina. Tickets for the ferry, either to Puella or straight through to Argentina, can also be bought at the Andina del Sur and Lago del Sur offices in Puerto Varas and Puerto Montt.

PUELLA

Lago Todos los Santos changes colour as you approach Puella and pass through a narrow stretch of deep-blue water which changes to emerald green before Puella. Puella has a hotel, customs post, school, post office and that's about it. Despite its size, it's a busy place in summer with numerous tourist groups passing through on their way to Argentina.

Things to See

Cascadas Los Novios is a waterfall just a few minutes walk uphill from the Hotel Puella. Transporte Lagos del Sur sometimes have a bus trip from Puella which goes 17 km up the road towards Argentina. From there, you can see Volcán Tronador, an immense extinct volcano with a huge glacier rolling down one side. It lies on the Chilean border – one peak belongs to Chile, the middle peak marks no man's land and the other is Argentine. The road from Puella follows a river which has its source in the volcano's glacier.

Places to Stay & Eat

One km from the dock is the *Hotel Puella*. It's a large place with singles/doubles for US$28/35, which includes two meals a day. There's a bar and restaurant and during the tourist season there is a buffet in a big canteen.

Near the hotel is the *Residencial Rabanita* which has rooms for US$12 per person, which includes two meals a day. It's a very simple place.

There's a campsite opposite the CONAF office. It may also be possible to get a room with one of the local families. According to some reports, staying with a family is excellent value with dinner, a cosy bedroom and breakfast provided.

Getting There & Away

For details on transport to Puella, see the Ensenada, Petrohué, Puerto Varas and Puerto Montt sections in this chapter.

PUERTO VARAS

Puerto Varas is a friendly but ordinary town on the south-east shore of Lago Llanquihue. There's not much of interest and the town is really just a transit point. From Puerto Varas, you can leave the Lake District and make your way south to Puerto Montt, head east to Lago Todos los Santos and Argentina or north to Santiago.

Information

Tourist Office The tourist office is at Del Salvador 328, near the corner with San Francisco. It has free brochures about the entire area.

Banks The Banco de Chile and the Banco del Estado de Chile are both on Santa Rosa, opposite the Plaza de Armas. Change cash and travellers' cheques at Exchange, Del Salvador 257.

Places to Stay – bottom end

Puerto Varas is a fairly large town and a tourist destination, so there's no problem finding accommodation.

The *Residencial Unión* is at San

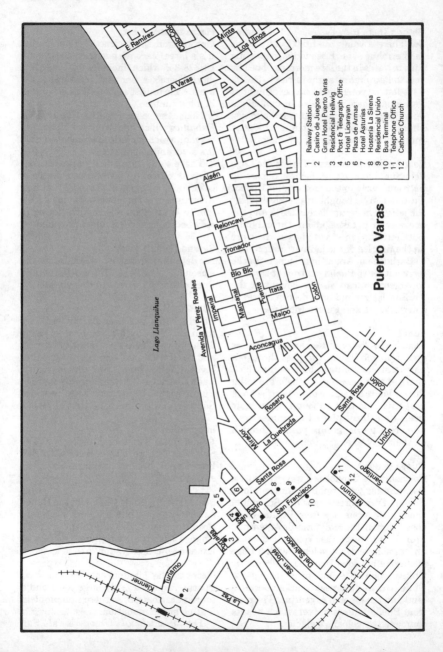

Puerto Varas

1   Railway Station
2   Casino de Juegos &
    Gran Hotel Puerto Varas
3   Residencial Hellwig
4   Post & Telegraph Office
5   Hotel Licarayan
6   Plaza de Armas
7   Hotel Asturias
8   Hostería La Sirena
9   Residencial Unión
10 Bus Terminal
11 Telephone Office
12 Catholic Church

Francisco 669, opposite the Varmontt bus terminal. It's very basic but clean and has hot showers. Rooms are US$6 per person, which includes breakfast. There's a cheap restaurant on the ground floor.

The *Residencial Hellwig*, at the corner of Portales and San Pedro, is also cheap. It's clean, bright and recommended, with reasonably spacious rooms at US$8 per person.

Places to Stay - middle

The *Hostería La Sirena* at Santa Rosa 710 is a fine place with a sweeping view of Puerto Varas. Doubles cost US$26, with a private bathroom.

Places to Stay - top end

The *Gran Hotel Puerto Varas* at Klenner 351 looks like a grand concrete bunker from the outside and gives the impression of having seen better days. Singles/doubles cost US$38/56.

Alternatives include the *Hotel Licarayan* which overlooks the waterfront and has rooms for US$41, or the *Hotel Asturias* at Del Salvador 322, which has singles/doubles for US$32/37.

Getting There & Away

Bus The best company for buses to Santiago or Puerto Montt is probably Buses Varmontt. Its terminal is on San Francisco and it has daily buses to Santiago and more than two dozen buses a day to Puerto Montt.

Several bus companies are in the town centre: Tur-bus Jedimar is at Del Salvador 322; LIT is at the corner of San Pedro and San Francisco; and Buses ETC and Buses Norte are both at the corner of San Francisco and Del Salvador. All operate buses to Santiago.

Typical fares from Puerto Varas are: Santiago US$32; Temuco US$12; Valdivia US$4; and Puerto Montt US$0.50.

For the bus/boat combination to Bariloche in Argentina, go to Andina del Sur at Del Salvador 243. It also has tours to Petrohué and Puella.

One Puerto Varas company has a daily bus from Puerto Varas to Petrohué via Ensenada, leaving every morning from the Residencial Hellwig. The bus stops briefly at Ensenada and Petrohué and then returns to Puerto Varas.

FRUTILLAR

Head north from Puerto Varas and follow the road which hugs the western rim of Lago Llanquihue. From Puerto Varas, take the Pan-American Highway as far as the little town of Llanquihue and then veer off on to the gravel road from Llanquihue to Frutillar.

The town is nothing, but the spectacle of sunbathers, swimmers, bright beach umbrellas and tiny tots in coloured floaties - all against a backdrop of the snow-capped Volcán Osorno on the horizon across the other side of the lake - is surrealistic.

Frutillar is noted for its well-preserved German houses and there is a Museum of German Colonisation a short walk up from the lakeside. It's extremely well laid out, with displays of old farming machinery and household artefacts.

Frutillar is divided into two parts: the resort area is by the lakeside beach and is referred to as Frutillar Bajo or Lower Frutillar, while the other part of town is Frutillar Alto or Upper Frutillar, which is an ordinary Chilean town, about two km uphill from the lakeside.

Information

There is a tourist kiosk by the beach, which is open during the summer holiday season.

Places to Stay & Eat

There are many hospedajes along the lakeside charging from about US$6 to US$10 per person. The most expensive hotel is the large *Hotel Frutillar* (you can't miss it) which has singles/doubles for US$41/52. There are many snack bars and a few restaurants along this stretch.

Getting There & Away

The drive from Llanquihue to Frutillar takes you through some interesting countryside, mainly grazing land with the lakeside occasionally sprouting salmon farms. If you're driving, turn off on to the Punta Larga road skirting a peninsula which juts into the lake. You can also reach Frutillar by bus from the direction of Osorno, but this means you miss out on the best countryside which is to the south of the town.

PUERTO MONTT

This is one of the largest towns in southern Chile and there are still many reminders of its German-influenced past. The area was settled by Germans in the mid-19th century and many houses are of northern-European design, faced with unpainted shingles, high-pitched roofs and quaint, ornate balconies.

Though timber houses make up a large share of Puerto Montt's housing, the pioneer image has long since faded. The large cathedral in the main square, built in 1856 entirely of redwood, is the oldest building in the city and one of the most important reminders of the city's early days.

Now Puerto Montt is the gateway to the southern end of the Lake District, to the island of Chiloé and Chilean Patagonia. It's the transport hub for buses, trains, planes and boats going north, east and south.

Information

Tourist Office The tourist office is a kiosk at the corner of Varas and O'Higgins, in front of the Plaza de Armas by the sea. It's open Monday to Saturday from 9 am to 1.30 pm and from 2.30 to 8 pm, and on Sunday from 10 am to 1 pm.

Post & Telecommunications The post office is at Rancagua 126.

Banks The Banco de Chile is at the corner of Urmeneta and Rancagua, and will change cash and travellers' cheques. Cash and travellers' cheques can also be changed at Exchange at Varas 595.

Argentine Consulate The Argentine Consulate is on the 2nd floor at Cauquenes 94, near the junction with Varas. It's open Monday to Friday from 9 am to 2 pm. It issues visas for Argentina.

Angelmo

The fishing village and market of Angelmo is about three km west of the town centre along the Portales. There are frequent local buses between the two which cost a few cents. Another attraction is the row of craft shops on Calle Angelmo just before you get to Angelmo. These sell a range of goods including sweaters, handmade boots, curios, copperwork, ponchos, woollen hats and gloves. Underneath the tourist junk there's some fine stuff. There's also a row of cheap seafood cafes along the sea front at Angelmo.

Museo Vicente Pérez Rosales

This museum has a collection of curios, small cannon and firearms and other implements of destruction from the colonial era as well as artefacts from the period of German settlement. The museum is at the corner of Varas and Quillota.

Places to Stay – bottom end

Many visitors to Puerto Montt stay in rooms in private houses. One of the best places is Raúl Arroya's house at Concepción 136. This is a very short street and his house is at the end, around the corner and against the base of the hill. Raúl and his family will make you very welcome. He often meets incoming buses and checks out the tourist office for visitors. The rooms are very clean and pleasant and cost about US$4 per person. There are hot showers. It's highly recommended and very popular.

Another private house used by visitors for many years is at Aníbal Pinto 328. It's warm, clean, friendly and good value.

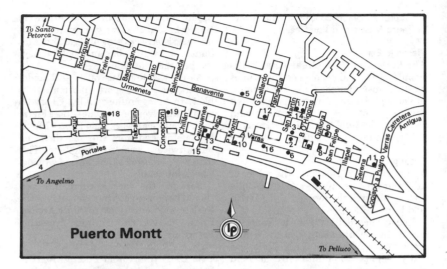

Puerto Montt

1	Railway Station
2	Plaza de Armas
3	Cathedral
4	Bus Terminal
5	Hotel Central
6	Tourist Office
7	Hotel Montt
8	Hotel Royal &
	Museum Vicente Pérez Rosales
9	Residencial Urmeneta
10	Hotel Burg
11	Hotel Punta Arenas
12	Banco de Chile
13	Hotel Colino
14	Ladeco
15	Argentine Consulate
16	Hotel Vicente Pérez Rosales
17	LAN-Chile
18	Residencial Embassy
19	Raul Arroya's House

The *Residencial Embassy* is on Valdivia, near the corner with Varas. It's a decent little place with rooms for US$6 per person.

The *Hotel Royal* is near the corner of Quillota and Varas. Despite the name, this is a moderately cheap hotel with singles/doubles for US$6/12, which includes breakfast. It's a bit rundown but otherwise reasonable. It also has a restaurant.

Places to Stay – middle
The pick of hotels in this price range is the *Hotel Montt* (tel 253651) at the corner of Varas and Quillota. It has small but cosy singles/doubles from US$15/22. Considerably more expensive rooms have private bathrooms.

The *Residencial Urmeneta* (tel 253262) is on Urmeneta, between Quillota and San Felipe. It has double rooms for US$16 and US$24, the latter with private bathrooms. It's a fairly good place, although rather dark and gloomy.

The *Hotel Colino* (tel 253502), at the corner of Talca and Portales, has good doubles for US$32, with a private bathroom.

Also try the *Hotel Punta Arenas* at Copiapó 119, near the corner with Varas. Singles/doubles cost US$12/20.

Places to Stay – top end
The *Hotel Vicente Pérez Rosales* (tel 252571) at Varas 447 is the city's top hotel. Singles/doubles cost US$48/70. Also try

the *Hotel Burg* (tel 253813) at the corner of Pedro Montt and Portales.

Places to Eat
The *Restaurant Bodegón* at Varas 931 is popular with local people and sometimes has live music at night. The *Club Alemán* at Varas 264 is also popular, especially as a drinking spot. For drinks, snacks and cakes try the *Café Central* at Rancagua 117, opposite the post office.

Getting There & Away
Air Ladeco (tel 253002) is at the corner of O'Higgins and Benavente and LAN-Chile (tel 253141) is at the corner of San Martín and Benavente.

Ladeco has daily flights to Santiago and flights several days a week to Osorno, Valdivia and Temuco. LAN-Chile has daily flights to Punta Arenas and Santiago.

Aeroregional SA (tel 254364), at Benavente 309, has flights three days a week from Puerto Montt to Bariloche in Argentina. The one-way fare is US$21. It has flights several days a week to Chaitén and Santiago.

Bus All bus companies operate from the huge central bus terminal on Portales.

Buses go to Santiago, to destinations in the Lake District, Chiloé Island, Chaitén on the Camino Austral, Punta Arenas and Argentina.

Typical fares from Puerto Montt are: Santiago US$15; Punta Arenas US$52; Bariloche US$25 via Osorno or US$33 via Lago Todos los Santos; Ancud US$2; Castro US$4; Puerto Varas US$0.50; Osorno US$2; and Chaitén US$10.

All the main companies, such as ETC, Tur Bus, Cruz del Sur and Buses Norte, have buses and bus cama to Santiago. Cruz del Sur has a dozen buses daily to Ancud and Castro on Chiloé Island.

Buses Andina del Sur and Varastur, both at Varas 437, have daily buses to Bariloche in Argentina via Ensenada, Petrohué and Puella. These depart Puerto

Montt in the morning and arrive in Bariloche in the early evening. This includes a ferry crossing of Lago Todos los Santos and various bus and boat journeys on the Argentine side.

As the Camino Austral is still under construction, transport information is likely to change quite rapidly. Check on details when you get to Chile. Buses Fierro has buses twice a week from Puerto Montt to Chaitén and from Chaitén there are buses twice a week to Coyhaique. This may have changed at the time of writing. Check for details.

Between the various companies you should be able to get a bus every day of the week from Puerto Montt to Punta Arenas. These go via Osorno and Argentina Patagonia. Try Buses Norte.

Train Daily trains from Puerto Montt to Santiago depart the train station on the waterfront at the eastern end of Avenida Portales. For fares and timetables, see the Getting Around chapter.

Boat An interesting way to get to the far south of Chile is by passenger ship from Puerto Montt. Using ships or bus/ship combinations can take you from Puerto Montt to Chiloé Island; to Chaitén and Coyhaique in the Aisén region; and to Punta Arenas. You can even reach truly remote spots such as the village of Puerto Edén and the Laguna San Rafael Glacier.

Navimag (tel 253754) is at the port, the Terminal de Transbordadores, in the Angelmo district of Puerto Montt. It has ships from Puerto Montt to Puerto Chacabuco (the starting point for Coyhaique) twice a week. It also has ships three times a month from Puerto Montt to Punta Arenas, a trip taking three days. Fares from Puerto Montt to Puerto Chacabuco cost from US$28 to US$48. Fares from Puerto Montt to Punta Arenas are from US$84 and US$112.

Empremar is on Portales, near the bus terminal. It has weekly ships from Puerto

Montt to Chaitén and Puerto Chacabuco, stopping at various ports on the way. Seats from Puerto Montt to Puerto Chacabuco are US$14 and US$19. A sleeper costs US$30.

Transmarchilay (tel 254654) at Antonio Varas 215 operates the ferries from the mainland to the northern tip of Chiloé Island (see the Chiloé chapter).

Getting Around

Cars can be rented from the Automobile Club (tel 252968) at Cauquenes 69, Budget (tel 254888) at the corner of San Martín and Benavente, Hertz (tel 55000) at Urmeneta 1036, AVIS (tel 253307) at Benavente 878 and National at Copiapó 30.

Car hire is definitely the way to go if you want to circumnavigate Lago Llanquihue as well as visit Petrohué and Lago Todos los Santos.

A local bus between the airport (El Tepuel) and the bus terminal connects with all outgoing and incoming flights.

Chiloé Island

About 180 km long by 50 km wide, Chiloé is one of South America's largest islands. It has a temperate climate, in comparison to the forbidding archipelago of islands and fjords immediately to the south. The climate enabled Indians to settle on the island at an early date and grow potatoes in its fertile, volcanic soil.

The interior harbours huge virgin forests, while the rest of the land has been turned over to wheat, vegetables and cattle. Fishing is also important.

The island is sparsely populated with only about 115,000 people, most of whom live within sight of the sea. About 60% of the population make a living from agriculture.

The Spanish took possession of Chiloé in 1567 and the following year founded Castro. The Jesuits dug themselves in, and early in the 17th century refugees from the Indian counterattack on the Chilean mainland also established settlements. The Spanish remained in Chiloé during the War of Independence, resisting attacks in 1820 and 1824 until they were finally defeated in 1826. The island was their last Chilean stronghold. In Ancud, one of the Spanish forts can still be seen.

Chiloé has a brooding quality, in some ways similar to the Scottish Hebrides. The difference is that instead of stone crofts, the houses are clapboard with corrugated iron roofs. It's a very relaxing place to visit. For much of the winter months the island is enveloped by mists and rain, but when the sun does break through the clouds it can be spectacularly green and beautiful, with views across the gulf to the snow-capped volcanos of the mainland.

There are only two towns of any reasonable size on the island: Ancud and Castro. Chonchi and Quellón are smaller towns. There are also small villages with distinctive churches up to 200 years old. In all there are about 150 churches on the island, of which nine have been declared national monuments. Those built in the 18th century are at Achao, Chonchi, Quilquico, Quinchao and Villipulli. Those at Dalcahue, Nercon and Rilán were built in the 19th century. The garish Iglesia San Francisco de Castro in Castro was built this century.

Chiloé also has some distinctive fishing villages, or *palafitos*. These are made up of rows of houses built over the water on stilts so that fishermen can park their boats underneath when the tide comes in. These can be found at Ancud, Castro, Quemchi, Chonchi and other ports.

ANCUD

Ancud was founded in 1765 as a fort town. Like Valdivia it was meant to defend the Chilean coastline from foreign intrusion. Now it's the largest population centre on the island, an attractive fishing and agricultural town built on a series of small hills overlooking a bay to the north. It doesn't look like much at first glance, but it can be interesting.

Typical Chiloé church

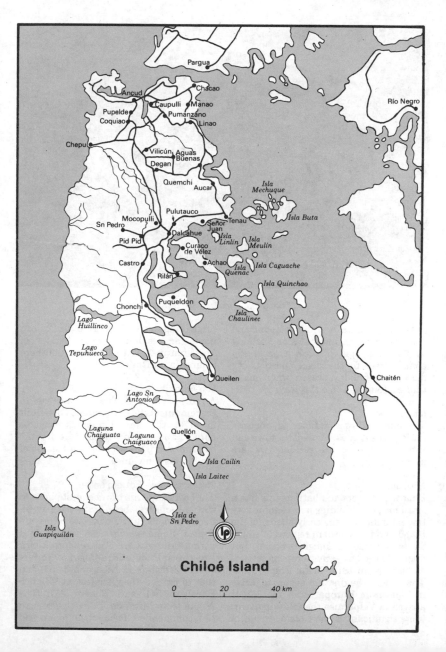

Chiloé Island

0   20   40 km

Fruit shop, Ancud, Chiloé Island

Ancud is a place for strolling around and relaxing, popping into cafés and talking with local people. There's a peculiarly amiable feel to the place, particularly during the holiday season when many Chilean tourists come this way.

Information
The tourist office is on Libertad, opposite the Plaza de Armas. Maps of the town and lists of hotels and residencials are available here.

Museum
Built with towers and battlements like a small fort, this building houses some very fine exhibits from the early history of the island and the southern regions of Chile. These include a rough wooden hut originally used by early European settlers and erected in 1815, 20 km from Ancud. There's also the first fire engine to arrive in Chile from Europe. Built in 1851, it arrived in Valparaíso the following year. More significant is the *Goleta Ancud*, a

tiny sailing ship which braved the Chilean fjords and sailed to the Straits of Magellan in 1843 to claim the southern peninsula for Chile.

San Antonio Fort
A short walk up Cochrane brings you to the remains of the San Antonio Fort. Built in 1770, the fort dominates Ancud's harbour and its cannon still stare over the battlements. This was the last bastion of the Spanish in Chile.

Places to Stay – bottom end
The hospedajes are the cheapest places to stay. All charge about US$4 per person. Look for signs in the windows of private houses. Some which seem to run on a permanent basis are: *Alojamiento Elvira Navarro* at Pudeto 361; *Alojamiento José Santos Miranda* at Moccopulli 753; and the unnamed hospedajes at Blanco Encalada 541 and Pudeto 357. The Alojamiento Miranda, in particular, can be recommended. It has clean rooms and

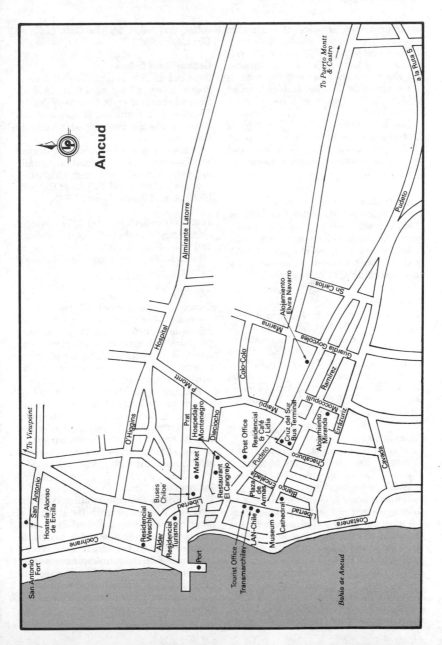

Ancud

San Antonio Fort
San Antonio
Hostería Alonso de Ercilla
Cochrane
To Viewpoint
O'Higgins
Residencial Weschler
Alder
Residencial Turismo
Market
Buses Chiloe
Libertad
Restaurant El Cangrejo
Port
Tourist Office
Transmarchilay
LAN-Chile
Plaza de Armas
Museum
Cathedral
Libertad
Blanco
Ensenada de Pudeto
Post Office
Residencial & Café Lidia
Hospedaje Montenegro
Dieciocho
P Montt
Hospital
Colo-Colo
Maipu
Cruz del Sur Bus Terminal
Chacabuco
Alojamiento Miranda
Mocopulli
Erräzuriz
Caveda
Costanera
Bahía de Ancud
Marina
Alojamiento Elvira Navarro
Guardia Goycolea
San Carlos
Ramírez
Almirante Latorre
To Puerto Montt & Castro
a la Ruta 5
Pudeto

bathrooms, hot showers and amiable hosts.

The *Hotel Lydia* (tel 990) at Casilla 371, doesn't look like much from the outside, but the rooms are clean and the hotel is quite agreeable. Singles/doubles start at US$12/17. More expensive rooms have private bathrooms.

The *Residencial Turismo* (tel 415) at Libertad 491 has little boxes for rent at US$4 per person. There's a bar and restaurant downstairs and the people are quite friendly.

Places to Stay - middle

The *Residencial Weschler* (tel 318) at Cochrane 480 used to be a very cheap place, but renovations have moved it more up-market. Double rooms cost US$15 or US$25, with a private bathroom. It's a very comfortable, attractive hotel.

Places to Stay - top end

Ancud's top hotel is the *Hostería Alonso de Ercilla* (tel 340) at San Antonio 30, overlooking the sea and the San Antonio Fort. It's a beautiful place that looks like a giant log cabin. Even if you can't afford to stay there you should at least have a drink at the bar overlooking the sea. Singles/doubles cost US$38/48, which includes breakfast and a private bathroom.

Places to Eat

One of the cheapest places is the *Cocinería Real* behind the Municipal Market. Good, cheap food is also available in the market.

The *Restaurant El Cangrejo* at Dieciocho 155 is a seafood restaurant. Judging from the business cards and other scrawls on the walls it seems that just about every visitor to Ancud has eaten here. Try their *paltina de mariscos* – a meal in itself. The staff are very friendly and the service is great.

Despite its appearance, the *Café Grill Jardín* is also relatively cheap and dishes up enormous slabs of meat. For good coffee and cakes try the *Café Lidia* at Chacabuco 650.

Getting There & Away

Bus Cruz del Sur at Chacabuco 672 has a dozen buses a day to Puerto Montt. Several continue on to Osorno, Valdivia, Temuco and Santiago. It has a dozen buses a day to Castro and several to Chonchi.

Buses Chiloé is at the corner of Libertad and Dieciocho. It has several buses daily to Castro, Chonchi and Puerto Montt.

Fares to Castro are US$1.50, to Chonchi US$2.50 and Puerto Montt US$3.

Boat Transmarchilay (tel 317) operates ships from Chonchi to Puerto Chacabuco and Chaitén. Its Ancud office is at Libertad 669, opposite the Plaza de Armas.

CASTRO

Castro is the capital of the Chiloé Province. Although it's a very old town, its principle attraction – the bizarre wooden cathedral in front of the main plaza – was only built this century. Like Ancud, this is a resort town during the holiday season with large numbers of Chilean tourists.

Dominated by its unusual cathedral, Castro has a lively atmosphere. It's an interesting town with some intriguing architecture. At first glance, it may not look like much but it's a likeable place, at its best in the summer evenings when the streets are filled with people.

Information

Tourist Office The tourist office is on the Plaza de Armas, beneath the stage of a small pavilion which looks like a cross between a bomb shelter and a spaceship. Maps of the town are available and there's information on the surrounding area. Also ask about tours to Dalcahue, Curaco and other places of interest. Boat trips to the small islands are sometimes organised if there are enough people.

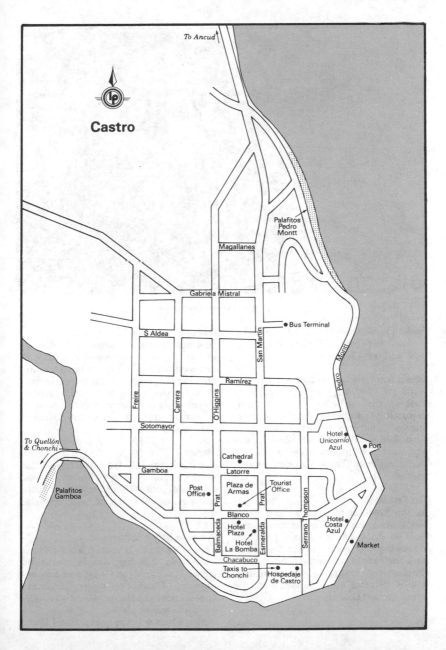

Castro

To Ancud

Palafitos
Pedro
Montt

Magallanes

Gabriela Mistral

Bus Terminal

S Aldea

San Martín

Ramírez

Freire

Carrera

O'Higgins

Sotomayor

Pedro Montt

Hotel
Unicornio
Azul

Port

To Quellón
& Chonchi

Cathedral

Gamboa

Latorre

Post
Office

Prat

Plaza de
Armas

Tourist
Office

Prat

Serrano Thompson

Palafitos
Gamboa

Blanco

Balmaceda

Hotel
Plaza

Hotel
La Bomba

Esmeralda

Hotel
Costa
Azul

Market

Chacabuco

Taxis to
Chonchi

Hospedaje
de Castro

Fishing village, Castro

Banks The Banco del Estado de Chile is at the corner of Prat and Latorre. It changes cash and travellers' cheques.

Iglesia San Francisco de Castro
Built in 1906 and the centrepiece of Castro, the cathedral is a lurching monstrosity painted in a dazzling shade of orange. The interior is of attractive varnished wood. The cathedral houses some incredibly bloody representations of the crucifixion. There are even wierder statues.

The Palafitos
At the junction of Gamboa and Pedro Montt are a number of fishermen's houses built on stilts over the edge of the river. When the tide comes in the fishermen park their boats between the stilts. From the street they look no different from other houses. Several other palafitos can be found around Castro.

Regional Museum
Ransack all the old farms in the district and this is what you come up with – an extraordinary collection of Indian relics, farming implements from the early days of settlement and even a rough wooden bicycle only used for travelling downhill. The museum is on Thompson, between Blanco and Latorre.

Market
The market on Lillo is good for buying fine woollen ponchos and pullovers, gloves, caps and basketwork. Bundles of dried seaweed and chunks of peat are also sold.

Places to Stay – bottom end
The *Hotel La Bomba* (tel 2300) at Esmeralda 270 has simple rooms for US$6. It's bright and airy and has hot showers. Despite it's very ordinary appearance from the outside, it's actually quite a pleasant place.

Much better is the cheap *Hotel Costa*

Top: Indian bullock cart, Chol Chol, near Temuco, Lake District
Bottom: Futrono, Lake District

Top: Petrohué, Lake District
Bottom: Chol Chol, near Temuco, Lake District

Azul (tel 2440) which is above the Restaurant Octavio at Lillo 67. It's a clean, decent place with a good, cheap restaurant.

The *Hotel Plaza* (tel 5109) is on Blanco, facing the main plaza and opposite the tourist kiosk. Singles/doubles cost US$6/12, without a private bathroom. Some of the rooms are OK, but others are windowless, dark and depressing.

Places to Stay – middle
The most appealing of Castro's hotels is the *Hotel Unicornío Azul* (tel 2359) at Pedro Montt 228, on the shorefront. Exactly where the unicorn pictures are I don't know, but the hotel is painted a brilliant shade of azul. Rooms are quite simple but the hotel does have a certain appeal. Singles/doubles cost US$26/32, which includes breakfast.

Places to Stay – top end
The *Hospedaje de Castro* (tel 2301) at Chacabuco 202 is easily identifiable due to its high sloping roof. Singles/doubles cost US$34/40.

Places to Eat
Try *Chilo's* at San Martín 449 for meat and fish dishes, the *Plaza* at Blanco 336 for parrillada and *Sacho* at Thompson 213 for curanto.

Getting There & Away
Bus The Bus Terminal Rurales is just off San Martín near the junction with Sergio Aldea. Usually a couple of buses a day go from here to such places as Dalcahue, Curaco and Achao.

Cruz del Sur is at San Martín 681. It has a dozen buses a day to Ancud and Puerto Montt, several of which continue on to Osorno, Valdivia, Temuco and Santiago. It has several buses daily to Chonchi.

Buses Chiloé at Esmeralda 252 has several buses daily to Ancud, Chonchi and Puerto Montt.

The fare from Castro to Puerto Montt is US$3.

CHONCHI
Chonchi is the starting point for ferries to Chaitén and Puerto Chacabuco. It's memorable for the impressive Iglesia San Carlos de Chonchi, at the junction of Centenario and Pedro Montt, with its tall three-stage spire and archways at the front. Jesuits founded the town and the original church was constructed in the 18th century. The structure you see now dates to the middle of the last century – its size being completely out of proportion to the small population of the time.

Information
The tourist office is at the corner of Candelaria and Centenario.

Places to Stay
There are several cheap hospedajes. Try the *Hospedaje Chonchi* at O'Higgins 379 and the *Residencial Turismo* on Pedro Andrade.

Iglesia San Carlos de Chonchi

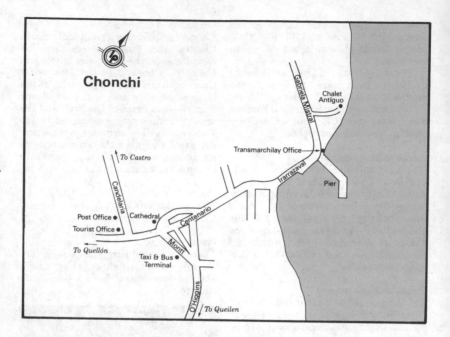

Getting There & Away

Bus Cruz del Sur and Buses Chiloé have several buses daily from Castro to Chonchi. In Chonchi the Transmarchilay office is at the end of Centenario by the port.

Taxi The best way to get to Chonchi is with a taxi colectivo from Castro. In Castro these leave from Chacabuco, near the corner with Esmeralda. In Chonchi they leave from Pedro Montt, opposite the cathedral. The fare from Castro to Chonchi is US$1 per person.

QUELLÓN

Not to be confused with Queilén, Quellón is the most southerly port of Chiloé, a rather drab little town from which the Transmarchilay ferries sail to Puerto Chacabuco.

Places to Stay

A few doors from the Transmarchilay office on the waterfront is the *Hotel Playa* (tel 278) at Pedro Montt 255. It's a decent little place with rooms for US$3.20 per person. There's hot water available and there's a good cheap restaurant.

The *Pensión Vera*, Gómez García 18, is US$2.50 per person. Despite it's tatty appearance from the outside, it's quite OK inside. It's very spartan, but it does have hot water.

The *Hotel La Pincoya* (tel 285), La Paz 64, is a comfortable place with friendly people, and hot water. It costs US$6.50 per person, including breakfast.

Getting There & Away

The bus ride from Castro to Quellón takes about 1½ hours depending on the road conditions. To be on the safe side, take an early bus. The fare from Castro is about US$2. The ferry runs to a timetable but it is often late to leave, depending on how long it takes to get all the cars and trucks on board.

In Quellón, the Buses Cruz del Sur office is at Aguirre Cerda 52 around the corner from the pier. The Transmarchilay office is on the waterfront at Pedro Montt 261, in front of the pier.

GETTING THERE & AWAY

Chiloé is connected by ferry to Pargua, a port close to Puerto Montt, and to the ports of Chaitén and Puerto Chacabuco in the Aisén region.

To/From Puerto Montt

Frequent, daily buses go from Puerto Montt to Ancud and Castro, crossing the straits between the mainland and the northern tip of the island by ferry. The ferries cross between Pargua on the mainland and Chacao on the northern tip of Chiloé. Buses board the ferries so there's no need to change or wait in Pargua or Chacao.

(See the Puerto Montt section in the Lake District chapter.) Ferries are operated by Cruz del Sur and there are frequent departures all day. The passenger fare is minimal. Cars are transported for US$5.

To/From Puerto Chacabuco

The Aisén region can be reached by a ferry from Chiloé to either Chaitén or Puerto Chacabuco. Puerto Chacabuco is the getting off point for Coyhaique. Ferries are operated by the Transmarchilay company and leave Chiloé from the port of Chonchi.

El Colono, a car ferry, sails between Chonchi and Puerto Chacabuco twice a week, departing Chonchi in the afternoon. The trip takes 18 hours. Depending on the size of your vehicle, it costs between US$58 and US$68 to transport a car from Chonchi to Puerto Chacabuco.

Apart from cabins there are four classes of travel on ferries:

1. *Camarote* (sleeper) costs US$98 per bed.
2. *Pasajes Pullman Proa con asiento reclinable* (reclining aircraft seats) cost US$28.
3. *Pasajes Pullman Popa con asiento reclinable* (reclining bus seats) cost US$23.
4. Tourist Class has fixed seats and two divisions. The first is *Pasajes Turistas con asiento fijo* which costs US$20 and gives you a place indoors in a large room with tables and upright bench seats. The second is *sin acomodación*, which costs US$12. With this you must try to find a place to camp on deck or squat in a corridor. Regardless of how warm it may be in Chiloé, it can be absolutely freezing camping out on deck! If you want to enjoy the trip, at least take the Pasajes Pullman Popa class.

To/From Chaitén

La Pincoya, also a car ferry, sails between Chonchi and Chaitén two or three days a week. There is only one class and the one-way fare is US$4. The ferry departs Chonchi in the afternoon. The trip takes about eight hours and arrives in Chaitén near midnight. Depending on vehicle size, it costs between US$28 and US$36 to transport a car. From Chaitén you can bus south to Coyhaique.

The Aisén District

South of Chiloé and Puerto Montt, Chile is wild and beautiful, quite unlike anywhere else in the world, with the possible exception of the south island of New Zealand and south-east Alaska.

The Camino Austral (Southern Highway) has recently been completed, linking Puerto Montt with Coyhaique and Puerto Ibáñez and Cochrane. It is planned to extend the road as far south as Villa O'Higgins, although it will be some years before that stretch is finished.

The natural scenery of the Región Aisén del General Ibáñez del Campo, of which Coyhaique is the capital, is built on monolithic proportions. The road edges its way along cliffs that drop into immense river valleys, walls of water stream down huge rock faces, ravines open up into vast valleys, lakes change colour halfway across and, in the distance, the Andes form a continuous barrier gashed by glaciers. On a clear day even the short stretch from Coyhaique to Puerto Ibáñez provides some of the most eye-boggling panoramas in Chile.

CHAITÉN

Chaitén is a quiet port town, military base and settlement towards the northern end of the Camino Austral. Just a few thousand people live here and the town is vaguely reminiscent of old photographs of pioneer towns in eastern Australia during the 19th century. From Chaitén there is a Transmarchilay ferry to Chonchi on Chiloé Island and an Empremar ferry to Puerto Montt.

Information & Orientation

The jetty for ferries to Chiloé is about a 10-minute walk from the town. Most of the town is comprised of a few wide streets laid out in a grid, with the inevitable plaza marking the division between the civilian and military areas. The hotels, restaurants and shops are around O'Higgins, Todesco, Portales, Riveros and Independencía – all within easy walking distance of each other.

Tourist Office There is a tourist office in the Centro Commercial, on the way in from the jetty. It has a few leaflets and may be able to suggest hospedajes to stay in.

Banks The Banco del Estado de Chile is on

Chaitén

Independencia

Banco del Estado de Chile
Empremar
Aerobus
Hostería Schilling & Transmarchilay
Todesco
ASA
Hotel Continental
Hostería Mi Casa
Centro Commercial y Mercado/Tourist Office

Libertad
Almirante
Riveros
Portales
O'Higgins

Libertad, but it does not change foreign cash or travellers' cheques.

Places to Stay & Eat

The cheapest accommodation is in private houses, so look for handwritten hospedaje signs in windows.

Permanent hotels include the highly recommended *Hostería Mi Casa* on a hill overlooking the town. It's a large place with simple, but clean, spacious singles/doubles for US$16/31. There's also a restaurant.

The *Hotel Continental* is at the corner of O'Higgins and Todesco, diagonally opposite the Centro Commercial y Mercado. If you're arriving by boat you'll see it as you come in from the jetty. It's a simple, cosy place with rooms for US$16. It also has a restaurant. Also try the *Hostería Schilling* which is a few doors away on O'Higgins.

Getting There & Away

Air Aeroregional SA (ASA) (tel 275) is at Todesco 41, near the corner with O'Higgins. It has flights from Chaitén to Puerto Montt four days a week. So far there are no flights between Chaitén and Coyhaique.

Bus Transport details for the Camino Austral are likely to change rapidly as the road undergoes improvements. At the time of writing, there were at least two regular buses a week from Chaitén to Coyhaique and one or two departures per week from Chaitén to Puerto Montt.

For buses to Coyhaique, enquire at the Aerobus office at the corner of Portales and Independencia. The fare is US$26 and the trip takes between 11 and 12 hours. The Camino Austral is a gravel road, cut through by many rivers. Vehicles are carried across the rivers by barges.

Boat The Transmarchilay (tel 272) office is at O'Higgins 243, by the Hostería Schilling. (See the Chiloé chapter for ferries to Chonchi.)

The Empremar office is on Independencia. It has a weekly boat from Chaitén to Puerto Montt. (See the Puerto Montt section in the Lake District chapter.)

PUERTO CHACABUCO

Apart from Chaitén, another popular entry port to the Aisén region is Puerto Chacabuco. This is the starting point for Coyhaique, the capital of the region. Puerto Chacabuco can be reached by ferry from Chaitén or from Chonchi on Chiloé. The tiny port lies at the eastern end of a very narrow fjord. Just up the road, on the way to Coyhaique, is Puerto Aisén which has a silted-up harbour and is no longer a port, despite the name.

Places to Stay

There are two small hotels in Puerto Chacabuco, just outside the harbour compound on the road leading to Coyhaique.

Getting There & Away

Bus There are regular buses from Coyhaique to Puerto Aisén and Puerto

Chacabuco. These also meet incoming and outgoing ferries (see the Coyhaique section). The trip from Puerto Chacabuco to Coyhaique takes about two hours.

For most of the way the road follows the river along the base of a deep, rocky gorge. There are waterfalls and vast walls of steep rock. Great sheets of water stream down from high above to the river below. Eventually the road climbs up the gorge and passes through a narrow, artificial tunnel (officially opened by President Pinochet in early 1986). Soon Coyhaique can be seen, nestled in a valley far below against a backdrop of monumental, barren mountains.

COYHAIQUE

Coyhaique is a sizeable town with a floating population of about 40,000 people. It was founded as recently as 1929 and is one of the largest Chilean towns south of Puerto Montt. It's mainly a military and government administration centre, though tourists find it a useful base for hiking in the surrounding mountains. It's connected by Puerto Aisén and Puerto Chacabuco in the west, Puerto Ibáñez in the south and Chaitén in the north.

Information

Tourist Office The tourist office (tel 221752) is at Cochrane 320, between Bilbao and Freire.

Post & Telecommunications The post office is at Cochrane 202 by the main plaza. International and long-distance phone calls can be made from the Compañia de Telefonos at the corner of Barroso and Bolívar.

Banks Cash and travellers' cheques can be changed at the Cambio Moneda Rosas, Office 208, 2nd floor, Prat 340. Also try the Banco del Estado de Chile at the corner of Morateda and Condell.

Places to Stay - bottom end

The *Residencial Puerto Varas* (tel 21212) at Ignacio Serrano 168 is very good value at US$6 per person. The rooms are quite small but the place is clean and thoroughly recommended. There are hot showers and a restaurant.

Places to Stay - top end

Try the *Gran Hotel Chile* (tel 21643) on José de Morateda. Singles/doubles cost US$33/50, with a private bathroom. There's a rather *gran* restaurant (by Coyhaique standards) on the ground floor.

The *Hotel Los Nires* (tel 22261), at the corner of Baquedano and Carrera, has singles/doubles for US$23/35, including breakfast and a private bathroom. There are mixed reports about this place, with some people thinking it's not worth the money.

Places to Eat

Prat is the street to visit for restaurants as there's a string of places from Lautaro all the way down to the plaza.

The *Samoa* at Prat 653 is a cosy little bar and restaurant with cheap meals and snacks. The *Café Restaurant Ricer* is a nifty snack bar on Horn (which changes to Prat) by the main plaza. Also try the *Café La Moneda de Oro* which is diagonally opposite the Ricer. The *Café Peña Quilantal* at Lillo 145 has live music some nights of the week – look for the house with the cow skull nailed above the entrance.

Getting There & Away

Air Ladeco (tel 221188) is at the corner of General Parra and 21 de Mayo. It has flights to Puerto Montt and Santiago six days a week.

ASA (Aeroregional SA) (tel 21889) is at Lillo 315 and has daily flights from Coyhaique to Puerto Montt.

The road south from Coyhaique only runs as far as Cochrane. To go further you must fly. Aerotaxi Don Carlos (tel 222981) at Cruz 63 has planes from Coyhaique to

Coyhaique

1 Hotel Los Nires
2 Gran Hotel Chile
3 Telex Chile
4 Transmarchilay
5 Plaza de Armas
6 Banco de Chile
7 Post Office
8 Museum
9 Telephone Office
10 Buses Giobbi
11 Residencial Puerto Varas
12 Tourist Office
13 Residencial La Bomba
14 Taxis/Jeeps to Puerto Ibáñez
15 Bus Terminal

Cochrane and Chile Chico three days a week, and to Villa O'Higgins twice a month.

Bus & colectivo The bus terminal is at the corner of Lautaro and Magallanes. Most bus companies operate from this terminal.

La Cascada has several buses a day to Puerto Aisén and Puerto Chacabuco. The fare is US$1.50.

Surray has weekly buses to La Junta, which is on the way to Chaitén.

BAP has buses several days a week to Puerto Ibáñez. The fare is US$6 and the buses meet the ferry to Chile Chico.

For buses to Comodoro Rivadavia in Argentina, go to Giobbi SA Transporte at Simon Bolivar 194. It has buses three days a week to Comodoro Rivadavia. The fare is US$24 and the trip takes all day, leaving Coyhaique in the morning and arriving in Comodoro Rivadavia in the early evening.

Aerobus at Bilbao 968 has buses two days a week to Chaitén. The fare is US$30 and the trip takes between 11 and 12 hours.

There are taxi colectivos from Coyhaique to Puerto Ibáñez. These cost US$6 per person and are a bit faster than the buses.

Boat The nearest port is Puerto Chacabuco, about two hours by bus from Coyhaique.

Transmarchilay (tel 221971) is upstairs at 21 de Mayo 417, Coyhaique. It has ferries from Puerto Chacabuco to Chonchi on Chiloé Island (see the Chiloé chapter).

Empremar is at 21 de Mayo 758, Coyhaique. It has ships from Puerto Chacabuco to Chaitén and Puerto Montt. (See the Puerto Montt section in the Lake District chapter.)

Navimag (tel 223306) is on Dussen, a few doors up from Coyhaique's main plaza. It has ships from Puerto Chacabuco to Puerto Montt (see the Puerto Montt section in the Lake District chapter).

Getting Around
Cars can be rented from Hertz (tel 23456) at Morateda 420, the Turismo Prado

travel agency at 21 de Mayo 417 and the Automobile Club (tel 21847) at Arturo Prat 348.

PUERTO IBÁÑEZ
Puerto Ibáñez is named after the president who initiated the settlement of this area. It's a tidy little place on the shores of an emerald-green lake, walled in by barren mountain ridges and lightly vegetated hills. From here you cross the lake to Chile Chico and then the border to Los Antigos in Argentina.

Things to See
While there is nothing much in the town, there is a great deal in the surrounding area for which you need a car to explore. Drive up the road which leads to Puerto Levican for panoramic views of the whole Río Ibáñez Valley. Pink flamingos and black-neck swans can be seen in the river. The land around this area is mainly used for cattle and sheep grazing. You can still see *hausos*, clad in the traditional ponchos and thick, furry pants, droving herds of livestock along the roads. Long lines of tall poplar trees, planted as wind breaks, divide the fields.

Places to Stay & Eat
The two places to stay are both opposite the ferry dock. The *Residencial Ibáñez* is at Buenos Aires 201, at the corner with Dickson. Rooms are US$3 per person and there's a cheap restaurant.

Next door is the *Hotel Monica* which is a friendly place with rooms for US$3 per person. It's clean and comfortable and its restaurant dishes up enormous meals.

Getting There & Away
For transport from Coyhaique to Puerto Ibáñez, see the Coyhaique section in this chapter.

From Puerto Ibáñez there is a Transmarchilay car and passenger ferry to Chile Chico on the other side of Lago Carrera. Departures occur three mornings a week. Check departure times at the Transmarchilay office in Coyhaique. The fare from Puerto Ibáñez to Chile Chico is US$2.50 per person.

VILLA CERRO CASTILLO

If you've rented a car, detour to Villa Cerro Castillo. The village takes its name from Cerro Castillo, the Castle Mountains, a massive fortress of glacier-slashed rock which looms up in jagged pinnacles and casts shadows over the village below. The village is a short drive down a gravel road from the Coyhaique to Puerto Ibáñez main road.

The Pension El Viajero is the only place to stay. It has a few rooms for US$2 per person and a bar and cheap restaurant. Otherwise, the village itself is an archetypal pioneer settlement of corrugated tin shacks and fibro-cement houses.

CHILE CHICO

Chile Chico was founded in 1928 by immigrant fortune-seekers who included Brazilians, Argentines, Chileans, Germans, Italians and French. A row of flags on a hill crest above the town represents each nationality. Chile Chico's early prosperity was based on a copper mine and you can still see blue-tinged copper ore in the rocky hills behind the town.

It's not hard to imagine the optimism and hopes of the first settlers, but these days there is only one reminder of the great city which was expected to rise here – the dusty main street, built as wide as any in Chile to accommodate the streams of traffic that never came. When the mine was exhausted the town began to decline. Only fruit growing has kept it from disappearing in recent years.

Chile Chico means 'little Chile' and for some reason it has a micro-climate which is especially warm and sunny almost year round – quite different from the colder climes you find around Coyhaique.

The fruit growers produce apples, pears, red and yellow plums and guinda (a cherry-like fruit), all of a quality equal to the fruit produced in the Chilean heartland. Most of the locals live in mud-brick houses surrounded by alamo trees, the tall and very dense trees which are used as windbreaks around the fruit tree plantations.

But life has been ebbing from the town

Chile Chico

1 Post Office
2 Harbour Master's Office
3 Café Elizabeth y Loly
4 CONAF
5 Restaurant Rapanui
6 Residencial Aguas Azules
7 LADECO Agent
8 Museum & Tourist Office
9 Police Station
10 Residencial Nacional

for years. Families have moved away and abandoned houses have fallen into ruins. Government houses remain unoccupied because there is no work and no one to fill them. Fruit growing is not profitable. The farmers cannot sell their produce to Argentina because the Argentines ship their own fruit to the border. Nor can they sell to Coyhaique because transport fees, a tax on their profits plus other taxes (apparently designed by the government to protect fruit growers in the Chilean heartland) mean they cannot produce fruit at a profit. Instead, they attempt to make a living selling their fruit in the town or to tourists. Otherwise the fruit falls off the trees, rots on the ground or is fed to pigs.

Because the town has no other industry many people have left Chile Chico and gone to work in Argentina. The population of the town was 6000 in the 1960s. Now it is about a third of that. The remittances of the expatriate workers, or those who have gone to work in other parts of Chile, seem to be the main source of income for the town. Others make a living catering to the small tourist trade and the passing traffic in Chileans and Argentines who cross the unbridged river which marks the border.

Information
Tourist Office There's a tourist office, occasionally open, at the corner of O'Higgins and Gana. The tiny museum here contains some Indian skeletons and artefacts. The spherical stones on display were used in slings for hunting.

Post & Telecommunications The post office is at the corner of Rodríguez and Balmaceda.

Police The police station is at the corner of O'Higgins 506 and Lautaro. The police keep a record on who's going to Argentina, so they may be able to help arrange transport if you can't find anything.

Places to Stay
There are a couple of cheap residencials in

Chile Chico, all charging a few US dollars per person.

Try the *Residencial Nacional* at Freire 24. Another decent place is the *Residencial Aguas Azules* at O'Higgins, which has rooms for about US$4 per person.

Places to Eat
For snacks and drinks, try the *Café Elizabeth y Loly* on Gonzáles, opposite the plaza. Also try the *Restaurant Rapanui* at the corner of O'Higgins and Alberto Blest Gana.

Getting There & Away
Air The Aerotaxi Don Carlos airline has three flights a week from Coyhaique to Chile Chico.

Boat There are regular ferries from Puerto Ibáñez to Chile Chico (see the Puerto Ibáñez section in this chapter).

Road From Chile Chico you can cross to Argentina. The Argentine border town is Los Antigos (also spelt Los Antiguos), just four km away. You can walk, hitch or find someone to take you by jeep. The problem is that there is a wide, unbridged river between the two towns. It is possible to walk across it – at least in the summer months – but it's very wide and there is no distinct route across. You can't even see the Argentine border post on the other side (look for a communications aerial). A hired jeep will cost a few US dollars per person. The Chilean checkpoint is at the edge of the river about a km out of Chile Chico. The Argentine checkpoint is on the other side just before entering Los Antigos. From Los Antigos you can hitch or get a bus to Perito Moreno and Caleta Olivia.

ONWARDS TO ARGENTINA
Unless you fly or take a ship, the only way you can get from the Aisén region to the far south of Chile is overland through Argentine Patagonia. What makes the detour so interesting is the striking

contrast between the land on the eastern and western sides of the Andes.

Here is a brief rundown on the main places along these routes, as well as some practical information on travelling in Argentina. For full details, see Lonely Planet's *Argentina – a travel survival kit*.

Visas Visas for Argentina are required by everyone except citizens of most western European countries, Canada, Japan and some Latin American countries. Australian, American and New Zealand citizens do require visas, which are valid for three months and allow you to leave and enter the country as often as you like within that time. It's renewable for an additional three months. A visa costs about US$15 in Chile and you can pay in Chilean pesos. There are Argentine consulates in Santiago, Punta Arenas, Puerto Montt, Arica and Antofagasta.

Customs Going from Chile to Argentina, the Argentine customs will probably only check your bags to make sure you're not taking fruit into Argentina. However, customs can be extremely thorough if you are entering Argentina from other countries, such as Paraguay or Bolivia, in which case they will be looking for illegal drugs.

Money The unit of currency is the Austral (A) which replaced the peso in mid-1985. The notes used are A1, A5, A10, A50, A100 and A500. There are no coins. Due to inflation it is likely there will be A1000 (or even larger) notes by the time you get to Argentina.

Quoting exchange rates is pointless. At the start of 1986, the rate was about one Austral to the US$. Two years later it had climbed to about five Australs to the dollar and was expected to double within a year. In fact, in another year the rate had skyrocketed to about 40 Australs to the dollar.

As you can imagine, trying to keep track of prices for hotels, transport, and so on, is almost impossible given the ludicrous

currency situation. When writing, Argentina was quite a cheap country to visit for any foreigner who had dollars to spend, but it's impossible to say what the situation will be in the future.

Hotels and travel agents usually give the best exchange rates and it's generally possible to exchange US dollars just about anywhere you go. Changing travellers' cheques, even in main towns such as Comodoro Rivadavia, is much more difficult. Make sure you have a decent supply of US dollars with you!

Health No vaccinations are required to enter Argentina from any country. There is a malaria risk from October to May in a tiny piece of Argentine territory in the far north of the country bordering Bolivia. Typhoid and polio vaccinations are recommended.

Getting Around
Air Argentine Patagonia, you may soon discover, pales very quickly. Distances are immense and the scenery becomes monotonous after the initial novelty wears off. If you intend doing a lot of travelling, it's worth flying occasionally.

The three airlines; Líneas Aéreas del Estado (LADE), Austral and Aerolíneas Argentinas have extensive networks in southern Patagonia and Tierra del Fuego. Their fares are often the same and in some cases they're even cheaper than the bus fare! The only catch is that there's heavy demand for tickets and all three airlines are often booked out two weeks in advance. Typical airfares for Argentine Patagonia and Tierra del Fuego are provided in the airfare chart in the Getting Around chapter.

Bus Argentine buses are similarly organised and are of much the same standard as buses in Chile. Most of the buses in Argentina are modern, comfortable and fast. Most large towns and cities have a central bus terminal though some bus companies operate from their own private

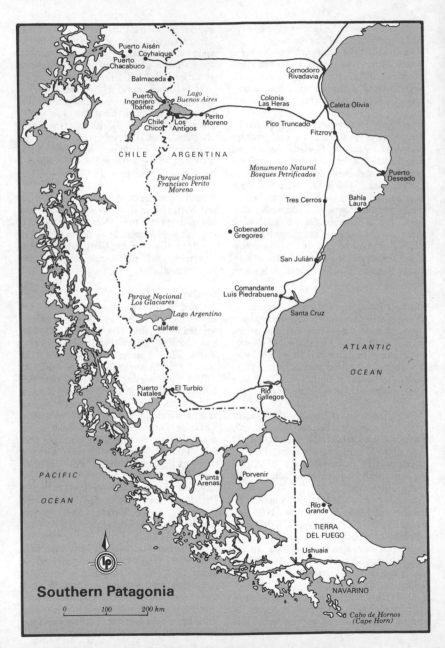

Southern Patagonia

0   100   200 km

terminals. Buses are few and demand is heavy in some of the more remote and less populated parts of Patagonia. Be prepared for some slow travelling in these regions.

Train There is an extensive railway network in northern Argentina with frequent services between towns. There are, however, no passenger railways in Patagonia and the main forms of transport are the buses and planes.

Hitching This is fairly easy in Argentina. However, in Patagonia and Tierra del Fuego you may have to wait much longer to hitch a lift as traffic is very thin on the ground. It might take a couple of days to hitch a few hundred km! If you do intend hitching then make sure you have warm, wind-proof clothes. The usual warnings about hitching apply, of course, especially where women travellers are concerned.

Routes through Argentine Patagonia

There are several points where you can cross between Chilean and Argentine Patagonia and Tierra del Fuego. The main routes are: Coyhaique to Comodoro Rivadavia; Chile Chico to Caleta Olivia via Perito Moreno; Río Gallegos to Puerto Natales via Río Turbio; Río Gallegos to Punta Arenas; and Ushuaia to Punta Arenas via Río Grande and Porvenir.

Coyhaique to Comodoro Rivadavia One of the main routes from Chilean to Argentine Patagonia takes you from the southern Chilean town of Coyhaique to the Argentine city of Comodoro Rivadavia. Buses run about three days a week (see the Coyhaique section in this chapter).

Comodoro Rivadavia is an oil town of 100,000 people and the largest city in Patagonia. The fields in the surrounding area supply about 30% of Argentina's crude oil. For foreign visitors, it's really just a transit point on the way to the north or the far south, though if you're a gregarious Spanish speaker you may find it interesting.

Since Comodoro Rivadavia is a transport hub it's easy to get to other places in Argentina. Aerolíneas Argentina, Austral and LADE have flights from Comodoro Rivadavia to northern Argentina and to southern destinations such as Calafate, Río Grande and Río Gallegos. Several companies have daily buses to the north and at least one has daily buses to Río Gallegos.

Chile Chico to Caleta Olivia The journey from Chile Chico to Caleta Olivia starts in Coyhaique. From Coyhaique you fly or take a bus/ferry combination to the Chilean village of Chile Chico.

From Chile Chico, you cross the border to the Argentine village of Los Antigos. Then you take a bus (about two departures per week) to Perito Moreno. From Perito Moreno, you take a bus to the town of Caleta Olivia on the coast. There are daily buses in summer, but at other times there are buses only two days a week. From Caleta Olivia, there are daily buses to Río Gallegos and frequent buses making the short hop to Comodoro Rivadavia.

Los Antigos is a dusty little town set on the shores of the beautiful Lago Buenos Aires. In the setting sun, the soft colours on this vast lake, rimmed by the distant mountains, make it look like an imagined scene from another planet.

Perito Moreno is a real frontier town where you still see elderly gauchos, dressed in their riding boots and enormous baggy trousers called *boleadoras*. LADE has a once a week flight from Perito Moreno to Ushuaia via Calafate, Río Gallegos and Río Grande.

Caleta Olivia is an astoundingly ugly oil town with few redeeming features. It's a smaller version of Comodoro Rivadavia and is really just a transit town on the road north or south.

Río Gallegos to Chile Heading south from either Comodoro Rivadavia or Caleta Olivia, you eventually come to Río

Gallegos. This is a sizeable town close to the southern tip of the Patagonian Peninsula. It's the starting point for trips to Calafate and Ushuaia, the latter in Tierra del Fuego.

From Río Gallegos there are daily buses to Puerto Natales and Punta Arenas in Chile. Aerolíneas Argentinas, LADE and Austral have daily flights to Comodoro Rivadavia, Río Grande and Ushuaia. LADE has daily flights to Calafate.

If you've made it to this part of the world, then you can't miss Calafate and the Moreno Glacier. In the nearby Parque Nacional de Los Glaciares is the spectacular Moreno Glacier. The glacier is a km wide and 60 metres high and descends to the surface of the lake. There's a second glacier, the 30-metre high Upsala Glacier, at the end of the lake. This can be visited by motorboat. In addition to the glaciers, the nearby Fitzroy Mountains provide incredible trekking country.

There are daily buses to Calafate from Río Gallegos. During summer, there are buses about three days a week from Calafate to Puerto Natales in Chile. This trip is not possible during winter when snow sometimes cuts the road from Calafate to Chile. The road from Calafate to Puerto Natales passes through the spectacular Parque Nacional Torres del Paine.

Another way of crossing from Argentina to Chile is by bus from Río Gallegos to Puerto Natales, via the coal mining town of Río Turbio. Take one of the daily buses from Río Gallegos to Río Turbio, then catch one of the frequent worker buses from Río Turbio to Puerto Natales. LADE has flights three days a week from Río Turbio to Río Gallegos.

Magallanes

Patagonia was given its name by the Portuguese navigator, Ferdinand Magellan. The name refers to the huge area of land occupying the southern cone of South America, generally considered to be the area south of the Río Colorado and north of the Straits of Magellan, the strait which separates the island of Tierra del Fuego from the mainland. Most of it belongs to Argentina. On the other side of the Andes is a thin and geographically very different slice which belongs to Chile.

This chapter is concerned with a small but spectacular slice of Patagonia called Magallanes, the southernmost region of the Chilean mainland before striking the island of Tierra del Fuego. Magallanes is a wild and beautiful area unlike anywhere else in the world with perhaps the exception of Norway. It's a land of virtually unspoilt mountains, glaciers, forests and lakes, with many national parks, including the spectacular Parque Nacional Torres del Paine near Puerto Natales.

History

Chile's takeover of Magallanes has its origins in the 1830s. The brief civil war of 1831 delivered Chile into the hands of the landed aristocracy of the central valley. Three conservative presidents came to office during the next 30 years, each of whom served two five-year terms: Joaquín Prieto in the 1830s, Manuel Bulnes in the 1840s and Manuel Montt in the 1850s.

Yet the strong man of the period was Diego Portales, who ranked no higher than a cabinet minister but ruled as a virtual dictator until he was assassinated in 1837, having just fought a successful war against Peru and Bolivia.

Pride in the nation's military prowess matched by triumphs at home gave the Chilean upper class a certain satisfaction. Trade was booming, Valparaíso was developing into the main port on the west coast of South America, mines were being opened, the old families were finding new wealth and a class of nouveaux riches arose. Chilean nationalism, spurred by the successful war, led to a wave of expansion which embroiled Chile in conflict with Argentina.

In 1843, President Bulnes laid claim to the territory around the Straits of Magellan, Tierra del Fuego and much of southern Patagonia. In that year, the first Chilean stake in Patagonia was established with the founding of Fuerte Bulnes on the Straits of Magellan, and five years later the city of Punta Arenas was founded nearby. The Lake District to the south of Valdivia was also opened for settlement, despite the tentative hold of the Mapuche Indians on this area. German immigrants began to arrive in the late 1840s.

Fuerte Bulnes and Punta Arenas might have remained nothing more than token gestures had it not been for three things – the discovery of gold in California in 1848, the industrial age in Europe and the development and increasing use of steamships in the second half of the

Ferdinand Magellan

175

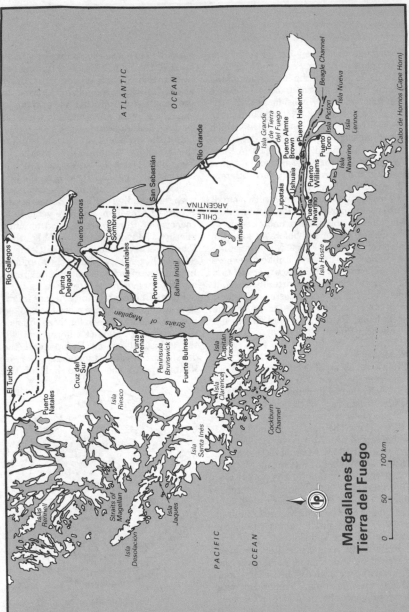

Magallanes &
Tierra del Fuego

Top: Rural scene, Aisén region
Bottom: Fishing village, Castro, Chiloé Island

Top: Southern Patagonian landscape, Argentina
Bottom: Penguins, near Punta Arenas, Magallanes

century. Since the Panama Canal had not yet been built, one way of getting from eastern USA to the goldfields in the west was a five-month wagon ride across the continent. The other was to sail to Panama, cross the isthmus by mule, then sail to California. It was cheaper and potentially quicker to sail via the tip of South America, a journey which could take anything from three to seven months.

Punta Arenas became a port of call for giant sailing ships and a coal stop for steamships. Migrants were not the only cargo. By the 1880s, these ships were also transporting Chilean nitrates and Australian meat as well as American wheat, oil and petroleum to Europe. Tools were transported from Europe to Australia, while machinery, railroad tracks and iron went from Europe to America. When the Americans dug their trench across Panama, shipping around the Horn declined dramatically and the Chilean ports on the western coast of South America were bypassed. The golden age of Punta Arenas was over.

PUNTA ARENAS
At the very end of the Chilean mainland, looking across the Straits of Magellan to Porvenir and Tierra del Fuego, Punta Arenas is a city of about 80,000 people. It once resembled Puerto Montt and the towns of Chiloé Island, with its wooden buildings, but most of these have been replaced with concrete and brick. Much of its recent development has been fuelled by the discovery of oil in the region, making Punta Arenas a surprisingly large and well-developed city and an important Chilean naval base.

All around Punta Arenas are reminders of bygone days. Monuments are lined up along Bhories like beads on a string, including memorials to the early Yugoslav settlers and to hardy farmers who pioneered the area. The enormous cemetery on Bulnes contains many large family crypts and numerous tombstones and graves of early British and Yugoslav settlers.

Information
Tourist Office The tourist office (tel 24435) is at Waldo Sequel 689, diagonally opposite the Plaza de Armas. It has maps of the city and the staff are friendly and helpful.

Post & Telecommunications The post office is at the corner of Menéndez and Bhories. International phone calls can be made from TELEX Chile at the corner of Fagnano and Nogueira, diagonally opposite the plaza.

Banks There are several places around the town centre where you can change Chilean and Argentine currency. Try La Hermandad at the corner of Roca and Lautaro Navarro, Sur Cambio at the corner of Pedro Montt and Lautaro Navarro and Casa Stop at Nogueira 1170.

Consulate The Argentine Consulate is at 21 de Mayo 1878.

Regional de Magallanes Museum
Being mainly a place of wooden buildings with corrugated tin roofs, the many gracious mansions of the city centre betray the early importance of Punta Arenas on the trade route around South America.

One of the finest mansions ever built belonged to what was once the city's most important family, the Braun-Menéndez, whose name still crops up in the higher circles of both Chilean and Argentine society.

Their former mansion is now known as the Centro Cultural Braun-Menéndez and houses the Museum Regional de Magallanes. The owners of vast areas of Patagonia and Tierra del Fuego at the turn of the century, the Braun-Menéndez moved to Buenos Aires when their lands were expropriated and when Punta Arenas went into decline after the opening of the Panama Canal.

The displays depict the European

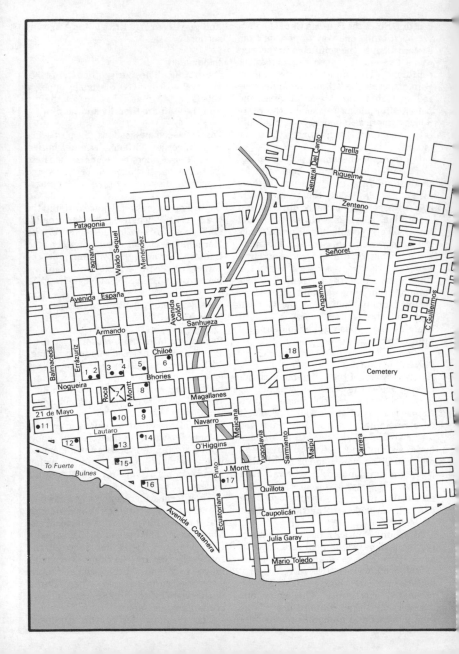

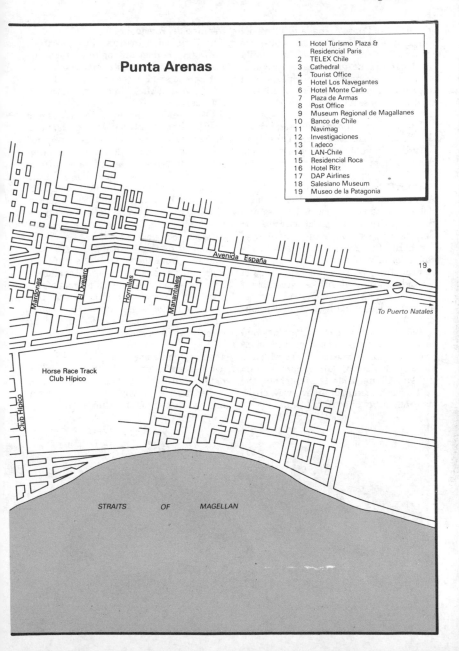

Punta Arenas

1 Hotel Turismo Plaza &
   Residencial Paris
2 TELEX Chile
3 Cathedral
4 Tourist Office
5 Hotel Los Navegantes
6 Hotel Monte Carlo
7 Plaza de Armas
8 Post Office
9 Museum Regional de Magallanes
10 Banco de Chile
11 Navimag
12 Investigaciones
13 Ladeco
14 LAN-Chile
15 Residencial Roca
16 Hotel Ritz
17 DAP Airlines
18 Salesiano Museum
19 Museo de la Patagonia

Avenida España

19

To Puerto Natales

Mardones
El Ovalero
Hornillas
Manantiales

Horse Race Track
Club Hípico

Club Hípico

STRAITS   OF   MAGELLAN

settlement of Punta Arenas and Tierra del Fuego. The front rooms of the house are preserved as they were when the family lived here and the furnishings are original. Almost every piece of furniture was imported from Europe (mainly France) to produce a house no less palatial than any in Santiago.

The museum is on Magallanes, just off the Plaza de Armas. It's open Tuesday to Saturday, from 11 am to 4 pm and during holidays from 11 am to 1 pm.

Salesian College

A curious museum in the Colegio Salesiano, at the corner of Bhories and Sarmiento, the Salesian College collection depicts the geography, fauna and flora of southern Patagonia and harbours a collection of stuffed animals and the relics of dead Indians. Large dioramas depict the Indian way of life before the coming of the white man. The depressing before-and-after photos hardly require captions or explanations.

Ten-thousand-year-old droppings and unidentifiable fragments of the giant ground sloth, uncovered in the Milodon Cave near Puerto Natales, are also on display. All that aside, this is probably the best place to come for an overview of the natural history of southern Chile.

Instituto del Patagonia

The Patagonian Institute has an extraordinary collection of old farming machinery, including steam tractors built in England and Europe and used in Tierra del Fuego and Magallanes in the 19th and 20th centuries.

Other vehicles include a wooden wagon used by the early settlers before permanent houses were built, horse-drawn wagons and coaches, early petrol-fuelled farm tractors and vintage cars. More surprising are the simple wooden horse-drawn ploughs used in southern Patagonia and Tierra del Fuego until the 1930s. There is also a reconstructed settler's house from the Punta Arenas area dating back to between 1875 and 1880.

To get to the institute, take a taxi colectivo from the front of the Museum Regional de Magallanes, on Magallanes near the plaza, then stop off in front of the institute. Across the road from the institute is the Zona Franca (Free Zone) where duty-free goods are sold, including everything from sacks of rice to trucks.

The Penguin Colony

The best sight outside Punta Arenas is the *pingüineros*, the penguin colony. This is rather like a colony of hobbits, with burrows dug in the shoreline's soft, sandy

soil, into which the penguins disappear when lumbering tourists come by. They're surprisingly amiable, although they will bite if you prod them too closely. Penguin beaks can inflict a nasty cut. The drive to the penguin colony takes you through sheep-grazing country, also inhabited by wild guanacos, rheas and ibises. To get there (hire a car or take a tour), see the Getting Around chapter.

The penguins near Punta Arenas are *spheniscus magellanicus*, named after the Straits of Magellan where they live. The common name for them is 'jackass penguin' because they bray. All species of spheniscus bray, but the term is more frequently applied to particularly vocal African species. The magellanic penguins nest in burrows which they dig themselves near the shoreline. When frightened, they will run on all fours using their flippers as front legs, dashing into the safety of their burrows. They spend roughly April through to August at sea (during which time they move northwards) and September through to March at or near their breeding grounds.

Fuerte Bulnes
Although Bernardo O'Higgins may have planned to annex the southern tip of South America for Chile, it was not until 1843 that the Chileans finally claimed the area. In October of that year, the first rude buildings of Fuerte Bulnes were slapped up from logs, thatch and mud and the lonely outpost was given the respectable status of a fort by the addition of cannon and a fence of pointed stakes. The fort is 55 km from Punta Arenas. It's been partly restored and is now a national monument. To get there, see the Getting Around section.

Places to Stay – bottom end
On Nogueira, a few doors up from the Plaza de Armas, is the *Residencial París* (tel 23112). It has rooms for US$6 per person, without a private bathroom, and is a very basic but clean place. A few rooms have no windows and most have no locks on the doors.

The *Residencial Roca* (tel 23803) is at the corner of Roca and Emilio Korner. It's a decent place with singles/doubles for US$6/9, including breakfast. It seems popular with overseas visitors.

Another cheap place recommended is the *Hotel Monte Carlo* (tel 23448) at Colón 605, on the corner with Chiloé. Singles/doubles are US$8/12. More expensive rooms have a private bathroom.

Places to Stay – middle
The *Turismo Plaza* (tel 21300) is on Nogueira, near the plaza and in the same building as the Residencial París. It has singles/doubles for US$22/27, with private bathrooms. It's spotlessly clean, bright and the front rooms overlook the town.

The *Hotel Ritz* (tel 24422) is at Pedro Montt 1102. This is one of the best hotels in Punta Arenas, being clean, comfortable and quiet. Singles/doubles are US$15/19 and it has a restaurant.

Places to Stay – top end
The *Hotel Los Navegantes* (tel 24677) at Menéndez 647 is the best place to stay. Singles/doubles are US$50/60, which includes a North American breakfast. The *Cabo de Hornos* (tel 22134) faces the Plaza de Armas and has singles/doubles for US$64/75.

Places to Eat
The *Bar Restaurant Stotito* at O'Higgins 1138 is good for moderately priced Italian-style seafood. Try the raw sea urchin, but be prepared to run!

Possibly better is the *Bar Grill Beagle* on O'Higgins, near the corner with Roca, which has large servings of seafood and is moderately expensive.

The *Nandu Café Grill*, Waldo Seguel 670, opposite the tourist office, is still as sleazy as ever. It's more a bar than a restaurant – not bad.

For wine and song there's the *Peña de Trovador* at Pedro Montt 919, near the corner with Lautaro Navarro.

If all else fails there's a good smorgasbord

restaurant in the Zona Franca – go to the first building on the right as you enter the compound.

Getting There & Away

The tourist office keeps a list of all road, sea and air transport out of Punta Arenas, Puerto Natales and around Tierra del Fuego, including connections to Argentina.

Air LAN-Chile (tel 23460) is at the corner of Pedro Montt and Lautaro Navarro, Ladeco (tel 22665) is at Roca 924 and DAP (tel 23958) is at Ignacio Carrena Pinto 1022.

Both LAN-Chile and Ladeco have daily flights from Punta Arenas to Puerto Montt and Santiago.

DAP flies from Punta Arenas to Puerto Williams once a week. It has daily flights between Punta Arenas and Porvenir.

The Aeropuerto Presidente Ibáñez is 20 km from Punta Arenas. DAP has its own bus to take passengers from the city to the airport while Ladeco and LAN-Chile use a local bus company to transfer passengers to the airport.

Bus There are direct buses from Punta Arenas to Puerto Natales, to Río Gallegos in Argentina and to Puerto Montt and Santiago via Argentine Patagonia.

Typical fares from Punta Arenas are: to Río Gallegos US$12; Puerto Montt US$52; Puerto Natales US$4; and Santiago US$70.

Buses Sur at Menéndez 565 has buses to Puerto Natales twice daily. The trip takes about four hours. It also has buses twice a week to Puerto Montt and buses several days a week to Calafate (in Argentina) via the Parque Nacional Torres del Paine.

Expresso Vera, at the corner of 21 de Mayo and Boliviano, has daily buses to Río Gallegos.

Buses Fernández at Chiloé 930 has buses to Puerto Natales twice daily. It also has three-day tours to the Parque Nacional Torres del Paine.

Buses Río Gallegos and El Pingüino are

Club de la Union, Punta Arenas

both at Lautaro Navarro 971 and have daily buses to Río Gallegos.

Buses Ghisoni, also at Lautaro Navarro 971, has buses twice a week to Río Gallegos. These continue through Argentine Patagonia to Osorno and Puerto Montt in Chile. For other buses to Puerto Montt, try Buses Norte at Gamero 1039 and Turibús at Menéndez 647.

Boat There are regular passenger ferries from Punta Arenas to Puerto Montt and Porvenir.

For ships to the north, enquire at Empremar (tel 21608) at Lautaro Navarro 1338 and at Navimag (tel 226600) at Independencia 840. Navimag has passenger ships to Puerto Montt about three times a month. (See the Puerto Montt section in the Lake District chapter.)

There are daily ferries across the Straits of Magellan to Porvenir, leaving Punta Arenas in the morning. These are operated by Transbordadora Austral Broom at Roca 924. The passenger fare is about US$2. Vehicles can be transported for US$21. I've even seen people take horses across. The trip takes about three hours. In Punta Arenas, the ferries leave from Puerto Trente about one km past the Zona Franca – take a local bus or a taxi colectivo.

Getting Around
Air Ask at DAP and travel agents about plane rides over the surrounding region. These take you over Tierra del Fuego, the Marinelli Glacier, the Beagle Channel, Puerto Williams and even as far south as Cape Horn.

Bus & Colectivo Punta Arenas has taxi colectivos and buses. Fares and destinations are posted on the outside of each bus and taxi. Although much of Punta Arenas is small enough to walk around, you'll need the buses and colectivos to get to places further out, such as the Patagonian Institute and the Salesian College.

Car Rental Cars can be hired from Hertz (tel 222013) at Lautaro Navarro 1064, Budget (tel 225696) at O'Higgins 964 and the Automobile Club (tel 21888) at O'Higgins 931. Budget should have the cheapest rates.

Tours For tours to the penguin colony, Fuerte Bulnes and other places in the vicinity of Punta Arenas, try Arka Patagonia at Lautaro Navarro 975. Other travel agents are around the centre of town. Typical prices for tours to the penguin colony are US$10 per person; likewise for Fuerte Bulnes.

For tours to the Parque Nacional Torres del Paine try Buses Fernández. Its tour costs US$120, lasts three days and the price includes transport, accommodation and meals.

PUERTO NATALES
Puerto Natales is a cool and tidy town of timber and corrugated iron houses. It's the last town of any size on the southern Chilean mainland, save for Punta Arenas on the Straits of Magellan. While unspectacular in itself, some of the most astonishing sights in southern Chile can be found in the vicinity of Puerto Natales. It's very popular with trekkers and climbers during the summer months as it's the gateway to the spectacular Parque Nacional Torres del Paine. It's also the starting point for the Balmaceda Glacier and the Milodon Cave.

Information
Post & Telecommunications The post office and TELEX Chile are in the same building on Eberhard, facing the main plaza.

Banks There are several moneychangers in Puerto Natales, where you can interchange Argentine and Chilean currency. Some of these may also change foreign cash. Try the one at Encalada 226, at the junction with Eberhard. There are others in the vicinity.

1 Buses to Río Turbio
2 Banco del Estado de Chile
3 Buses Fernández
4 Ladeco
5 Buses Sur
6 Post Office
7 Investigaciones
8 Hotel Natalino
9 Captain Eberhard Hotel
10 Hotel Palace
11 Residencial Grey
12 Harbour Master's Office

Puerto Natales

The Meat Factory

The miniature steam engine in the Plaza de Armas was built in Bristol (UK) in 1920 and was used at the British-owned meat-packing and tanning factory, established early this century outside Puerto Natales. The meat and hides were taken from the factory along a railway line laid along a pier, where they were loaded on to ships.

The factory still operates, though the scale of operations is much smaller than it was during its heyday when several thousand sheep were slaughtered weekly. Then some of the sheep ranches in the area each ran as many as 80,000 to 120,000 sheep.

Some of the land now included in the Parque Nacional Torres del Paine was once a sheep ranch, owned by a Chilean-Italian up until the early 1970s. Sheep no longer graze in the park. Instead there are herds of guanaco and flocks of rheas and pink flamingos. Rheas are now a protected species. Their meat is said to taste like turkey.

The meat-processing factory is just

outside Puerto Natales, by the road to Torres del Paine. Much of the original steam-driven machinery is still there but is no longer used, as now the compressors used to freeze the meat are electrically powered. The wooden buildings in front of the factory are used to dry the hides. Narrow spaces occur between the slats of the walls to allow air to circulate.

The Balmaceda Glacier

This impressive glacier slides down a mountain into one of the many estuaries and fjords of jagged southern Chilean coastline. Huge blocks of ice break off and wallow around in the lagoon in front of the glacier wall.

The glacier lies to the north-east of Puerto Natales. During January and February a boat called the *21 de Mayo* takes groups to the glacier almost every day. The fare is about US$20 per person. Several travel agents in Puerto Natales

Balmaceda Glacier

Balmaceda Glacier

sell tickets for the boat. Try the Monte Everest agency at Encalada 296. Bring something to eat, as only drinks are provided.

The tub is about 40 or 50 years old and the pioneering spirit is maintained by the provision of two inadequately sized lifeboats and two life preservers. There are no life jackets!

The winds that roar through the narrow channel leading to the glacier can be so strong that sometimes the boat has to turn back or does terrifying rolls in the choppy sea. Console yourself with the knowledge that it has done many successful trips. Small waterfalls, condors and bands of seals can be seen on the voyage. At the glacier, the boat pulls into a small jetty and you can get off and walk along a trail very close to the glacier. The Torres del Paine can be seen in the distance.

The Milodon Cave

The milodon was a giant ground sloth, larger and more ferocious looking than a full-grown bull and of a class unique to South America. The naturalist, Charles Darwin, found the bones of a similar milodon in South America and sent them back to England. The animal was so big that rather than putting it in a tree like smaller sloths, zoologists of the day imagined it rearing up on its haunches and using its long, extendable tongue to scoop up leaves and grubs.

The Milodon Cave forms an enormous cavity in a mountain at the back of what was once a sheep ranch on Last Hope Sound. It was settled in 1893 by a Prussian, Herman Eberhard. The story goes that in early 1895 he took a look at the giant cave and found a human skull and a piece of skin sticking out of the floor. A year later, a Swedish explorer visited the cave and found more skin as well as the eye-socket of an enormous mammal, a claw, a human thighbone of giant size and some stone tools.

As pieces of the animal and other milodon bones found their way to England and Europe, the inevitable conclusion was drawn that some species of giant sloth had managed to survive into recent years! As there were Indian stories and travellers' tales of grotesque creatures inhabiting South America, a British expedition was launched to find one, but had no success.

Meanwhile the cave was excavated. In the uppermost layer were the remains of human settlement, in the middle were the remains of the now-extinct American horse and in the bottom layer were the remains of the milodon. One excavator even devised the bizarre theory that the milodon was a domesticated beast, kept by the Indians at the rear of the cave like a horse in a corral. The modern verdict is that the giant sloth lived about 10,000 years ago. Indians may have killed it in a battle for possession of the cave but, sad to say, they did not keep it as a pet.

The cave is not far from Puerto Natales, just off the road to Torres del Paine. A full-size model of the milodon stands in the cave. For a rundown on the history of the cave and the discovery of the creature's remains, see Bruce Chatwin's book *In Patagonia*.

Places to Stay - bottom end

Very spartan and a bit dilapidated, the *Pensión La Busca* is at Valdivia 845 – there's no sign. Basically it's OK and one of the cheapest places you'll find at just US$3 per person, including breakfast. There are hot showers.

The *Residencial Grey* (formerly the *Burnier*) is at the corner of Bulnes and Ladrilleros. It's a fairly spartan place, a bit dreary and rundown, but the rooms are large and have heaters. Rooms are US$2.50 per person.

Places to Stay - middle

The *Hotel Natalino* on Eberhard, near the corner with Tomas Rogers, is great value. It's one of the best little hotels in Chile. It's very clean and comfortable, has room heating and is run by a lively, friendly woman. Singles/doubles without a private bathroom are US$10/14 or US$14/19 with a private bathroom.

Another fine place is the *Austral Hotel* at Valdivia 955. It's run by Eduardo Scott, a very friendly man and the best local tour guide. Singles/doubles are US$8/12 or US$12/16 with a private bathroom. It's very clean and well run and it has a restaurant. Try the piping hot seafood soup – a meal in itself. Highly recommended.

Places to Stay - top end

One of Puerto Natales' most commodious hotels is the *Hotel Palace* near the corner of Eberhard and Ladrilleros. Singles/doubles are US$40/45.

The town's best hotel would probably be the *Captain Eberhard Hotel*, on the waterfront at the corner of Ladrilleros and Senoret. Singles/doubles are US$42/46.

Neck and neck with the Captain

Eberhard is the *Hotel Juan Ladrilleros*, on the waterfront at Pedro Montt 161. It's a very bright hotel with singles/doubles for US$27/45.

Places to Eat
The *Restaurant Midas* at Tomas Rogers 169, facing the main plaza, is a fine place for seafood and surprisingly cheap. It's very popular with young local people. There's also Eduardo Scott's restaurant in the Hotel Austral, which is very good. There are many small, nondescript restaurants around town.

Getting There & Away
Air Ladeco have an office at Bulnes 530 for bookings only, as there are no flights out of Puerto Natales. The nearest airport is at Punta Arenas. If you don't want to visit Punta Arenas you can arrange for the bus from Puerto Natales to drop you at Punta Arenas' airport.

Bus Buses Sur at Baquedano 534 and Buses Fernández at Eberhard 555 have buses twice daily to Punta Arenas. The fare is US$4 and the trip takes about four hours.

Buses Sur also has daily buses to Torres del Paine during summer. The fare is US$6. Buses take you to the Hostería Petrohué and the Posada Río Serrano in the park.

During summer, Buses Sur also has buses four or five days a week from Puerto Natales to Calafate in Argentina. These go via the Parque Nacional Torres del Paine . The fare from Puerto Natales to Calafate is US$36.

For buses to Argentina, try Buses Alvaro Gomez at Baquedano 244, near the corner with Valdivia. It has buses to Río Gallegos via Río Turbio, three days a week.

Empresa Turis-Sur is at the corner of Baquedano and Valdivia and has daily buses to Río Turbio in Argentina. The fare is US$1. From Río Turbio you can catch another bus to Río Gallegos.

Alternatively, go to the corner of Phillippi and Baquedano and catch one of the local workers' buses to Río Turbio. Departures occur daily at half-hour or hourly intervals, from early morning to early evening.

PUERTO EDÉN
The south coast of Chile, with its hundreds of islands, looks like a demolished jigsaw. On the voyage between Puerto Montt and Puerto Natales is Puerto Edén, one of the most isolated settlements in the world. The ship may pull in briefly, otherwise ask the captain if it would be possible to do so. If enough people ask he may make an unscheduled stop.

About 500 people live in Puerto Edén, making a living solely by fishing and selling some of their catch to passing ships. They have chickens but no other animals. The soil is clay so they cannot grow crops of any kind. There is at least one policeman and, even in this remote place, the inevitable bust of the naval hero Arturo Prat.

PARQUE NACIONAL TORRES DEL PAINE
The granite Towers of Paine make a sudden and dramatic appearance on the horizon in the midst of a flat, dry, windswept plain – they're so extravagantly beautiful that superlatives soon fail you. This is, despite the almost constant cold

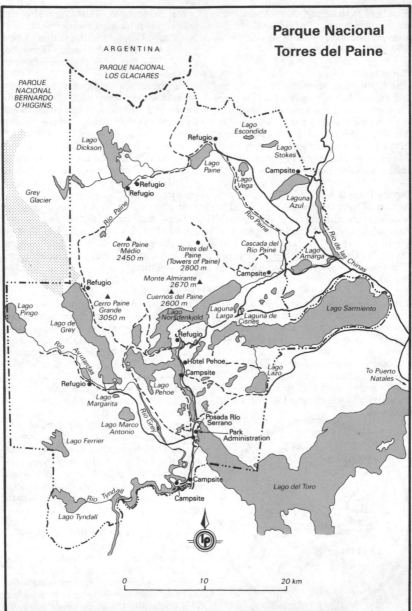

Parque Nacional
Torres del Paine

ARGENTINA

PARQUE NACIONAL
LOS GLACIARES

PARQUE
NACIONAL
BERNARDO
O'HIGGINS

Lago
Dickson

Refugio

Lago
Escondida

Lago
Stokes

Campsite

Lago
Paine

Grey
Glacier

Refugio
Refugio

Lago
Vega

Laguna
Azul

Río Paine

Río Paine

Cerro Paine
Médio
2450 m

Torres del
Paine
(Towers of Paine)
2800 m

Cascada del
Río Paine

Lago
Amarga

Río de las Chinas

Lago
Pingo

Refugio

Cerro Paine
Grande
3050 m

Monte Almirante
2670 m

Cuernos del Paine
2600 m

Campsite

Lago
de Grey

Lago
Norsdenkjold

Laguna
Larga

Laguna de
Cisnes

Lago Sarmiento

Río
Avutardas

Refugio

Hotel Pehoe

Lago
Lazo

To Puerto
Natales

Refugio

Lago
Margarita

Lago
Pehoe

Campsite

Río Grey

Lago Marco
Antonio

Posada Río
Serrano

Park
Administration

Lago Ferrier

Campsite

Río Tyndall

Campsite

Lago del Toro

Lago Tyndall

0   10   20 km

wind, some of the finest trekking country in Chile. It is endowed with mountains, lakes, waterfalls and glaciers, as well as herds of guanacos, flocks of pink flamingos, condors and large Patagonian hares.

The park was established in 1959 as the Parque Nacional Lago Grey. Prior to this, shepherds grazed their flocks here and their fires occasionally burnt out of control. You can still see the devastation that was wrought near Lago Grey, with large areas of burnt-out forest and charred logs extending up the hillsides as far as the snowline.

More land was added to the park in 1962 and the name was changed to its present one. It is said that the towers and park were named after a woman climber or settler (or both) named Paine, although *payne* is also an Indian word for blue. Estancia El Paine, a sheep-grazing property, was added to the park in about 1974.

Guanacos, Torres del Paine National Park

With a bit of planning, trekkers could spend weeks exploring the park, but it's possible to see a good deal of it on a day trip from Puerto Natales. A rough but motorable track extends up to Lago Grey, and you can see enormous blue icebergs which have broken off from the glacier at the other end of the lake and floated down. Some of the lakes are also accessible by road and the towers, when not shrouded by low cloud, are always present in the background.

Geography
The Paine Mountain Range is made up mainly of granite rock which was pushed up and folded by tremendous pressure about 12 million years ago. This area was once under water. The yellow-orange rock is granite and the dark rock at the top is sedimentary rock. The whole range would now be covered in sedimentary rock, but a lot of this has been worn away by ice, wind and rain.

The range takes its name from the three *torres* or towers which are tall pinnacles of rock. The Torres Sur rises 2900 metres above sea level, the Torres Central is 2850 metres high and the Torres Norte is 2600 metres.

The towers are just to the north of a group of structures known as the Cuernos del Paine or the Horns of Paine. Cuerno Norte rises 2400 metres, Cuerno Principal is 2600 metres and Cuerno Chico (the Little Horn) is 2200 metres.

To the west of the Cuernos del Paine is a massive range, the Cerro Paine Grand, which rises 3500 metres above sea level. The other big mountain range is the Monte Almirante Nieto. Another important feature is the 17-km long Grey Glacier, one of the last reminders of the ice age about 15,000 years ago.

Entrance
There is an entrance fee to the park of about US$1. You pay at the CONAF (Corporación Nacional Forestal) office at

the entrance to the park on the road up from Puerto Natales.

Maps

The best map is the CONAF map, *Parque Nacional Torres del Paine*, which has all the refugios, roads, tracks, ranger stations and picnic areas marked. You can buy it at the CONAF office at the entrance to the park. You should, however, check with the rangers as to the present condition of the refugios and campsites. Refugios sometimes burn down and it may take a long time before these are repaired. Don't go wandering off into the wilderness expecting to find huts that are no longer there – even if they're marked on the CONAF maps.

Books

If you intend trekking you should go to the park armed with Hilary Bradt & John Pilkington's *Backpacking in Chile & Argentina* which has a chapter on the park.

Horse-riding

Horses can be hired from CONAF for US$18 per day. A pack horse costs US$32 per day, with a maximum load of about 60 kg.

Clothing

Take warm clothes with you even if you're not trekking! The weather can be stormy throughout summer (though there are also beautiful days of warm sunshine and light wind). At Lago Grey, where the wind sweeps off the glacier, it can be very cold. You must have rain and wind protection and a change of clothing.

Places to Stay & Eat

There are two hotels in the park. The *Hotel Pehoe* is on an island in Lago Pehoe and is connected to the shore by a footbridge. It faces the Cuernos del Paine (the Horns of Paine) and is one of the most beautiful settings in the park. Singles/

doubles are US$37/42. It has an OK, although rather expensive, restaurant.

The other hotel is the *Posada Río Serrano* which is near Lago del Toro at the start of the road leading to Lago Grey. Singles/doubles are US$15/22 or US$28/35 with a private bathroom. The rooms are simple, but clean and comfortable. My main complaint is the ridiculously noisy generator which goes on in the early evening and stays on until midnight. You can also camp in the hotel grounds and use the hot water for US$4 per tent.

There is a small shop in the hotel where you can stock up on food, although it may be an idea to bring essentials from Puerto Natales. Gasoline can also be bought here. Bookings for the hotel can be made at the office at Arturo Prat 270 in Puerto Natales.

A refugio near the hotel costs US$2 per person. There are other refugios, campsites and shelters in the park. Most are free and can be located using the CONAF map. The refugios are not like European refugios. To use them you must have your own sleeping bags, ground sheet and cold-weather gear. Some refugios are very dilapidated.

If you intend trekking you must bring all your own food as there is none available in the park other than what's at the hotels.

Getting There & Away

If your time is limited or if you don't have the equipment or the urge to trek and camp out, then consider taking a tour to the park. Eduardo Scott, a Falklander who speaks both Spanish and English, is the person to contact for tours of the surrounding area and especially of the Parque Nacional Torres del Paine. He takes people for day trips to the park in his van. He can also arrange a visit to the old meat-packing and tanning factory outside of Puerto Natales. Contact him at the Hotel Austral in Puerto Natales. He's very informative and knowledgeable, as he used to work on the Estancia El Paine which is now in the park.

Outside of summer, transport to the park is likely to be more haphazard. You may have to hitch, but there will be few vehicles, or you could hire a taxi to take you from Puerto Natales to the park.

Bus Buses Sur in Puerto Natales has daily buses to the park during summer. These take you to the Hotel Pehoe and the Posada Río Serrano. The fare is US$6.

Buses Fernández in Punta Arenas has three-day tours to the park costing US$120 per person, which includes transport, meals and accommodation.

Tierra del Fuego

History

When Ferdinand Magellan came to the great island at the tip of the American continent he observed the Indian campfires and called the island *Tierra del Humo*, the Land of Smoke. Later his patron, the King of Spain, Charles V, reasoned that there could be no smoke without fire and renamed the island *Tierra del Fuego* – the Land of Fire.

Having sailed across the Atlantic, in October 1520, the fleet entered the strait separating the mainland of South America from what is now known as Tierra del Fuego. It took more than a month to get through this tempestuous strait, with its nightmarish seas, into the Pacific. The fleet headed west and finally came to the Philippines where, as fate would have it, Magellan was killed in a minor skirmish with some of the indigenous inhabitants.

Since no one else on the voyage would risk returning through the terrible Straits of Magellan they pushed on westwards. The dismal voyage not only caused Magellan's death but also the deaths of most of his crew. Three years after the voyage had begun, just one ship of the original five, the *Victoria*, limped into Spain with a few survivors. In a voyage akin to Homer's Odyssey, they had inadvertently become the first people to sail around the world. Only about 30 men survived the expedition.

Magellan's ships had found a western route to Asia, but they may not have been the first to sail through the Straits of Magellan. That honour may actually belong to a Portuguese expedition which may have sailed through the strait and back in 1514, or even to Egyptian sailors who may have come this way in the first and second centuries AD. In fact, the prize should be awarded to the Indians who have lived in Tierra del Fuego since about 7500 BC.

The Straits of Magellan cut Tierra del Fuego off from the rest of South America. Tierra del Fuego is, in fact, not one island but a whole archipelago. The largest of the islands is the Isla Grande de Tierra del Fuego and is usually the one which is referred to when speaking of this region. The other islands of the archipelago include Navarino and Dawson, and the three small islands at the mouth of the Beagle Channel (which separates Isla Grande from Navarino).

When Magellan came by, the archipelago was home to four distinct groups of Indians. The oldest of these groups was the Haush who were pushed to the eastern tip of the island by the more numerous Ona and Yahgan. Like the Ona, the Haush hunted guanaco with bows and arrows, dressed in guanaco skins, and lived in huts made of sticks, branches and sometimes skins. Like the Yahgan, they used spears and harpoons to fish and also gathered mussels from the beaches at low tide. The nomadic Ona were similar to the Haush, but were much more numerous and ranged over most of Isla Grande in search of guanaco which provided them with all their needs.

Further south, along the beaches of the Beagle Channel and the islands southward to Cape Horn, lived the Yahgan. This group was also nomadic, but lived by hunting otter, fish and seals from canoes with harpoons and spears. They used slings and snares to catch birds and clubs against each other. They used tree bark to make their canoes and seal skin for clothing.

The fourth group were the Alacaluf who ranged from Puerto Edén, in the forbidding fjords of southern Chile, to the Beagle Channel. They were similar to the Yahgan, but their language was different. They also used bows and arrows and had sails on their canoes. Unlike the Indians

Top: Fuerte Bulnes, near Punta Arenas, Magallanes
Bottom: Balmaceda Glacier, near Puerto Natales, Magallanes

Top: Guanacos in the Torres del Paine National Park, Magallanes
Bottom: Torres del Paine, Magallanes

further north, none of the Fuegian Indians had chiefs or organised religion.

Magellan's voyage brought on what for those days was a veritable stampede – Spanish, Dutch, French and English ships passed through the strait. To keep these interlopers out, the Spanish contemplated building forts on the straits as early as 1580. Although this plan didn't come to fruition, in 1584 two colonies were established on the northern side of the strait, only to be wiped out by famine. Voyages of exploration, scientific expeditions, English pirates and increasing numbers of sealers and whalers, all came this way.

In 1843, Chile (through the guise of the Englishman John Williams) officially took possession of the Straits of Magellan and founded Fuerte Bulnes on its western shore near the present city of Punta Arenas. Had it not been for the discovery of gold in California, this settlement might well have remained a distant outpost at the end of the earth. But the same metal that drove the Spanish to South America now provoked an enormous migration to North America. Punta Arenas, which was founded on the west side of the strait, was suddenly an important port on one of the world's busiest shipping routes.

In the same year, Chile also laid claim to southern Patagonia. The renunciation of this claim and the division of Tierra del Fuego between Chile and Argentina was made in 1881 when Chile was fighting the War of the Pacific with Bolivia and Peru. This war made it imperative for Chile to keep the peace and finalise borders with Argentina. It was not until 1899, however, that the northern boundaries of the two countries were settled, and it was 1902 before the southern boundaries were finalised. This 'perpetual accord' inspired the famous statue of Christ which was erected on Mt Aconcagua to celebrate the decision and symbolise peace between the two countries.

The first farms were cleared on Tierra del Fuego in the 1880s, from when the history of the island is one of who owned the turf. In the years following, less and less land was owned by Yahgans, Onas, Haush and Alacalufs and more and more by foreigners. The first white residents were English missionaries who stayed on as farmers, followed by Germans, Argentines, Chileans, Yugoslavs, Italians and other immigrants. For a few years the island even had a Rumanian dictator, who printed his own money and stamps and maintained his own gold mines and a private army until his death in 1893.

The Indians, meanwhile, were forced to prey on the settler's livestock as the herds of guanacos and other animals which they hunted became increasingly scarce. The settlers arranged punitive expeditions against the Indians and eventually bounties were placed on Indian heads resulting in them being hunted down like animals. Others were simply wiped out by foreign diseases. Now there are no pure-blooded Fuegian Indians, although there are some mestizos, such as those at Puerto Williams on Navarino Island. Many Indians were killed either by the white settlers, in fights among themselves or more commonly by measles, tuberculosis and other diseases brought by the whites. It is hard to say when the last full-blooded Fuegian Indians died. The last sizeable groups of full bloods were those who worked on the estancias in Chilean and Argentine Tierra del Fuego in the 1930s.

Sawmills, meat-salting and tallow-making factories, whaling stations, meat warehouses and crab and mussel-canning industries were established on the island from the 1880s to the 1920s.

The estancias, now grazing sheep and cattle, are enormous properties because of the large amount of land required to graze even small flocks and herds. The latest fires in the Land of Fire are those that flicker from the oil fields – the San Sebastián refinery produces liquefied petroleum gas. Río Grande is a large town, dependent on the petroleum industry, meat exports and farming. During the last decade, tourism has also boomed in Tierra del Fuego. Aided by its magnificent trekking country, and the duty-free status of the biggest town Ushuaia, the island is a favoured holiday resort for Argentines.

Geography

Altogether the archipelago covers an area slightly smaller than Ireland, about 70% of this belongs to Chile. The border between Chile and Argentina on the Isla Grande is a straight line running north to south and then along the Beagle Channel. The northern part of the island is a windswept land of rolling hills and vast plains bare of trees. Sheep grazing and oil extraction are important. The central region includes mountains which are covered in snow from April to November and is too rugged for farming or grazing. The Beagle Channel separates Isla Grande from Navarino and the narrow strip of land on Isla Grande bordering the channel has a comparatively mild climate with cool summers and snow in winter (this usually melts quickly). The channel never freezes and there are no icebergs.

The eastern part of the island has less snow and ice, but much more rain and cloudy weather. In the west the climate is sub-Antarctic with fierce winds, cloudy skies and frequent rain. These distinct climatic areas influence the type of fauna and flora found on the island. In the north are treeless plains. The mountains and shores of the Beagle Channel are covered in forest and swampland which merge to the east and to the west with the rainforests of the even wetter areas. Cape Horn and the other outer islands have a sub-Antarctic flora of hardy bog plants and dwarf trees and bushes, but only in sheltered places.

The chief settlement on the Chilean side is Porvenir from where you can get a ferry to Punta Arenas. On the Argentine side Río Grande and Ushuaia are two large, well-developed towns. The main crossing point between the two halves is at San Sebastián on the road between Río Grande and Porvenir. As the Germans settled in Valdivia, the British and Yugoslavs settled in Tierra del Fuego and there are still sizeable populations of their descendents in the area. Immediately south of Tierra del Fuego, separated by the narrow Beagle Channel, is the Chilean island of Navarino. Puerto Williams is a Chilean naval base. It's the only settlement on Navarino and can be visited.

Fauna

Tierra del Fuego is home to several of the world's largest birds, the rhea (akin to an ostrich or emu), the condor and the albatross, and to large animals such as the guanaco (which is the most commonly seen), otter and several varieties of seal and sea lion.

PORVENIR

The sign at the Punta Arenas dock says it all. You are now 18,662 km from Yugoslavia. With some 4500 people, Porvenir is the only settlement of any size in Chilean Tierra del Fuego. Its predominant ethnic group is of Yugoslav descent.

Places to Stay & Eat

The *Hotel España* has double rooms for US$10, including a private bathroom. For good meals, try the *Yugoslav Club*. The *Restaurante Puerto Montt* is good for seafood.

Getting There & Away

Air If rough weather causes the ferries to be cancelled you can fly to Porvenir. DAP has daily flights to Porvenir from Punta Arenas.

Bus Buses Senkovic is at Carlos Bories 201 and has buses from Porvenir to Río Grande in Argentine Tierra del Fuego. Departures are every Wednesday and Saturday afternoon. The fare is US$15 and the trip takes about eight hours.

Boat There is a daily ferry to Punta Arenas, departing Porvenir in the afternoon. The

Sign at Porvenir, Tierra del Fuego

ferry is operated by Transbordadora Austral Broom Ltda at Roca 924 in Porvenir. (See the Punta Arenas section in the Magallanes chapter.)

RÍO GRANDE

On the east coast of Tierra del Fuego, Río Grande sits on a flat, windswept plain and is essentially an oil refinery centre and service town for the estancías. For foreign visitors, it's mainly a halfway house between Punta Arenas or Río Gallegos and Ushuaia.

Places to Stay – bottom end

Most cheap accommodation in Río Grande is permanently occupied by workers, so it's difficult to find low-budget rooms.

One of the cheapest hotels is the *Hospedaje Argentina* on San Martín, between 11 de Julio and Libertad. Dormitory beds are a few US dollars a night.

The *Hospedaje Irmary* at Estrada 743 (near the corner with San Martín) is clean, pleasant and conveniently located. Rooms are about US$6 per person.

The *Residencial Rawson* is at Estrada 750. It's a good place, if rather sterile. Singles/doubles are US$14/18, with private bathrooms.

Try the *Hotel Anexo Villa* at Piedrabuena 641. It's a decent place but it's often full. Beds cost about US$6.

Places to Stay – middle

Possibly the best hotel in the whole city is the *Hospedaje Miramar* at the corner of MacKinley and Belgrano. Singles/doubles are US$9/14. The hotel is very clean, has heating in the rooms and passageways and is quite cosy. Since it's a bit more expensive than other hotels there's a good chance it'll have a room.

The *Gran Hotel Villa* is at San Martín 281. It's a good place with singles/doubles for US$15/20, with private bathrooms. There are slightly cheaper rooms without

1	Hospedaje Argentina
2	Gran Hotel Villa
3	Hotel Federico Barra
4	LADE and Aerolíneas Argentinas
5	Hospedaje Irmary
6	Residencial Rawson
7	Buses Senkovic
8	Hotel Anexo Villa
9	Hotel Atlantido
10	Transporte Los Carlos
11	Hospedaje Miramar
12	Hotel Yaganes
13	Post Office

private bathrooms. The hotel has a good, cheap restaurant.

Places to Stay – top end
The *Hotel Yaganes* is on Puy, at the junction with Belgrano. Singles/doubles are US$31/40, including breakfast. Similarly priced is the *Hotel Federico Barra* on Rosales, facing the main plaza. Also try the glittering *Hotel Atlantido* at the corner of Belgrano and Rosales.

Places to Eat
The *Restaurant El Castor* is a parrillado on Lasserre near the corner with Fagnano. Otherwise you'll find the meals at the *Gran Hotel Villa* to be fairly cheap and very filling. Also try the *Restaurant El Porteñno* on Lasserre, near Belgrano.

Getting There & Away
Air LADE and Aerolíneas Argentinas (tel 22749) are at the corner of San Martín and Belgrano. LADE has daily flights to Calafate, Río Gallegos and Ushuaia. One flight a week continues on from Calafate to Perito Moreno. Aerolíneas has flights several days a week to Ushuaia, Río Gallegos and Comodoro Rivadavia.

Bus Buses Senkovic at San Martín 959 have buses to Porvenir every Wednesday and Saturday. The trip takes about eight hours and the fare is about US$15. The bus connects with the ferry to Punta Arenas.

Buses Los Carlos is at Estrada 568 and has daily buses from Río Grande to Ushuaia. Buses are less frequent in winter. The trip takes about five hours and costs US$11.

USHUAIA
The world's southernmost town began, not with a brave band of hardy colonisers, but with a prefabricated mission hut put

up in 1869 by an Anglican bishop. He lived there for six months alongside the huts of the Yahgan Indians.

The following year an Anglican minister named Thomas Bridges, together with his wife and baby daughter, set up a mission and became Tierra del Fuego's first permanent white settlers. Perhaps his greatest achievement was the compilation of a large dictionary of the Yahgan language, which described its phenomenal complexity.

Sixteen years later, the Argentine navy paid a visit and the Indians dropped dead of imported pneumonia and measles. After serving as a naval base, Ushuaia was used as a convict station with a jail masterfully built from stone and concrete.

Ushuaia has been called a romantic kind of place, but it would have to be a bitter love affair. Some people find the area reminiscent of parts of Canada, while others liken the mountains, the drizzle and the biting wind to Scotland. You can forget any images you have of some isolated backwoods town inhabited by weather-beaten frontierspeople. The city at the end of the world is a modern, duty-free port of concrete houses, sprawling up hills overlooking the Beagle Channel. This is a tourist resort town, a sort of Antarctic version of Cairns or Brighton, and a good place to base yourself to explore the many tranquil lakes and mountains of Tierra del Fuego.

Ushuaia is actually the second-last resort, as from here you can travel south to Puerto Williams, the Chilean naval base and the most southern settlement in the world barring those in Antarctica. Otherwise you can head from Ushuaia to Punta Arenas in Chile, via Río Grande, Porvenir and the stormy straits that separate Tierra del Fuego from the mainland.

Information
Tourist Office The tourist office is at San Martín 524, near the corner with Lasserre. The staff are friendly and speak some English. They have plenty of information about hotels and tours.

Post & Telecommunications The post office is at the corner of San Martín and Godoy.

Bank Change cash and travellers' cheques at the Banco de la Nación Argentina at the corner of San Martín and Rivadavia.

Consulate The Chilean Consulate is at the corner of Malvinas Argentinas and Jainen.

Books For a round-up of Tierra del Fuego, see *Tierra del Fuego* by Rae Natalie. It's in English and Spanish and can be bought in the bookshops in Ushuaia. Also, take a copy of *Backpacking in Chile & Argentina* by Hilary Bradt & John Pilkington (Bradt Enterprises), which has an excellent description of the treks in the area.

Trekking
Most of what there is to see around Ushuaia demands time and funds. There are few marked trails and you need appropriate equipment, but the area is a trekker's paradise. A trek to the Martial Glacier (the Martial Mountains overlook Ushuaia) is one possibility.

For trekking information, enquire at the tourist office or at Onas Tours on 25 de Mayo. There are various other agencies in the centre of town. If you don't intend trekking, there are tours to various places of interest in the surrounding area.

Boat Tours
During summer, daily boat trips go to the sea lion colony on the Isla de los Lobos. The trip costs US$13 and takes six hours. A nine-hour trip takes you to Gable Island at the mouth of the Beagle Channel and day trips to Río Grande include visits to an estancia and a meat-processing factory.

It's even possible, at least during summer, to charter yachts on a weekly basis and cruise around the region, even as far south as Cape Horn. Half-day yacht

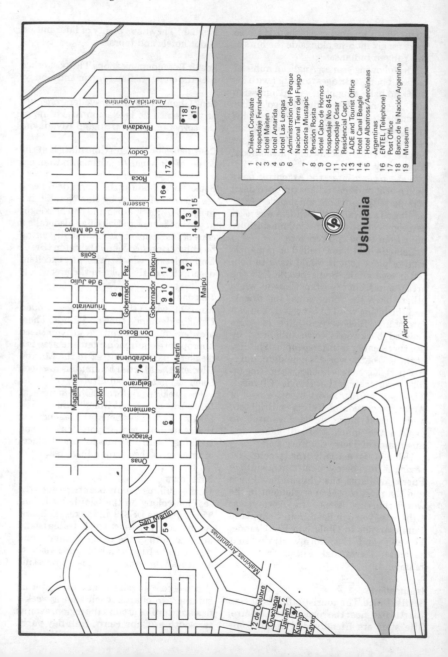

Ushuaia

1 Chilean Consulate
2 Hospedaje Fernández
3 Hotel Maiten
4 Hotel Antárida
5 Hotel Las Lengas
6 Administration del Parque
   Nacional Tierra del Fuego
7 Hostería Mustapic
8 Pensión Rosita
9 Hotel Cabo de Hornos
10 Hospedaje No 845
11 Hospedaje César
12 Residencial Capri
13 LADE and Tourist Office
14 Hotel Canal Beagle
15 Hotel Albatross/Aerolíneas
   Argentinas
16 ENTEL (Telephone)
17 Post Office
18 Banco de la Nación Argentina
19 Museum

Airport

trips are also possible at about US$35 per person. Full-day trips are about US$60 per person.

Places to Stay – bottom end

It's worth trying to find somewhere to stay in a private house in Ushuaia, especially during January and February. The tourist office has a list of these places and will telephone around to try and find a room or a bed for you. Don't expect too much. Chances are that at the height of the tourist season you'll wind up sharing someone's attic.

One place that's been recommended is the hospedaje at Deloqui 400. The people are friendly and there are cooking facilities. It costs a few US dollars per bed.

Another good place is the *Pensión Rosita* on Paz, between 9 de Julio and Triunvirato. Beds are US$6. It's run by a friendly woman and is recommended.

There is a hospedaje above the restaurant at the corner of Maipú and 9 de Julio. Beds are about US$6. There is a similarly priced hospedaje at San Martín 845, also above a restaurant. Also try the unfortunately-named *Kau-pen* at Piedrabuena 118.

Places to Stay – middle

One of the cheaper hotels is the *Residencial Capri* (tel 91833) at San Martín 720, between 9 de Julio and Soliás. It has bunk beds and hot water, is fairly clean, but is often full of long-term residents. Singles/doubles are US$13/32.

Another reasonably cheap place is the *Hospedaje Fernández* (tel 91453) at Onachaga 68, where singles/doubles are US$25/32.

One place that's been recommended is the *Hospedaje Malvinas* (tel 92626) at Deloqui 609, where doubles are US$30. The people are said to be friendly and helpful.

Other places in this price range include the *Hospedaje César* (tel 91460) at San Martín 753, the *Hostería Mustapic* (tel 91718) at Piedrabuena 230 and the *Hotel Maiten* (tel 92745) at 12 de Octubre 140.

Places to Stay – top end

At the top of the range is the *Hotel Canal Beagle* (tel 91117) at the corner of Maipú and 25 de Mayo on the waterfront. Singles/doubles are US$31/40, which includes breakfast.

Only very slightly cheaper, the *Hotel Albatross* (tel 92504) is next door, at the corner of Maipú and Lasserre.

Also, try the *Hotel Cabo de Hornos* (tel 92187) at the corner of San Martín and Triunvirato.

Places to Eat

The *Restaurant Los Canelos*, at the corner of Maipú and 9 de Julio, is the best in Ushuaia with very large servings of seafood. Also try the *Sloggert Pub* (that's its name) on Godoy, between Maipú and San Martín. The *Cafetería Ideal*, at the corner of San Martín and Roca, is an ideal eating place. It has main courses of *cholga* (giant mussels) and pretty good pizzas.

Getting There & Away

From Ushuaia, you can take a bus to Río Grande and continue on to Punta Arenas via Porvenir. Otherwise, you can fly from Ushuaia to Río Grande and beyond.

Air LADE is at San Martín 542 and has daily flights to Calafate, Río Gallegos and Río Grande. One flight a week continues on from Calafate to Perito Moreno.

Aerolíneas Argentinas (tel 91218) is at the corner of Maipú and Lasserre. It has flights several days a week from Ushuaia to Río Grande, Río Gallegos and Comodoro Rivadavia.

Ushuaia's airport is on the opposite side of the harbour to the town. Get there by a local bus or taxi. The local buses run down Maipú before heading out to the airport.

Bus Buses Los Carlos is at the corner of San Martín and Triunvirato. It has daily buses to Río Grande (less frequently in winter). The fare is US$11 and the trip takes about five hours.

Boat There used to be a weekly ferry between Ushuaia and Puerto Williams, the Chilean naval base on Navarino Island. This service had been discontinued at the time of writing, but check to see if this has changed.

PUERTO WILLIAMS

For almost 40 years, Puerto Williams on Navarino Island has been waving the Chilean flag at the toenails of Argentina. It was established in 1953 as a naval base – which it still is. The forerunner of this settlement was the world's most southerly sawmilling operation. The last people of identifiable Yahgan Indian descent can be found here and there is a fine museum. Trekking is limited since there are few trails and only two roads.

Museo Martín Gusinde

The museum has a fine display on the natural history of the region, the Indians who once lived here and European exploration and settlement.

Ukika

The last people of Yahgan Indian descent live in a small enclave of several houses called Ukika, by the road a short distance east of the settlement. Further along, on a clear day you can get good views across the Beagle Channel to Gable Island and the mountains to the north. West of town, a branch road runs about four km to a waterfall.

Places to Stay & Eat

In the central block of buildings behind the gymnasium is a small, cheap hotel. It's a spartan little place, but clean and decent with its own restaurant. There's

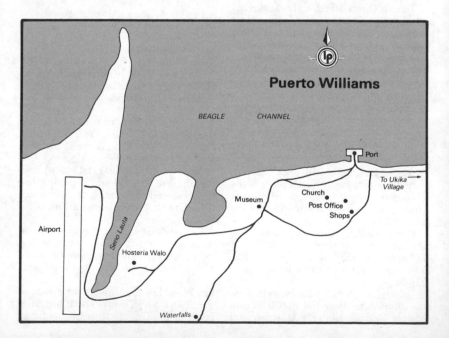

Puerto Williams

BEAGLE   CHANNEL

Port

To Ukika Village

Church

Museum

Post Office

Shops

Airport

Cerro Lauta

Hosteria Walo

Waterfalls

another small restaurant beside it and a supermarket a few doors away. The up-market place is the *Hostería Walo* on the road in from the airport. It's surprisingly comfortable, with a good restaurant and blazing fireplace. It runs tours to the museum, the waterfalls and the Ukika village, which are worth taking if it's a cold, wet day.

Getting There & Away

DAP flies Puerto Williams to Punta Arenas once a week. There used to be a weekly ferry from Puerto Williams to Ushuaia, but this has been discontinued. Check to see if this has changed.

Easter Island

How the world's most isolated island was discovered by early seafarers is as baffling a problem as how these people were able to carve hundreds of enormous statues (*moai*) from hard volcanic basalt, transport them several km from quarry to coast, and erect them on great stone platforms.

All sorts of theories have been concocted about who the original Easter Islanders were: ancient Egyptians, red-haired caucasian North Africans on their way to the Pacific via South America, Greeks, Hindustanis, Andean Indians, Melanesians, Polynesians, or the survivors from a sunken continent. Some say the moai were moved by the magical powers of a now extinct race of priests, others believe they were moved using aerial ropeways, or with the aid of extraterrestrial construction workers!

The island is also called Isla de Pascua, which is simply Spanish for Easter Island, and Rapa Nui, which is its Polynesian name.

HISTORY
Polynesia versus America

Easter Island has been given a number of other names: San Carlos (after King Carlos III of Spain) by the first Spanish to land on the island; Davis's Land, given to it when it was confused with land named by English buccaneer Edward Davis in the 17th century; and Rapa Nui, which it is often called today, was the name given to it by Polynesians. But you only need to climb to the top of Terevaka, the island's highest point, and scan the sea in all directions to understand why the natives of Easter Island called it Te Pito o Te Henua – the Navel (Centre) of the World.

The island is just 117 square km and there is no inhabited land within about 2000 km, so the chances of just finding the island in the first place seem exceedingly small. The South American coast lies 3700 km to the east. Some 1900 km to the west lies Pitcairn Island, which was once inhabited by Polynesians but was abandoned or depopulated prior to the arrival of the first group of Europeans (mutineers from the *Bounty*) in 1790. The nearest inhabited islands to the west are the Mangarévas (Gambier Islands) 2500 km away and the Marquesas 3200 km away.

Unless they were spontaneously generated on the island, where did the original Easter Islanders come from? If they came from the east then they must have had their origins in South America. Traditional stories told on Easter Island describe the original homeland as a place where, during certain seasons, the burning sun scorched and shrivelled plants – which fits in very well with the formidable climate of northern Chile and the coastal plains of Peru, but which does not fit any possible points of embarkation to the west.

At the time of the Spanish invasion the Indians of Peru had some knowledge of the existence of distant islands in the Pacific. Centuries before, their ancestors had sailed to some of these islands, and it is possible the location of Easter Island was known to them. In 1947, a Norwegian adventurer and archaeologist, Thor Heyerdahl, proved that such voyages were possible when he and his companions sailed the *Kon-Tiki*, a balsa log raft designed according to what was known of these early vessels, from South America to Raroia in the Tuamotu Archipelago of Polynesia.

A European mariner on a voyage from Chile, who sailed past Easter Island in 1828 and 1834, described the strong southern branch of the Humboldt (or Peru) Current which, he said, could speed sailing ships from the coast of northern Chile and southern Peru towards this island even with vague winds. He

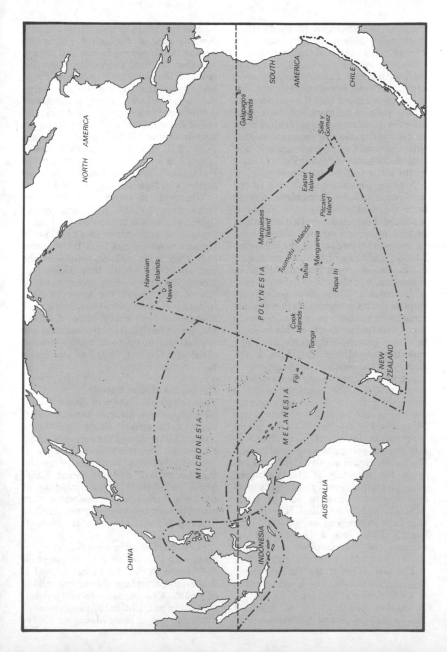

therefore recommended that all sailing ships follow this particular route on a voyage to the islands of the South Seas.

So it is certainly possible that early South American Indian mariners were carried to Easter Island on their rafts. But it has been argued that if voyagers from South America did reach Polynesia, they did so by deliberate voyages of exploration rather than by allowing their rafts to drift with the winds and ocean currents, and that the chances of finding Easter Island by the latter method are almost nil.

Another possibility is that the island was populated by Polynesians coming from the west. These people somehow managed to spread out over a multitude of islands, covering a gigantic triangle with its apexes at New Zealand, the Hawaiian Islands, and Easter Island, together with a scatter of small islands deep in Melanesia, and along the southern border of Micronesia. There have been many theories about the origin of the Polynesians: some thought they were survivors from a lost continent reduced to rubble by some immense catastrophe, others that they came from the Middle East, India, South-East Asia, Indonesia or the Americas.

It's probably fair to say that orthodox opinion within the academic world is currently in favour of an Asian origin for the Polynesian peoples, and that it was Polynesians who built the Easter Island monuments. Details may vary, but it is now generally thought that migration into the Pacific region began 50,000 years ago when the ancestors of the Australian Aboriginals and New Guinea highlanders first crossed the open sea to settle Australia and New Guinea. It is thought that Papuan-speaking people settled the islands of New Britain, New Ireland and perhaps the Solomons, no later than 10,000 years ago – possibly much earlier.

The settlement of the Pacific islands beyond the Solomons was the achievement of a different ethnic group – the Malay-Polynesian speakers who had colonised the western islands of Micronesia, Fiji,

Samoa and Tonga by about 1000 BC. It is thought that a distinctive Polynesian culture developed on Samoa and Tonga, and that the final Polynesian migration probably started from Samoa and Tonga early in the first millennium AD. Large double canoes, able to carry the food and domestic animals required for colonisation, sailed eastwards to settle the Marquesas Islands around 300 AD – perhaps as early as 100 AD. From the Marquesas, Easter Island was settled by about 400 AD, the Hawaiian Islands by 800 AD or even earlier, and New Zealand by 900 AD.

Whatever, it seems that both the Polynesians to the west and South American Indians to the east did launch voyages of exploration into the Pacific Ocean in search of new land. It also seems that they were able to establish the position of the islands they discovered, record the information, pass it on to others, and revisit the same locality. Interestingly, traditional stories of Easter Island tell of the arrival of two different peoples – the first from the east and the second from the west – and of the division of the islanders into 'Long Ear' and 'Short Ear' groups.

The Legend of Hotu Matua

The traditional history of Easter Island falls into three distinct periods. First, there was the arrival of King Hotu Matua and his followers, and the period of initial settlement. This was followed by a period of rivalry between two groups of people, the 'Long Ears' and the 'Short Ears', which ended with the extermination of the Long Ears. Lastly, there was a more recent tribal war between the people of the Tuu region and the people of the Hotu-iti region.

Hotu Matua ('the prolific father' – *matua* is a Polynesian word for 'ancestor' and means 'father' on Easter Island) is said to have come from the east and landed at Anakena on the island's north coast. According to tradition, 57 generations of kings succeeded Hotu Matua on Easter

Island – from which it is estimated that Hotu Matua landed on the island around 450 AD. A second group of immigrants is supposed to have arrived later, coming from the west and led by a chief called Tuu-ko-ihu.

The problem is that by the early part of the 20th century, European visitors were bringing back different versions of the story. A number of different starting points for Hotu Matua's voyage were now proposed: the Galapagos Islands to the north-east, the Tuamotu Archipelago roughly to the north-west, Rapa Iti to the west, and the Marquesas to the north-west. Some versions of the story even have Tuu-ko-ihu arriving on Hotu Matua's boats.

Trying to date events using genealogies is fraught with problems. A number of lists of the kings descended from Hotu Matua have been collected – all of them different. One estimate, working on a figure of 20 to 30 generations of kings descended from Hotu Matua until the last died after a slave raid in 1862, concludes that Hotu Motua arrived at Easter Island as late as the 16th century.

Long Ears & Short Ears
In the old stories, there is a sudden leap from the arrival of Hotu Matua to the division of the islanders into Long Ear and Short Ear groups. It has been suggested that the Long Ear immigrants may have come from some part of Polynesia, where the custom of ear lobe elongation was practised. But since no one knows the actual direction from which the original inhabitants of the island came, it's equally possible that the custom was brought by Indian immigrants from Peru, where ear lobe elongation was also a custom.

It has also been tempting to speculate – in order to fit the old stories in with theories of migrations from both South America and Polynesia – that the Long Ears arrived with Hotu Matua from the east, followed by Short Ear arrivals under Tuu-ko-ihu from the west. Some theories suggest that the Long Ears were the first to build the great *ahu* (altars or platforms) and that the Short Ears began to carve the moai and place them on the ahu. Other stories hold that the Long Ears began to carve the moai and that the Short Ears helped them.

At some time though, there appears to have been a war between the two groups which resulted in the extermination of the Long Ears, bar one solitary survivor. Counting back the generations from the Easter Islanders who claimed descent from the last Long Ear, who had married a Short Ear woman after the end of the war, one estimate puts that survivor as having lived in the second half of the 17th century. Oddly enough, the islanders are known to have practised ear lobe elongation into this century, possibly because the religious or class barriers to it were removed once the original Long Ears were done away with.

The Toppling of the Moai
After the victory of the Short Ears over the Long Ears, there is said to have been a long period of peace, but dissensions arose between different families or clans, bloody wars broke out and cannibalism was practised, and many of the stone moai were toppled from their platforms. According to one account, the tribes or clans each had their own area and were proud of their moai, so an enemy tribe would topple the moai to insult and anger the owners. The only moai standing today have been restored this century.

The Dutch Arrival – 1722
Spanish ships began entering the Pacific from South America in the 16th century, but it was the members of a Dutch expedition under the command of Admiral Jacob Roggeveen who, in April 1722, became the first Europeans to land at Easter Island, having sailed from Chile. Their observations are recorded in Roggeveen's log and in a narrative

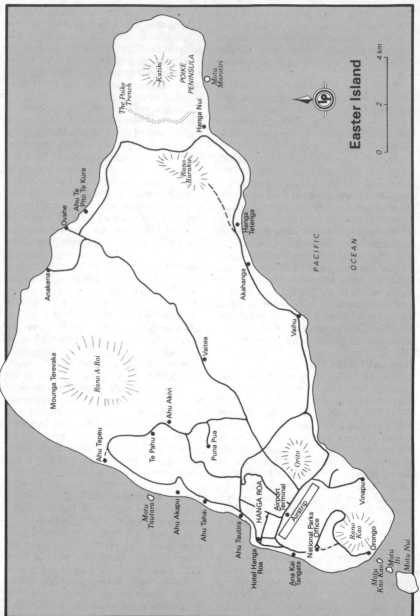

Easter Island

published by one of his companions, Carl Behrens. The island was named in honour of the day of its discovery, Easter Sunday.

The Dutch found the native inhabitants friendly, and living primarily on agricultural produce as the island was very extensively and neatly cultivated. But what baffled the Europeans were the great stone moai, which they thought had some religious significance. Roggeveen wrote:

What the form of worship of these people comprises we were not able to gather any full knowledge of, owing to the shortness of our stay among them; we noticed only that they kindle fire in front of certain remarkably tall stone figures they set up; and, thereafter squatting on their heels with heads bowed down, they bring the palms of their hands together and alternately raise and lower them.

Behrens recorded that the natives:

. . .relied in case of need on their gods or idols which stand erected all along the sea shore in great numbers, before which they fall down and invoke them. These idols were all hewn out of stone, and in the form of a man, with long ears, adorned on the head with a crown. . .

Behrens mentioned how some of the natives wore a block of wood or a disk in their artificially extended ear lobes. Some were so long that, after taking out the plugs, the natives often hitched the rim of the lobe over the top of their ear to stop it from wobbling during work. He concluded that those who wore the wooden blocks or disks were probably priests because they paid more reverence to the gods than the others did, and could also be distinguished by their shaven heads. Roggeveen noted that those who did not cut their hair wore it long, either hanging down the back or else plaited and coiled on the top of the head.

The Spanish Expedition – 1770

It was not until 1770 that another European ship came to Easter Island, this time a Spanish expedition from Peru led by Don Felipe González de Haedo who claimed the island for Spain and renamed it San Carlos.

The Spanish found that the male Easter Islanders were generally nude, wearing only plumes on their heads, whilst a few wore a sort of coloured poncho or cloak. The women usually wore hats of rushes, a short cloak around the breasts and another wrap from the waist downwards. Most of the natives dwelt in underground caves, but some lived in long, boat-shaped reed houses, probably of the type seen by the Dutch. The islanders' only weapons appeared to be sharp-edged stones, probably made of obsidian, the hard black volcanic rock found on the island. But the absence of goods and metal implements suggested there had been no trade with the outside world. Plantations of sugar cane, sweet potatoes, taro and yams were being grown. An officer of the expedition recorded that the islanders' appearance:

Islander, Cook's 1774 visit

. . .does not resemble that of the Indians of the Continent of Chile, Peru or New Spain in anything, these islanders being in colour between white, swarthy and reddish, not thick-lipped nor flat nosed, the hair chestnut coloured and limp, some have it black, and others tending to red or a cinnamon tint. They are tall, well built and proportioned in all their limbs; and there are no halt, maimed, bent, crooked, luxated, deformed or bow legged among them, their appearance being thoroughly pleasing, and tallying with Europeans more than with Indians.

Captain Cook's Arrival - 1774

After the Spanish, the next European ships to visit the island were those under the command of an Englishman, Captain James Cook, in 1774. Cook, already familiar with the inhabitants of the Society Islands, Tonga, and New Zealand, concluded that those on Easter Island were of the same general origin. Later accounts also suggested a Polynesian origin. In 1864 Eugene Eyraud, the first European missionary on the island, commented that:

These savages are tall, strong, and well built. Their features resemble far more the European type than those of the other islanders of Oceania. Among all the Polynesians the Marquesans are those to which they display the greatest resemblance. Their complexion, although a little copper-coloured, does neither differ much from the hue of the European, and a great number are even completely white.

Cook believed that, whatever the moai may have been at the time of the Dutch visit, they were no longer regarded as idols but appeared to be used as burial places for certain tribes or families. It appeared that the moai were still held in some sort of veneration and Cook thought that they were erected in memory of former kings.

But most importantly, it is mentioned for the first time that though some of the moai were standing and still carrying their topknots, others had been toppled and the platforms on which they stood had been damaged. Cook found the islanders in a poor and distressed condition, describing them as small, lean, timid, and miserable. It, therefore, seems possible that some great war had raged on the island since the Spanish visit in 1770, reducing the population to misery and causing a number of the moai to be overturned. Another theory is that no such decimation of the population had taken place at all, but that most of the islanders had become wary of foreigners and hidden themselves from Cook's sailors in underground caves. It's also possible that a number of moai had already been toppled at the time of the Spanish and Dutch visits but that sailors from these ships did not visit the same sites Cook did.

Only one more European visit was made to the island in the 18th century – the Frenchman La Perouse, whose two ships crossed from Chile in 1786. He found the population of Easter Island a happy one with what seemed a prosperous economy, suggesting that, if some great catastrophe had struck the island just before Cook's landing, the people had recovered very quickly.

There were a number of visits by European vessels in the early 19th century. From the visit of a Russian ship in 1804, it is known that more than 20 moai were then still standing, possibly including some of those at Vinapu on the south coast. Accounts from visitors over the following years suggest that another period of moai overturning began about this time and that perhaps only a few moai still stood a decade later.

Colonialism in the Pacific

Whether or not the native inhabitants of Easter Island had indeed fallen into a period of self-inflicted havoc and bloody wars, their discovery by the outside world resulted in their almost total annihilation.

The first catastrophe was the Peruvian slave raid of 1862, which directly or indirectly led to the death of most of the island's inhabitants. This was followed by

Top: Ahu Nau Nau, Easter Island
Left: Statue designs, Ahu Nau Nau, Easter Island
Right: Long-eared statue, Ahu Nau Nau, Easter Island

Top: Statues, Rano Raraku quarry, Easter Island
Bottom: Ahu Ko Te Riku, Easter Island

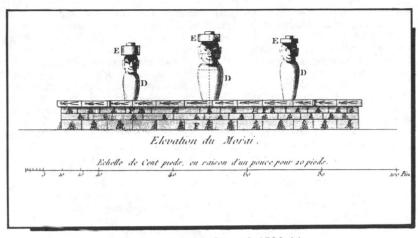

Elevation du Morai.

Echelle de Cent pieds, en raison d'un pouce pour 20 pieds.

Ahu drawn during La Perouse's 1786 visit

a brief and violent period which involved the transportation of many islanders to foreign mines and plantations, the assaults of diseases previously unknown on the island, emigration induced by missionaries, and a substantial disintegration of indigenous culture on the island.

The Peruvian raid came at a time when European and American entrepreneurs were beginning to enter and loot the Pacific, hard on the rudders of the initial European voyages of discovery in the late 18th century. First came the whalers – many of them North American – who ranged the Pacific from Chile to Australia. Then came the planters who set out to build up a long-term source of income by supplying the growing demand in the western world for tropical agricultural products like rubber, sugar and coffee. This usually resulted in the people becoming wage labourers on what was once their own land, and foreign labour being imported where local labour proved insufficient, inefficient or difficult to control.

Then came the slaving ships which either kidnapped Polynesians or – to give the trade in human bodies an aura of legality – compelled or induced them to make contracts committing themselves to work in foreign lands as far afield as Australia and South America. Many died from the rigours of hard labour, poor diet, disease, and ill-treatment.

Missionaries also entered the Pacific, introducing their own variations of Christianity to the islanders, importing European-American culture and morality, and breaking down and degrading local culture.

What happened on Easter Island in the 19th century was not so different from what was happening in other parts of the Pacific at the time. The history of Easter Island since the 1860s can be split into three periods: the first when the island was ruled by a French sea captain; the second from 1888 to 1952, when almost the entire island was leased to a Chilean-Scottish sheep-grazing concern; and the third the ongoing control by Chile.

The Peruvian Slave Raid

There were raids on Easter Island by slavers in the first half of the 19th century and other violent incidents associated with the visits of European and American ships (even the first Dutch visit left several islanders dead or wounded), but these were nothing compared to the Peruvian raid.

About a thousand islanders were kidnapped in this raid, including the island's king and nearly all the learned men (*maori*), and taken to work on the Chincha Islands off the coast of Peru. Protests by Bishop Jaussen of Tahiti to the French representative at Lima resulted in the Peruvian authorities ordering the return of the islanders to their homeland. But by that time disease and hard labour had killed about 900 of them. Smallpox killed most of the others on the return voyage and only about 15 made it back to Easter Island. These 15 brought a smallpox epidemic to the island which resulted in the decimation of the surviving population, leaving perhaps only a few hundred survivors.

The first recorded attempts at Christianising the island occurred in the wake of this disaster. Eugene Eyraud, from the Chilean branch of the French Catholic *Société de Picpus*, charged with the Christianisation of the Eastern Pacific, landed on the island. Eyraud met with a hostile reception and was badly treated by the islanders. He left the island in 1864 but returned in 1866, and with the assistance of other missionaries the islanders were converted to Christianity within a few years.

The Dutroux-Bornier Period

The first attempt at commercially exploiting the island began in 1870 when a French sea captain, Jean-Baptiste Dutroux-Bornier, settled at the site of the old Mataveri settlement at the foot of Rano Kau. Setting up as a sheep rancher, his intention was to turn the whole island over to grazing and ship the excess islanders off to work on the plantations of Tahiti. The missionaries, who planned to ship the islanders to mission lands in

southern Chile or the Mangarévas, stood in the way of his claims to ultimate sovereignty over the island and its people.

Dutroux-Bornier armed his native followers and raided the missionary settlements, burning houses and destroying crops, probably leaving a number of dead and injured, and eventually forcing the missionaries to evacuate the island in 1870 and 1871. Most islanders were induced to accept transportation to Tahiti and others went to the Mangarévas, leaving about 100 on the island. Easter Island was ruled by Dutroux-Bornier until he was, apparently, killed by the remaining islanders in 1877.

Annexation by Chile

Spain had not kept up much interest in its original 1770 annexation and, in any case, lost most of its possessions in South America the following century. Chile officially annexed the island in 1888 during a period of aggressive Chilean expansion.

With its vigorous and effective naval force, Chile was capable of expanding into the Pacific. It valued Easter Island for its agricultural potential, real or imagined; as a naval station; for its location on what was perceived to be the major future trading route between South America and east Asia; to prevent its use by a hostile power as a base to attack the Chilean coast; and no doubt for the prestige of having overseas possessions – any possessions – in an era of colonialism.

Williamson, Balfour & Company

Attempts to colonise the island after the Chilean annexation came to nothing, and with no clear government policy about the future of the island it had, by 1897, come under the control of a single sheep-grazing company run by Enrique Merlet, a businessman from Valparaíso who had bought up or leased the land. Control soon passed into other hands, however.

In 1851, three Scottish businessmen

founded S Williamson & Company in Liverpool, England, with a view to shipping goods to the west coast of South America. Williamson, Balfour & Company officially came into being as the Chilean branch in 1863, by which time a shipping fleet had been built up and the company had expanded its interests into an incredible range of products and countries. They took over Merlet's holdings on Easter Island in the first decade of the 20th century and controlled the island through their Compañía Explotadora de la Isla de Pascau (CEDIP), under lease from the Chilean Government. The company effectively became the government of the island and until the middle of the 20th century continued profitable sheep grazing and wool production.

How the indigenous Easter Islanders actually fared under this system depends on which reports of the period you choose to believe, but it seems that there were several uprisings of sorts by the islanders against the company. One interesting result of foreign control was the fairly rapid elimination of the Easter Islanders as a pure-bred race, as other immigrants inter-bred with them. By the 1930s, it was estimated that about three-quarters of the population of several hundred islanders were of mixed descent, including North American, British, Chilean, Chinese, French, German, Italian, Tahitian, or Tuamotuan stock.

The company's lease was finally revoked in 1953, at a time when the Chilean Government was seeking to extend its control over its far flung and rather unwieldy territories. In place of the company, the Chilean Navy was put in charge of the island, thus continuing the authoritarian (some would say dictatorial) rule to which the islanders had been subjected for 50 years.

Chilean Colonialism

The island continued under military rule until the mid-1960s. After that a brief period of civilian government followed until the military coup of 1973 when the island once again came under the direct control of the military. Since December 1984, the island's governor has been Sergio Rapu; Rapu is a civilian, a native of Easter Island and a professional archaeologist who was trained in the USA.

During the 1960s, the island was as much a colony as any other. The islanders' grievances included unpaid labour, travel restrictions, confinement to the Hanga Roa area, suppression of the indigenous language, ineligibility to vote (universal suffrage in Chile did not extend to Easter Island) and arbitrary decisions on the part of the navy administration against which there was no appeal. Coupled with this were increased opportunities for contact with the outside world, particularly after the opening in 1967 of a regular commercial air link between Santiago and Tahiti via Easter Island.

Perhaps because of the islanders' unrest, international attention on the island, the tourism potential, increased immigration from the mainland, feelings of guilt after 80 years of neglect, or the coming to power of President Frei, the Chilean Government did undertake some improvements on the island during the 1960s and 1970s. These included improvements to the water supply, medical care, education, and electrification.

Although livestock are still grazed on the island, the chief industry seems to be tourism - a fairly recent phenomena which only got going with the institution of regular air services between Easter Island and mainland Chile. Tourism will certainly have some sort of long-term impact on the island, but the really substantial changes to the island occurred under the onslaught of inter-tribal wars, slavers and foreign looters.

There may, however, be one more radical change to the island this decade. In August 1985, President Pinochet approved a plan allowing the USA to use Easter Island as an emergency landing site for the space shuttle. Others believe that Easter Island is to be turned into a US military base for long-range bombers. This would inevitably make the island, and possibly mainland Chile, a nuclear target in the event of war. There is opposition both on the mainland and on Easter Island to the establishment of this base, but the island is still treated like a colonial outpost by the military government. The indigenous people have no say in major decisions such as these.

GEOGRAPHY

Easter Island is a small, hilly island of volcanic origin, roughly triangular in shape with a volcano at each corner, none of which are active. The total area of the island is just 117 square km; its maximum length is 24 km and maximum width 12 km.

The largest volcano, Terevaka, rises 600 metres above sea level in the northern corner of the island and makes up the largest mass of the island. Katiki, about 400 metres high, forms the eastern headland known as the Poike Peninsula. Rano Kau, about 410 metres high, forms the south-west corner of the island.

There are several smaller craters, including Rano Raraku, from whose hard basalt (the chief type of rock found on the island) the giant moai were carved, and Puna Pau, a small crater north-east of Hanga Roa, from whose red rock the topknots of the moai were carved. Orito is a volcanic cone where black obsidian was quarried to make spearheads and cutting tools.

The craters of Rano Kau and Rano Raraku both contain freshwater lakes. Rano Kau's lake is about one km in diameter and is partly covered by a thick floating bog of reeds and peat. The surface of the lake is about 120 metres above sea level and is bounded by crater walls which rise 400 metres above sea level on the inland side, with a lower saddle on the southern edge facing the sea.

For the most part, the slopes of all these volcanos are gentle and covered in grass, except where cliffs have been formed either by the action of the sea (as at Rano Kau) or by quarrying (as at Rano Raraku). In contrast, the larger stretches of the island are covered in very rugged lava fields. There are several areas where there is thick soil suitable for cultivation. These are mainly in the Hanga Roa and Mataveri areas of the west coast, Vaihu on the south coast, the plain south-west of Rano Raraku, and inland at Vaitea.

There are numerous caves formed by volcanic action, many of them located in the cliffs by the sea. Some of the caves extend for considerable distances into the lava rock, and generally consist of large and small rooms connected by tunnels through which a person can barely squeeze. Some of these caves were used as refuges in time of war, others as secret storage or burial places, and others appear to have been used as long-term homes.

There are no coral reefs around Easter Island, although some areas of coral occur where the water is sufficiently shallow. The lack of reefs has enabled the action of the sea to produce huge cliffs in parts of the island, some of them rising over 300 metres. Those cliffs composed of lava are usually lower but are also extremely hard, torn and rugged. There is no natural sheltered harbour on the island and Anakena on the north coast is the only wide sandy beach, although there are a few shallow bays.

Some theories have it that the island once belonged to a much larger land mass, home of an advanced civilisation which sunk into the ocean through some catastrophic volcanic eruption, like a Pacific version of Atlantis. The island rests on a platform some 50 or 60 metres below sea level, but at about 15 to 30 km off the coast the platform ends and the ocean bottom drops off to between 1800 and 3600 metres, reaching over 7000 metres as the coast of South America is approached. It also seems to have been very stable geologically, and was pretty much its present shape and form when the great moai were carved. In any case, most of the moai were erected around the coast, suggesting little change in the shape of the shoreline since.

There are three tiny islands just off Rano Kau: Motu Nui, Motu Iti and Motu Kao Kao. Motu Nui is the largest and has more level ground than any of the others. It is (or was) the nesting ground of thousands of sea-birds and, along with the ceremonial village of Orongo on the crest of Rano Kau, became the focus of a peculiar 'birdman' cult which persisted until the middle of the 19th century.

There is sufficient rainfall on Easter Island to maintain a permanent covering of coarse grasses, but the volcanic soil is very porous and the water quickly finds its way underground. There are no permanent streams on the island and water for use by people and livestock is drawn either from the volcanic lakes or from underground. It seems possible that the island vegetation was once much more luxuriant – perhaps including forests with palms and conifers and species no longer found on the island – but much of it was cut down by the inhabitants long ago. Most of the trees you see on the island today, like the eucalypts, were planted only within the past century.

Like other isolated islands, whole families of both plants and animals are completely absent, whilst some species appear to be unique to the island. Small animals like chickens and rats were brought by the original immigrants. The Norway (or brown) rat was brought by European ships; horses and other large animals were also introduced by Europeans, initially by missionaries in the 19th century.

CLIMATE
Although Easter Island lies just to the south of the Tropic of Capricorn (the same latitude as central Queensland in Australia) its subtropical climate is profoundly influenced by winds and ocean currents.

The hottest months are January and February, and the coolest are July and August. The average maximum summer temperature is around 28°C and the average minimum is around 15°C, but these figures belie what can often be a fierce sun and formidable heat. The average maximum winter temperature is around 22°C and the average minimum around 14°C. But it can get very cold when Antarctic winds lash the island with rain.

Light showers are the most common form of rainfall. The wettest month is May but heavy tropical downpours can occur during all seasons.

BOOKS
One of the most substantial works on the island is *Reports of the Norwegian Archaeological Expedition to Easter Island & the East Pacific. Volume 1: Archaeology of Easter Island* (George Allen & Unwin, London, 1962). This was the expedition led by Thor Heyerdahl in 1955 and 1956. It's fully illustrated and gives a detailed description of all the important sites, although none of them had been restored when the expedition did its work on the island. Copies of reports on the restoration of certain sites are sold by one of the shops at Hanga Roa's Mataveri airport.

Father Sebastian Englert's *Island at the Center of the World* (Charles Scribner's Sons, New York, 1970) relates the history of the island according to some versions of the Easter Islanders' traditional stories. A Bavarian, Englert was the island's priest from 1935 until his death nearly 35 years later. If you can read Spanish then get *La Tierra de Hotu Matúa* (Editorial Universitaria, Santiago, 3rd edition 1983), which is his main book about the island and was first published in 1948. Also in Spanish is his *Idioma Rapanui – Gramatica y Diccionario del antiguo idioma de la Isla de Pascua* (Universidad de Chile, 1978). Both books can be bought in Santiago.

To add colour to mystery, you can't go past Thor Heyerdahl's *Aku-Aku: The Secret of Easter Island* (George Allen &

Unwin, London, 1958). Written rather like a detective story, this is his popular account of Easter Island and the work of the Norwegian expedition.

There are a number of accounts of early expeditions and visits to the island. The first archaeological expedition was a private venture in 1914 headed by an English woman, Katherine Routledge. All the scientific notes of the expedition were lost but she did write *The Mystery of Easter Island: the Story of an Expedition*, first published in 1919. Other interesting accounts include J MacMillan Brown's *The Riddle of the Pacific* (published in 1924) and *Easter Island* (published in 1957) by French archaeologist Alfred Metraux, who first went to the island on a French-Belgian expedition in the 1930s.

If Easter Island is the navel of the world then it's also the centre of the Polynesian versus South American Indian debate: from which direction was the Pacific colonised and who built the enormous moai on Easter Island? Thor Heyerdahl's *American Indians in the Pacific: The Theory Behind the Kon-Tiki Expedition* (George Allen & Unwin, London, 1952) is an enormous book which makes a comparative study of American Indian and Pacific cultures, legends, religious ideas, stone sculpture, boat building, physical characteristics and cultivated plants. It includes a discussion on Easter Island. For the story of the Kon-Tiki expedition read his book *Kon-Tiki* (Rand McNally, Chicago, 1952).

Computer simulations have been done of both drift and navigated voyaging in the Pacific in an attempt to explain the distribution of the Polynesian people. One of these is *The Settlement of Polynesia: A Computer Simulation* (Australian National University Press, Canberra, 1973) by Michael Levison, R Gerard Ward and John Webb.

It is now generally thought that the original Easter Islanders were Polynesians who arrived at Easter Island from the west by way of the Marquesas. For a general review of current thinking on the migration of people across the Pacific try *The Peopling of the Pacific* (in *Scientific American*, Nov 1980, vol 243, No 5) by Peter Bellwood. For more reading try *Man's Conquest of the Pacific* (Oxford University Press, New York, 1979) by the same author, which also includes a lengthy section on Easter Island and the Polynesian-American argument, although you may find his conclusions rather shaky. Despite the book's title, presumably some women also went along for the ride.

The other alternative to the Polynesian-American debate is not to go sideways, but upwards. Erich von Daniken's theories about the origin of the island's moai can be found in his book *In Search of Ancient Gods* (Souvenir Press, London, 1974).

The Peruvian slave raid on Easter Island was not an isolated incident. The first few years of the 1860s saw many Polynesian islands raided and their populations decimated by the Peruvian slavers. For the story behind the slave trade read Henry Maude's *Slavers in Paradise: the Peruvian labour trade in Polynesia, 1862-1864* (published in Australia by the Australian National University Press, and in the USA by the Stanford University Press).

Largely ignored, as if it doesn't have one, is the modern history of Easter Island. For a blow-by-blow account of the island's history from the mid-1800s until the late 1970s try *The Modernization of Easter Island* (University of Victoria, British Columbia, Canada, 1981) by J Douglas Porteous.

If a picture book is what you want, then perhaps there is none finer than *Isla de Pascua* by Michel Rougie, published by the National Tourist Service of Chile. The beautiful photos record all the major sites and the text is in Spanish, French, and English.

MAPS

The only decent map of the island which is

readily available is called *Isla de Pascua, Rapa Nui – Mapa Arqueológico & Turistico*, available from some bookshops in Santiago. Most other maps of the island are so poor as to be virtually useless. Perhaps the best map available on the island itself is a relief map housed in the island's museum. It shows the town, all the roads, volcanos, and archaeological sites, and is very good for getting your bearings.

GETTING THERE

LAN-Chile is the only airline which has commercial flights to the island, with two to three flights a week from Santiago to Tahiti via Easter Island. This means that coming from Australia or New Zealand you can take a Melbourne/Sydney-Tahiti flight with Qantas or an Auckland-Tahiti flight with Air New Zealand and then change to LAN-Chile for the onward flight to Easter Island and Santiago. For details of fares, see the Getting There chapter at the start of this book.

GETTING AROUND

The town centre of Hanga Roa is about a 20-minute walk from the airport, but to get beyond the town you really need your own transport. Just how long you take to get around the island depends on what sort of transport you take and how long you want to spend at each site. A week is enough to take in all the major sites, but there are many minor places of interest on the island.

Rented horses, motorbikes and cars are your main transport options. Some books say you can walk around the island in two or three days or so. Theoretically, it's possible but there are some good reasons why you should not walk around Easter Island: it is fiercely hot in summer; there is almost no shade or water supply outside the settlements; and distances quoted from one site to the next are often grossly misleading. Maps and tourist leaflets often show distances to places of interest from Hanga Roa – but these are sometimes as the crow flies, not the distance you actually have to go to get there.

If you ride a horse or a motorbike around the island you need a day-pack. And regardless of how good a tan you got on the beach before you arrived you need a powerful sun block, otherwise you'll spend your time sheltering in a hotel room watching your skin peel off in sheets. A few general stores sell sun block but not the strength you really need.

Take a long-sleeved shirt with you, sunglasses, and a large hat or headgear which will cover your face and neck. Always carry a water bottle. Head-hunting is hot work!

Motorbikes & Cars

The locals will rent their motorbikes for about US$30 to US$35 a day. Motorbikes can be rented from the Hotel Hanga Roa for US$40 per day. Jeeps can be rented from the hotel for US$70 per day, and locals will rent you theirs for around US$50 or US$60 per day. Ask at the residencials and at the tourist office. All the roads on the island are unsurfaced – beware of potholes, rocks and deep ruts.

If you've never ridden a motorbike but need a convenient way to get around town then ask the Hotel Hotu Matua to fix you up with one of their 70 cc bikes. These will cost about US$20 per day. They're small three-speed bikes with no handle clutch control, so it's easy to ride if you've never ridden a motorbike before. All you have to operate is a hand brake and foot brake, accelerator, and a gear shift operated with your foot.

Horse-riding

Mangy horses can be hired for US$10 a day – but if yours isn't dead when you get it then it may well be by the time you've finished. Most horses hired from locals (some will approach you on the street; if not, ask at your hotel or residencial) will only have a rope for the reins and another holding on the stirrups and nailed to the saddle. That latter arrangement can be quite dangerous if you ride too fast and put too much pressure on a stirrup – the stirrup flies off and so do you. The Hotel Hotu Matua or the Hotel Hanga Roa seem to organise horse-riding excursions for groups, but may be able to get you a horse with proper stirrups and reins. Horses are good for visiting sites close to Hanga Roa like Ahu Tepeu, Vinapu, Ahu Akivi and Orongo, but to get to places like Rano Raraku and Anakena you really need some motorised transport.

Tours
A couple of people run tours around the island in minivans. If you're only in transit on the way to Tahiti or to the Chilean mainland then Anakena Tours often has a half-hour tour which takes you from the airport up to the impressive Ahu Tahai site and then back to the airport.

HANGA ROA
Just a few thousand people live on Easter Island. About 70% are Polynesians (they think of themselves as Polynesian, not as Chileans or South Americans) and the rest are mainly immigrants from the Chilean mainland. Almost the whole population lives in the township of Hanga Roa on the west coast of the island. How people make ends meet in this place is a mystery to the casual observer. There are some fishermen and some cattle and sheep grazing, but there seems to be no agriculture other than vegetable, banana and papaya gardens on the outskirts of the township. Government offices, general stores, a bank and post office soak up a fraction of the labour supply, but scraping money off the tourist trade seems to be the main industry.

Information
Tourist Office The tourist office is in Hanga Roa on Tuu Maheke. The staff usually speak Spanish, French, and English. The office at the airport is open when planes arrive or depart.

Bank The *Banco del Estado de Chile* is next to the tourist office. It will change some foreign currency and travellers' cheques, but charges a hefty 10% commission on US dollars travellers' cheques. Otherwise, US cash can be changed readily with the locals in Hanga Roa.

LAN-Chile The LAN-Chile office is in the Hotel Hanga Roa.

Film Take as much film as you can, as it's scarce and expensive on the island. You may be able to find some Fujicolor and Ektachrome 35 mm transparencies and perhaps some Kodak 110, but don't expect much else. Look in the general stores in Hanga Roa and in Hotel Hanga Roa or Hotel Hotu Matua.

Places to Stay
Easter Island is not a cheap place to visit. Room prices on the island are more or less fixed, although you may have some leeway for bargaining if a place is half empty. If you want to keep costs down you will have to find a room in one of the many residencials or with a family. You are expected to pay your bill in US cash.

The cheapest rooms you'll get in a residencial will be about US$15 a single and US$25 a double per night including breakfast. Meals may be as much as US$10 each. Occasionally, someone meets the incoming flights at the airport with a discount offer – say US$10 per person for bed and breakfast.

There are only a few places at the bottom end of the price range. The majority of residencials in Hanga Roa charge in the vicinity of US$45 a single and US$75 a double, though that's with full board.

The best way to find accommodation is to check out what's available at the tourist office at the airport. The locals and hotel proprietors flock there to meet the incoming flights and to rake in a tourist or two. The advantage of this is that you can find out which hotels and residencials

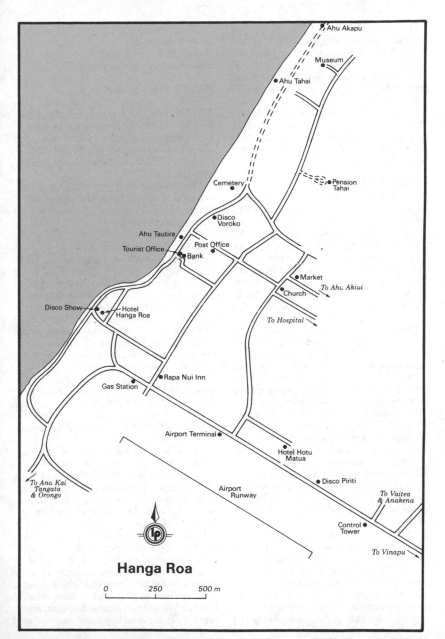

Ahu Akapu
Museum
Ahu Tahai
Pension
Tahai
Cemetery
Disco
Voroko
Ahu Tautira
Post Office
Tourist Office
Bank
Market
To Ahu Akiui
Church
Disco Show
Hotel
Hanga Roa
To Hospital
Rapa Nui Inn
Gas Station
Airport Terminal
Hotel Hotu
Matua
To Ana Kai
Tangata
& Orongo
Disco Piriti
Airport
Runway
To Vaitea
& Anakena
Control
Tower
To Vinapu

Hanga Roa

0   250   500 m

have spare rooms and this saves you tramping all over Hanga Roa looking for a place. You also get transport into the town which is useful – Hanga Roa is so spread out that just the walk from the airport to a place like the Pension Tahai would take you an hour.

If you don't like what you get you can always move the following day. The tourist office on Tuu Maheke should help you find a place. Most residencials are not sign-posted.

Places to Stay – bottom end

One place which has been enthusiastically recommended is the *Pension Tahai* run by Maria Hey. She charges US$10 per person, room only; meals are extra. You stay in a very clean bungalow set amidst a large garden. She's not as aggressive as the other people at the airport so she doesn't get to pick up that many customers. Her place is a bit out of town, on the road leading to Ahu Tahai, and it's very quiet and relaxing.

Another place which operates on a permanent basis is the *Rapa Nui Inn* near the corner of the main street and the airport road. Singles are US$10, or US$15 with breakfast; doubles are US$25 with breakfast. You get a large, clean room with a double bed and private bathroom.

Camping is allowed on the island, but officially only at Anakena and Rano Raraku. Rangers are stationed at Orongo, Rano Raraku, Ahu Tahai, and Anakena. Apparently, camping out other than in the official campsites is frowned upon – but I imagine that if you did so in some of the more remote areas nobody would come looking for you.

Places to Stay – middle

The *Hotel Apina-Nui* (tel 292), on Calle Apina Nui, has rooms for US$45 a single and US$75 a double, which include three meals per day. Rates with only two meals per day are slightly less. They may also cater for camping in their grounds.

One place that is recommended is the *Hotel Victoria* (tel 272), a small place with several rooms. It's on a hill overlooking Hanga Roa, about midway between the settlement and the airport.

Places to Stay – top end

The *Hotel Hanga Roa* (tel 299), on Avenida Pont, is a rather lengthy walk from the middle of town, but it does have a swimming pool, a bar and restaurant, and several souvenir shops. Single and double rooms are US$95, and considerably more with full board.

Moderately cheaper, and perhaps better, is the *Hotel Hotu Matua* (tel 242). You really need your own transport as it's a long walk out of town.

Places to Eat

Some residencials are prepared to rent you a room only but there isn't any advantage in doing this unless you're going to put your own food together with what you can buy at Hanga Roa market. Food at the few restaurants in Hanga Roa will cost you as much as it does at a residencial, and in any case the restaurants are more like snack bars and the food is not particularly sustaining.

You can bring in canned food from outside but fresh fruit and vegetables are not allowed. Your bags will be checked at the airport to ensure you're not bringing any in, whether you're coming from Tahiti or from Chile.

The island's water supply is safe to drink. It's all bore water and has a high mineral content, and it can take an appalling couple of days to adjust. Make it more palatable by squeezing in some orange juice or buying some flavouring from one of the general stores.

If you want to camp out or cook your own food there's no trouble getting enough provisions to do so. There are a couple of general stores and bread shops on the main street where you can buy canned food, bottled drinks (soft drinks, wine, beer) as well as fresh vegetables, fruit, and eggs. You can also buy fresh vegetables and fruit at the market (Mercado Municipal).

Things to Buy

There are a number of souvenir shops in Hanga Roa, most of them on the main street, and on the street leading up to the church. You can buy small stone replicas of the moai, as well as *moai kavakava* which are small famished-looking figures with protruding ribs, replicas of wooden *rongo-rongo* tablets, and fragments of obsidian from Orito. You can also get T-shirts with Easter Island motifs like rongo-rongo writing or moai. Some of the tackier ones are made in the People's Republic of China.

The Hotel Hanga Roa has a number of stalls set up by local souvenir sellers. Look for the work of a Chilean woman who makes cloth rubbings of the birdmen and rongo-rongo petroglyphs. Obsidian earrings are good cheap souvenirs. The locals set up a small market at the airport when planes arrive or depart, selling souvenirs and handicrafts.

THE ARCHAEOLOGICAL SITES

Giant, brooding stone moai buried up to their necks in dirt and rubble are the images that Easter Island brings to mind. But there are, in fact, several types of stonework found on the island. Apart from the moai, some of the other important sites include large ahu on which the moai were erected, burial cairns which are basically large piles of rock in which bodies were entombed, and the stone foundations of unusual boat-shaped village huts.

Although many of these structures were partially demolished or rebuilt by the original inhabitants and the moai were probably toppled during inter-tribal wars many years ago, a good deal of damage was done during the rule of the CEDIP. Many ahu, burial cairns, house foundations, and other structures were ripped apart and used to make the piers at Hanga Roa and Hanga Piko as well as stone fences to wall

off sheep-grazing areas. Windmills were constructed over the original stone-lined wells to provide a water supply for sheep, cattle and horses.

Not only have many of the ancient monuments been destroyed, but much has been pillaged. Only a few moai were carried off, but wooden rongo-rongo tablets inscribed with a forgotten script, painted wall tablets from the Orongo ceremonial village houses on the edge of the Rano Kau crater, small wood and stone moai, weapons, clothing, skulls and other artefacts have been taken from the island and can now be found in foreign museums and inaccessible private collections in Chile and elsewhere. Some sites, like the Orongo village, were wholly or partially dismantled by the islanders for building material.

A number of sites have been restored within the last 30 years or so including Ahu Tahai, Ahu Akivi, the Orongo ceremonial village, and Ahu Nau Nau. Others, such as Ahu Vinapu and Ahu Vaihu, lie in ruins but are nonetheless impressive sights.

Approximate distances to the important sites by road from Hanga Roa are:

Orito	2 km
Vinapu	5 km
Vaihu	9½ km
Akahanga	12½ km
Rano Raraku	18 km
Ahu Tongariki	20 km
Ahu Te Pito Kura	26 km
Ovahe	29 km
Anakena	30 km
Ahu Tahai	1½ km
Ahu Tepeu	2 km
Ahu Akivi	10 km
Puna Pau	2 km
Orongo	7 km

It's possible to take in all the major sites on three loops out of Hanga Roa – the South-West Route, Northern Loop, and Island Circle. The three routes are convenient ways to see the sites with a minimum of backtracking.

The South-West Route

From Hanga Roa take the road leading to the top of the Rano Kau crater and the Orongo ceremonial village. Backtrack to the township, then follow the road along the northern edge of the airstrip to Orito which is the site of the old obsidian quarries. From here head southwards to Ahu Vinapu with its impressive, finely-cut stonework.

The Northern Loop

Take the route from Hanga Roa to Puna Pau, the crater from whose red rock the topknots of the moai were cut. From here you continue inland to Ahu Akivi, which has been restored and its seven moai re-erected. From Ahu Akivi follow the track to Ahu Tepeu on the west coast which is said to be the burial site of Tuu-ko-ihu. You then head southwards to Hanga Roa, stopping off at Ahu Akapu, Ahu Tahai and Ahu Tautira which have all been restored and their moai re-erected. Because of the vagueness of the trail between Ahu Akivi and the coast, it's probably easier to go from Hanga Roa to Ahu Akivi and then cut cross-country to Ahu Tepeu rather than the other way round.

The Island Circle

From Hanga Roa, travel along the southern coast stopping off at the ruins at Vaihu and Akahanga with their massive ahu and giant toppled moai. Continue west from Akahanga and detour inland to the Rano Raraku crater, from whose hard basalt most of the moai on the island were cut, and where moai in all stages of production can still be seen. Leaving Rano Raraku, follow the road west to Ahu Tongariki, a ruined ahu whose moai and masonry were hurled some distance inland by a massive tidal wave after the Chilean earthquake of 1960. From here, follow the road to the north coast to Ahu Te Pito Te Kura, which boasts the largest

moai ever erected on an ahu. Continue east to the beach at Ovahe, and then to Anakena which is the island's main beach and the site of two more restored ahu. The excavation and restoration of Ahu Nau Nau at Anakena showed that the moai once had eyes and were not 'blind' as previously believed.

Ahu Tautira, Tahai, Akapu & Tepeu

Lined up along the west coast of the island are four large ahu complexes. Ahu Tautira is next to Hanga Roa's small pier; from here a road and track leads northwards to the Ahu Tahai complex, which is connected by another track along the coast to Ahu Akapu and Ahu Tepeu.

There are about 245 ahu on the island (the number differs according to various classifications) most of them forming an almost unbroken line along the coast except for some high cliffs around the Poike Peninsula and Rano Kau, though there are some by the cliff edges in other places. The ahu tend to be sited around good landing places and areas which are favourable for human habitation, although only a few were built inland.

There are several varieties of ahu, built at different times for different reasons, but the most impressive type are those on which the moai are placed, called *ahu moai*. Each is essentially a mass of loose stones held in place by retaining walls, and paved on the upper surface with more or less flat stones. Each structure has a perpendicular wall on the seaward side and usually around each end. The moai which were erected on these platforms range from two to almost 10 metres in height, although even larger moai were under construction in the quarry at Rano Raraku when work came to a sudden end.

Usually gently sloping ramps paved in various ways – often using rounded beach boulders or closely placed slabs of irregular stones – are built against the landward sides of the platforms. Adjacent to the ramps there are usually large flat plazas which may have been artificially levelled. In a few cases, these are outlined by earth embankments forming rectangular or irregular enclosures. Sometimes, there are small rectangular platforms built on the plazas which may be altars, and large circles paved with stones. In some places, a bit further inland, there are the remains of boat-shaped thatch-houses in which members of the priesthood who served the altars may have lived. It is known that the original Easter Islanders used one and two-person reed boats, and it's likely that much larger reed boats were launched from the stone ramps (apapa) leading into the sea by the side of the ahu.

Not much is known about the ceremonies once associated with these ahu complexes. One theory is that the moai represented ancestors of the clan owning the ahu, and that the ceremonies were part of a clan ancestor cult. Ahu were also places of burial; originally, bodies were buried in stone-lined tombs constructed in the ahu ramps and platforms. However, it seems that later on, after the moai had been toppled, the bodies were placed around the fallen moai and on other parts of ramps and covered with stones. Other bodies were cremated at the ahu sites, but whether these were bodies of deceased members of the clan or the remains of human sacrifices is unknown, though traditional stories do tell of human sacrifice by burning.

The large plaza in front of Ahu Tahai has been restored and there are several interesting features, including the foundation stones of the houses once used by the islanders, and which were probably the main type of housing right up until European-style houses were introduced. Long and narrow, the general appearance of this house has been likened to an upturned canoe. The floor shape is outlined by shaped rectangular blocks or curb stones with small cup-shaped depressions on their upper surfaces. A single narrow opening at the middle of one side served as the doorway. To form the walls and the roof, the ends of thin poles were inserted into the cup-shaped sockets of the stone foundations. These poles were arched across the centre of the structure and, where each opposed pole crossed with another, lashed to a ridge pole. As the space to be covered narrowed progressively toward the ends, the roofing poles decreased in length, thus lowering the roof level and producing a house shaped like an overturned canoe. A crescent-shaped, boulder pavement often covered the ground in front of the house. The size of these dwellings varied enormously; some were capable of housing over 100 people, while others could house only about six.

Ahu Tautira Ahu Tautira stands by Hanga Roa's tiny port which is only used by a few tiny fishing boats. The torsos of two broken moai have been re-erected on the ahu.

Ahu Tahai Although Ahu Tahai seems to be the name commonly given to the entire site, there are actually three restored ahu here: Ahu Tahai itself, Ahu To Ko Te Riku, and Ahu Vai Uri. The restoration work was done in 1968 under the direction of an American archaeologist, William Mulloy.

Ahu Tahai is the ahu in the middle of the group. It supports a large, solitary moai with no topknot.

To one side of Ahu Tahai is Ahu Ko Te Riku, which supports a large, solitary moai with its topknot in place. Regardless of its appearance, this is a relative lightweight. It's about a quarter of the weight of the giant moai at Ahu Te Pito Te Kura on the north coast of the island.

On the other side of Ahu Tahai is Ahu Vai Uri, which supports five moai of varying sizes.

Ahu Akapu Ahu Akapu, with its solitary moai, stands on the coast further to the north of Ahu Tahai.

Ahu Tepeu This large ahu is on the north-west coast between Hanga Roa and the North Cape. To the north-east rises

Terevaka, the highest point on the island, while to the south is a large grassy plain over a jagged lava sheet. To the west, the sea breaks against rugged cliffs up to 50 metres high.

The seaward side of the ahu is the most interesting feature of the structure. It has a wall about three metres high near the centre composed of large vertical slabs of stone. A number of moai once stood on the ahu but these have all been toppled. Immediately east of Ahu Tepeu is an extensive village site marked by the foundation stones of several large boat-shaped houses and the walls of several round houses, consisting of loosely piled stones.

Ahu Vinapu

Although the original structures at Ahu Tahai appear to belong to the earliest period of building on Easter Island, the restored complex looks something like the second last chapter of an unfinished mystery novel with the clues pieced together but the puzzle unsolved. To shed some light on how, why, and when the moai were carved you have to begin in the south-west corner of the island at Ahu Vinapu, in a small valley facing the coast.

To get to Ahu Vinapu, follow the road from Hanga Roa along the northern edge of the airstrip. At the end of the airstrip follow a road heading south between the airstrip and some large oil containers, until you see an opening in a stone fence. Here a sign points the way to nearby Ahu Vinapu.

There are two ahu next to each other on the valley floor. Both once supported moai but these have all been overturned, and most of them are broken and lying with their faces in the dirt and rubble in front of the platforms. Accounts by 18th and early 19th-century visitors to the island suggest that the moai were not all overturned at once, although they were all tipped over by the middle of the 19th century – some by undermining the

Stonework, Ahu Vinapu

foundation stones on which they stood, others perhaps being pulled down with ropes.

An interesting find at the Vinapu site is a long brick-red stone, shaped something like a four-sided column, which now stands in front of one of the ahu. It's obviously not one of the standard moai found on the island, but if you look closely you can see that it is in fact a moai of some sort with hands and arms, but minus its head. It also has short legs, unlike most other moai on the island which have no legs. It's rather reminiscent of pre-Inca column statues in the South American Andes.

Ahu No 1, with its perfectly carved and fitted stonework, is the most interesting ahu of the group and is usually referred to as Ahu Vinapu, although the name originally seems to have referred to the entire area and the ahu itself once went under a different name. Ahu No 2 has walls made of cut stone but is not as finely worked as Ahu No 1.

The Vinapu stonework is so reminiscent of the fine stonework of the Incas of the Cuzco Valley in Peru and that of the pre-Inca civilisation which once had its capital at Tiahuanaco near Lake Titicaca in Bolivia, that it was suggested that the Easter Island stonework had its origins in South America. However, it was generally accepted that the Easter Islanders could have developed the techniques to produce such perfectly carved blocks independently of South America, and that Vinapu represented the last and most advanced phase in the development of stone-carving on the island.

This theory was upset when the Norwegian expedition's excavations at Vinapu found that the central wall of Ahu No 1 – with its finely carved stonework – belonged to the very oldest building period. They concluded that the ahu had twice been rebuilt and added to by builders who were no longer capable of reproducing such stonework. From this and other evidence, it appeared that there

had been three clearly separate periods in the island's history: Early, Middle and Late.

During the Early Period, ahu were built of large stone blocks which were carved and fitted together without a crack or hole between them. No burials seem to have been placed in the structures and there were no moai standing on them. Carbon-14 dating of remnants of fires and other material found at various sites suggests that the Early Period began sometime before 400 AD and ended about 1100 AD.

During the Middle Period, most of these structures were altered or pulled down. A paved slope was built up against the wall of the ahu which faced inland, and giant stone figures carved at Rano Raraku were erected on the platforms which now often contained burial chambers. Less care was taken with the stonework of the ahu itself since the emphasis was now on the production of the moai. It is thought that this second period finished towards the end of the 17th century.

Then, for some unknown reason, the island entered into a period of bloody war and cannibalism and the production of the moai came to an end. During this Late Period, boulders and shapeless blocks were flung together to make funeral mounds along the walls of the ahu. The moai, all of which had been toppled by the middle of the 19th century, were often used as improvised roofs for new burial vaults. Many of the ahu were modified into semi-pyramid shapes by packing stones over and around the fallen moai, and the dead were buried amidst the mass of stones.

Others, however, did not find these categories quite so conclusive. Over two decades ago, just by re-interpreting the findings of the Norwegian expedition, it was argued that Ahu No 2 at Vinapu (which does not have the same finely cut stonework as Ahu No 1) was actually built before Ahu No 1. This suggests that Ahu No 2 could have been a development of the *marae* platforms found on other Polynesian islands. Eventually, masonry skills improved so much that it was possible for descendents of the original Polynesian immigrants to produce the finely-worked stones of Ahu No 1 – independent of any influence from South America. It's generally accepted that the main function of the ahu differed for each period, apparently serving as an altar in the Early Period, a base for moai in the Middle Period, and a burial place in the Late Period. However, the change from one to the other appears to have been more gradual than previously thought.

Rano Raraku

Otherwise known as 'the nursery', the Rano Raraku volcano provided the hard basalt from which the moai were cut. The mountain is littered with moai in all stages of completion, in quarries on both the exterior and interior sides of the southern slope and along the crater rim. Coming in from the south you'll see the slope of the volcano studded with moai,

Statues, Rano Raraku quarry, Easter Island

most of them standing upright but up to their shoulders or necks in the earth so that only the heads gaze across the grassy slopes. The volcano is surrounded by a stone fence and from the entrance gate a trail leads up the slope. Going straight up brings you to a 21-metre giant – the largest moai ever built. Follow a trail to the right to several other large moai still attached to the rock, or turn left along the trail which leads over the rim and into the interior of the crater.

Inside the crater stand about 20 moai, a number of fallen moai and others only partly finished – about 80 figures in all. Outside on the mountain stand about 50 moai. Below them, at the foot of the mountain and on the plain towards the sea lie almost 30 more, all of which have fallen and, with a few exceptions, lie face downwards. In the quarries above there are about 160 unfinished moai. That means that when work came to a stop some 320 moai were being carved or had been completed but not yet erected on ahu. The total number of moai made at the Rano Raraku quarries would appear to be well over 600.

Although all the moai are of a uniform type they are not all identical, contrary to popular belief. The standard Rano Raraku moai has its base at about the level of the hips. Arms hang stiffly at the sides and extended hands with long slender fingers are turned toward each other across the lower part of a protruding abdomen. The heads are elongated and rectangular with heavy brows and prominent noses, small mouths with thin lips, and prominent chins. The ear lobes are elongated and some are carved to show inserted ear ornaments. Hands, breasts, navels, and facial features are clearly shown, and the backs are sometimes carved to represent what may be tattoos. It is interesting to speculate where the makers of the moai got their models from, since the features of the moai – long straight noses, tight-lipped mouths, sunken eyes, and low foreheads – seem to

Top: Ahu Akivi, Easter Island
Left: Ahu Nau Nau at Anakena, Easter Island
Right: Squatting statue, Rano Raraku quarry, Easter Island

Top: Shattered statue from Ahu Tongariki, Easter Island
Bottom: Anakena Beach, Easter Island

be very un-Polynesian. Large stone statues have also been found on the Marquesas, Raivavae, and other islands of eastern Polynesia, but they can also be found in western South America.

Since the quarry shows all the stages of carving a moai it's easy enough to see how this process was conducted. Most were carved face up, and in a horizontal or slightly sloping position. A channel large enough to accommodate the workmen was excavated around and under each moai, leaving the moai attached to the rock only by a narrow keel along its back. Almost all the carving of the figure, including the fine detail, was done at this stage. The moai was then detached from its keel, and by some means transported down the mountain, sometimes down a perpendicular wall, avoiding moai on which work was still proceeding on a ledge below. At the foot of the cliff the moai were raised up into a standing position in trenches. The sculptors then carved the finer detail on the back and decorated the waist with a belt surrounded by rings and symbols. When the carving was finished they were moved to their ahu on the coast.

Modest moai can be found next to giants; some of the smallest are as little as two metres in length whilst the biggest is just under 21 metres. Overall there are very few moai here under three metres long, and the usual length is between 5½ and seven metres. The 21-metre colossus is unique; the face alone is just over nine metres long; it measures just over four metres across the shoulders, and the body is about 1½ metres thick. The story goes that it was destined for Ahu Vinapu but it is hard to believe that it could ever have been moved. Work has been completed on the front and both sides of the moai but it has not been freed from the rock beneath it.

The carving was done with basalt tools called *toki*, literally thousands of which have been found discarded at the quarry site. In *Aku-Aku: The Secret of Easter Island*, Heyerdahl recounts commissioning a number of the islanders to work at Rano Raraku carving a new moai. The work lasted for three days until the carvers gave up, but their efforts suggested that it would take maybe 12 to 15 months of work to carve a medium-sized moai (say four or five metres long) with two teams working constantly in shifts.

Among the many moai here, a few are of special interest. One moai exhibits a roughly carved three-masted sailing ship on its chest. From the bow, a line extends downwards to a circular figure with what might be interpreted as a head and four short legs. The figure is so roughly carved that it certainly had no connection with the making of the moai itself. The carving may represent a European ship, although it's also thought it may represent a large *totora* reed vessel. The figure below it may represent an anchor of some sort, although it might also be a turtle or tortoise held by a fishing line. Contrary to popular belief, there were a number of female moai made, some with carvings which clearly represent the vulva and others which have clearly defined breasts.

The most unique discovery at Rano Raraku made by the Norwegian expedition was a kneeling moai which at the time was almost totally buried. The moai, a little less than four metres high, now stands to one side of the outer slope of the mountain. Just standing it upright, according to the Norwegian expedition's report, required the aid of the 'expedition jeep, tackle, poles, ropes, chains, and 20 native workers'. It has a fairly natural rounded head, a goatee beard, short ears, and a full body squatting on its heels and with its forearms and hands resting on its thighs. It appears that the moai was made on the spot. The brow is low with curved eyebrows, the eyes are hollowed out and slightly oval, and the pupils are marked by small round cavities. The nose is considerably damaged, the cheeks round and natural, and the lips damaged but perhaps originally quite plump and pouting.

Imagine that, having carved a moai with toothpicks from hard basalt, you must lift it out of its cavity and lower it down the cliff face. This must have been difficult because a couple of broken moai suggest that ropes broke or workers slipped. Then you stand it up at the foot of the mountain, probably by sliding it downwards into a trench cut for the occasion, so that work on the back can be completed. When that's done, all you have to do is transport it several km to the coast, where you stand it upright on a raised platform. Easy.

Over 300 moai were either placed on ahu or are lying along the old roads in various parts of the island. Many explanations as to how this feat was performed have been suggested, but for any of them to be valid they have to be able to account for the transport and erection of the biggest moai ever placed on an ahu – the 10-metre tall giant at Ahu Te Pito Te Kura.

Ahu Te Pito Te Kura

On the north coast of the island, overlooking La Perouse Bay (look for the sign by the road), on the south-east side of a small, shallow cove called Hanga-ko-uri or Black Bay, can be found the largest moai ever moved from Rano Raraku and erected on an ahu. The name of the ahu comes from a particular stone called *te pito te kura* which means 'the navel of light'. Hotu Matua is said to have brought this stone to the island and it is believed to symbolise the island itself – the island is sometimes called Te Pito o Te Henua, the Navel of the World.

At first glance, little light seems to be shed on the mystery of Easter Island here. This moai is 9¾ metres long and lies face down upon the sloping surface on the inland side of the platform. Its ears alone are each 2¼ metres long. A topknot – oval rather than round like those at Vinapu – lies nearby.

Oral history relates that the moai was erected by a widow to represent her dead husband. It is also said to have been the last moai to have been toppled, although that claim has also been made of the moai re-erected by the Norwegian expedition at Anakena. In height and bodily proportions and in general appearance the moai at Ahu Te Pito Te Kura is similar to the tall moai still buried up to their necks at Rano Raraku. If those standing at the quarry site are the last to have been made then it seems likely that the Te Pito Te Kura moai was probably the last to be erected on an ahu.

To work out how they got the thing up in the first place it is worth considering the moai that was re-erected on Ahu Ature Huki at Anakena, just up the road from La Perouse Bay.

Anakena

Anakena is the island's largest white-sand beach and the legendary landing place of Hotu Matua. There are a number of caves in the area and one of them is said to have been the dwelling place of Hotu Matua while he waited for his boat-shaped house to be built near the beach, although the Norwegian expedition found no traces of very early habitation in the cave said to have belonged to Hotu Matua. Nearby, the remains of an unusually large boat-shaped house (*hare paenga*), probably originally about 25 metres long, is said to have been the house of Hotu Matua. But the Norwegian expedition failed to find anything of particular interest here. Of much greater interest are Ahu Ature Huki and Ahu Nau Nau.

Ahu Ature Huki On the side of the hill above Anakena Beach stands Ahu Ature Huki and its lone moai, re-erected when the Norwegian expedition was here. In *Aku-Aku: the Secret of Easter Island*, Heyerdahl described how the moai was raised back on to its platform using wooden poles:

...the men got the tips of their poles in underneath it, and while three or four men hung and heaved at the farthest end of each pole, the mayor lay flat on his stomach and pushed small stones under the huge face... When evening came the giant's head had been lifted a good three feet from the ground, while the space beneath was packed tight with stones.

The process continued for nine days, the giant on an angle supported by stones, and the logs being levered with ropes when the men could no longer reach them. After another nine days work, the moai finally stood upright and unsupported on its platform. The work had required the efforts of a dozen people.

Getting the moai to the site in the first place must have been an even greater problem. It was suggested at the time that the moai could have been moved using a Y-shaped sledge made from a forked tree trunk, pulled with ropes made from tree bark. Heyerdahl eventually got together 180 islanders to pull a four-metre moai across the field at Anakena, and he suggests in his book that a much larger moai could have been moved given wooden runners and enough people to do the pulling.

There is a story that the moai were moved by the power of the *mana* of the priests, who were able to make the moai walk a short distance every day until eventually they reached their ahu. Another explanation is that round stones were inserted under the moai and that they were pushed, pulled and rolled to their destinations like a block on marbles. If you look around the island you will find numerous round stones, so it is not an unlikely idea, but it doesn't explain how the moai were moved without harming the fine detail carved on them at the quarry.

There is one plausible explanation of how it could have been done, which was developed by American archaeologist William Mulloy, who was on the Norwegian expedition. The method he postulated would have been physically possible if enough workers were available (although very difficult), and it ties in with the shape and configuration of the moai. First, a wooden sledge would have

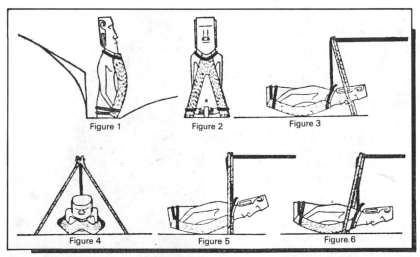

William Mulloy's statue-moving theory

been fitted to the moai (Figures 1 & 2). The distribution of the statue's weight would have kept the relatively light and fragile head above ground when it was tipped over. A bipod would then have been set up astride the statue's neck, at an angle to the vertical (Figures 3 & 4). A cable attached to the neck of the moai would be tied to the bipod apex and pulled forward. The head of the moai would rise slightly (Figure 5), and the moai would be dragged forward. When the bipod passed vertical, the statue's own weight would carry it forward along its belly (Figure 6). By moving the legs of the bipod forward, the entire process could be repeated.

It's interesting to consider that the figure is thus moved across the ground in a repetitive series of upward and forward movements, reminiscent of the islanders' legend that the moai walked to their ahu. It could also explain why broken moai can be seen along the old transport routes; the rope or bipod may have slipped or broken when the moai was in a raised position, sending it plummeting to the ground. There are a few problems with Mulloy's method (for a start, it requires very large tree trunks to make the bipods) but it's still theoretically possible.

But even with the moai at its ahu, it had to be stood up on an elevated platform. The restoration of seven moai in the 1960s by Mulloy and Gonzalo Figuero (described in the section on Aku Akivi) suggests that levering and supporting the moai with rocks may indeed have worked.

Ahu Nau Nau *Mata ki te rangi* is a term in the language of Easter Island which means 'eyes that look to the sky' and it is one of the names by which the island has long been known to Europeans. Some thought it was a reference to the craters of the extinct volcanos which lie at the corners of the triangular-shaped island. Other more imaginative interpretations thought it referred to the islanders looking to the skies in expectation of the return of their extra-terrestrial ancestors or building patrons.

But what makes the Anakena site so important was the discovery, during the excavation and restoration of the Ahu Nau Nau site in 1979, that the moai were not blind as was previously believed, but actually had inlaid coral and rock eyes – the eyes that looked to the sky – some of which were reconstructed from fragments found at the site. It's also thought the figures were painted and had inlaid earplugs.

There are seven moai at Ahu Nau Nau; four have topknots on their heads, whilst only the torsos remain of two others. Fragments of bodies and heads lie in front of the ahu.

Anakena Beach This beach is a little white-sand beach which is very popular with the locals. Oddly enough, tourist brochures don't do justice to the place and if you've got the time to spare (Easter Island is a long way to go just to go swimming) then this is a pleasant place to spend some time.

Ahu Nau Nau, Anakena

Ahu Akivi

This restored ahu sports seven moai. Unlike most other ahu on the island, Ahu Akivi is built inland with the moai looking out to sea. It was completely restored in 1960 by a group headed by William Mulloy and a Chilean archaeologist, Gonzalo Figueroa. They used a technique for re-erecting the seven moai similar to that used at Ahu Ature Huki. Some years later, Mulloy wrote:

... a surprising amount of skill was acquired with practice. The first moai at Ahu Akivi was erected in a little over a month, while the last was accomplished in less than a week. . . Clearly the prehistoric islanders with their hundreds of years of repetition of the same task must have known many more tricks than modern imitators were able to learn.

Mulloy suggested that the large number of stones found in front of Ahu Akahanga on the south coast were the leftovers of stones used to erect the moai, and that one moai appeared to have fallen sideways off the platform as it was being erected. He also pointed to the tremendous number of stones gathered near many ahu, including Ahu Te Pito Te Kura, as possible evidence that the moai may have been erected using stones to support the moai as it was gradually levered upwards.

He thought that the moai and topknot at Ahu Te Pito Te Kura could have been carved by 30 men working eight hours a day for one year; it could have been transported from the quarry to the ahu by 90 men over a previously prepared road in two months; and could have been erected by 90 men in about three months. But even if Mulloy is right there is still the problem of raising the topknots, carved from the red rock of the Puna Pau crater, to the heads of the moai.

Puna Pau

The cylindrical topknots of red stone which once capped a number of the moai have been variously thought to be hats, baskets, or crowns. The stone, quarried from the small volcanic crater called Puna Pau, is relatively soft and easily worked. Most have a clearly marked knot on the top and a depression carved into the

Horse and topknot, Puna Pau

underside which allows them to be slotted onto the heads of the moai. The original native name for this head decoration is *pukao* which means topknot, the usual hairstyle of the Easter Island males at the time the first Europeans came to the island.

The custom of capping the moai with topknots appears to have developed later in the piece as it seems many moai did not have topknots at all. Only about 60 moai are known to have had them, and about 25 topknots remain in or near the Puna Pau quarry. The topknots were carved in much the same way as the moai, and may then have been rolled to their final location. These topknots – each about the weight of two elephants – were then somehow placed on the moai, some of which were as much as 10 metres high. The first few Europeans to visit the island did record that moai were still standing on their ahu with the topknots on their heads.

It seems that the knot on top of the stone and the depression on its underside were carved after the stone had been transported to its ahu – probably to prevent the knot breaking off in transport and to allow the head to be measured in order to carve a depression of the right size. Oral tradition suggests that a long causeway of stones was erected to the head of the moai long enough to provide a grade up which the topknots could then be rolled. Mulloy suggested that the more probable method of getting it on to the top of the moai was to tie them together and raise the moai and topknot at the same time. This would eliminate the clumsy and time-consuming method of trying to roll the topknot up an enormous ramp.

The Poike Peninsula

By the time the first Europeans arrived at the island, construction work had ceased and the moai makers had disappeared off the face of the earth, as if they had been taken up into the heavens. It seems more likely though that they were, in fact, swallowed by the earth and consumed by fire.

The eastern end of the island is a high plateau called the Poike Peninsula. The western boundary of the peninsula is marked by a narrow depression called Ko te Ava o Iko, or Iko's Trench, running from one side of the island to the other. Legends record it was built by the Long Ears to defend themselves against the Short Ears. One version of the story begins with the Long Ear rulers deciding to clear the Poike Peninsula of all its loose rocks so that the whole area could be cultivated. The Short Ears tired of the work and decided on war, and the Long Ears – under the command of their chief Iko – gathered on the Poike Peninsula and dug a trench which separated Poike from the rest of the island. The trench was then filled with branches and tree trunks, ready to be set on fire should the Short Ears try to storm across.

But one of the Long Ears had a Short Ear wife who allowed the Short Ears to slip into the Poike Peninsula and surround the Long Ears. When another Short Ear army marched up towards the ditch the Long Ears lined up to face them and set fire to the pyre; the other Short Ears rushed down behind them and in a bloody fight the Long Ears were pushed into, and burned in, their own ditch. Only three of the Long Ears are said to have escaped; two of these were later killed, but the one who was permitted to live married a Short Ear and had children.

It was once thought that the ditch was a natural one and the story of the battle purely an invention. The Norwegian expedition, however, found thick layers of charcoal and ashes and carbonised wood, proving that there had once been a great fire here; and since much of the ash was red it must either have produced a very intense heat or else burnt for a long time. The topmost part of the trench was natural but this had been artificially enlarged further down to create a trench with a rectangular bottom, three or four metres deep, about five metres wide and running a couple of km across the hillside. It is not a continuous ditch but is actually made up of a number of separate trenches. Carbon-14 dating suggested that the great fire had burnt perhaps 300 to 350 years ago.

It's worth considering that though the Long Ears, suddenly forced to retreat to the Poike Peninsula, would perhaps have had time to fill the ditch with wood, they would certainly not have had time to undertake the heavy and time-consuming work of enlarging the ditch. In fact, dating the remains of earlier fires suggested that the ditch was originally dug out around 400 AD. It may not have been a defensive ditch originally, but may have been used as such in the 17th century. Whatever the case, the Late Period is marked by the absence of moai carving, and the only new ahu built seem to have been used specifically for burials.

Orito

Having done away, so it would seem, with their Long Ear rulers, the Short Ears are said to have entered into a long period of peace until tribal rivalries and conflicts arose, resulting in a period of bloody warfare involving the toppling of the moai.

The weapons used to fight these battles were made from hard black obsidian, some of which were quarried from Orito. The *mataa* is a common artifact turned up on the island – usually a crudely shaped blade of obsidian used as a spearhead. It's also suggested that the blades could have made highly effective weapons by fixing them in series in the edges of the flat wooden clubs which were once commonly used on the island. The quarry was also used for peaceful purposes; other artifacts found on the island include obsidian files and obsidian drill bits which would have been attached to a wooden shaft and used to drill bone, wood or rock.

From the vantage point of Rano Kau, the quarry looks like an enormous grey rectangle on the southern slope of Orito, but quarrying actually took place around the whole circumference of the mountain. This is not the only obsidian quarry on the island: there is one on the island of Motu Iti off the south-west tip, and another on the north-east edge of the Rano Kau crater.

The South Coast

Apart from Ahu Vinapu, the handiwork of the 'statue overthrowing' period is best seen along the south coast where a number of enormous ruined ahu and their fallen moai can be seen.

Vaihu One of the most impressive sights on the south coast, this ahu has eight large moai which have been toppled and now lie with their noses in the ground and several topknots scattered in front. One topknot has rolled into the small estuary next to the site.

Akahanga Akahanga is a large ahu with large fallen moai. Across the adjacent estuary stands a second ahu with several toppled moai. On the hill slopes opposite Akahanga are the remains of a village, including the foundations of several boat-shaped houses and the ruins of several round houses.

Hanga Tetenga Also on the coast, this almost completely ruined ahu has two large moai which have toppled and broken into pieces. From Hanga Tetenga, the road branches inland towards Rano Raraku. Along the track leading to the volcano, you will see several fallen moai making a bee-line towards the sea.

Ahu Tongariki To the east of Rano Raraku, there is a field in which several topknots and shattered moai were strewn by a tidal wave produced by an earthquake on the Chilean mainland in 1960. The ruined ahu from which these pieces were swept was called Ahu Tongariki; it was the biggest ahu built, and supported 15 massive moai. There are several petroglyphs cut into the flat rock outcrops in front of the scattered moai. These include a turtle with a man's face, a tuna fish, a birdman motif, and one which may represent a woman with her legs spread apart.

Orongo Ceremonial Village

Almost covered in a bog of floating totora reeds, the crater lake of Rano Kau looks like a giant witch's cauldron. Perched 400 metres up on the edge of the crater wall of Rano Kau, the ceremonial village of Orongo occupies one of the most dramatic pieces of real-estate on the island. This was once the most important ceremonial site on the island, but its significance seems to belong to a period after the construction of the great moai and ahu.

A seemingly endless winding road makes its way from Hanga Roa up the side of Rano Kau to Orongo, perched on the rim of the crater facing the sea. There are sweeping views of the whole island on the

Birdman petroglyphs, Orongo

way up. There is an entrance fee to Orongo – about US$1 – which you pay at the ranger's office outside the entrance to the site. There is also a small booklet on Orongo available here for US$1 that's worth getting.

The Orongo village seems to have been the centre of an island-wide bird cult linked to the gods Makemake and Haua, at least in the 18th and 19th centuries. Makemake, apparently the supreme deity of the island, is said to have created the earth, sun, moon, stars, and people. He rewarded the good and punished the evil, and when he was angry he made it known by thunder. During times of trouble, it is said he required the sacrifice of a child. Makemake is also credited with bringing the birds and presumably the bird cult to Easter Island, but he is said to have been aided in this venture by Haua.

There is no complete record of the ceremonies which took place here and accounts which do exist conflict with each other, particularly in regard to the time of the year when the ceremonies would begin and their duration. At the required time, the people involved with the ceremonies would move up to Orongo where they would live in stone houses. During this period, they made offerings and said prayers to their gods, conducted rites to propitiate the gods and held what may have been fertility dances in front of the houses.

The climax of the ceremonies was the attempt by each contestant or his representative, called a *hopu*, to obtain the first egg of the sooty tern, whose breeding grounds were on the islands of Motu Nui, Motu Iti, and Motu Kao Kao, just off the south-west tip of the island. When the word was given for the contestants or their hopu to leave, they would descend down the cliff face from Orongo and, with the aid of a small reed raft called a *pora*, swim out to the islands. The contestant who found the first egg became the 'birdman' of the year. If a hopu found it he called out the name of his master across to a man stationed in a cave in the cliff face below Orongo. The fortunate master's head, eyebrows and eyelashes were then shaved, and his face was painted red and black; he became the new birdman for the next year and went into seclusion in a special house. The advantage of becoming a birdman has never really been worked out, but it seems that whoever won the first egg also won the favour of Makemake. The last bird-cult ceremonies were held at Orongo about 1866 or 1867.

The Orongo ceremonial village has been partially restored and has a breathtaking setting. The Orongo houses were generally made by cutting a floor into the side of the slope. The walls were made using slabs of stone placed horizontally and overlapping each other, and the structure was roofed by laying overlapping stone slabs horizontally to produce an arch. The roofs were covered in earth and give the appearance of being partly underground. Because the walls were thick and the roof had to be supported by its own weight, the doorway is a low narrow tunnel, only high enough to crawl through. At the end of the site, where the crater suddenly drops away, is a cluster of boulders carved with numerous birdman petroglyphs which look something like a hybrid between a man and a bird, with a long beak and a hand clutching an egg.

THE MUSEUM

A few more mysteries are housed in the island's museum which is some distance inland from the coast, midway between Ahu Tahai and Ahu Akapu. A road from Hanga Roa leads to the museum – see the Hanga Roa map for directions.

Odd Moai

Just outside the museum stands a peculiar moai of red rock. The moai was uncovered not far from the modern cemetery outside Hanga Roa and was re-erected by the Norwegian expedition. The intact moai stands about 2½ metres high

and appears to be crudely made. The appearance may be somewhat deceptive since the moai appears to have been badly damaged and eroded, although it appears to have a triangular-shaped head with rather large sunken eyes.

This is not the only odd moai found on the island; the seated figure dug up at Rano Raraku is another. Inside the museum there are also several oblong-shaped stone heads, known as 'potato heads', which have eye-sockets and rudimentary features, including one with round ears. These are thought to be the oldest carvings on the island, pre-dating the Rano Raraku figures.

Artefacts

Other exhibits include skulls from bodies originally entombed in ahu; basalt fish-hooks and other implements; obsidian spearheads and other weapons; sketches of boat-shaped houses, circular beehive-shaped huts, and the ceremonial houses at Orongo; a moai head with reconstructed fragments of its eyes; moai kavakava; and replicas of rongo-rongo tablets.

The Moai Kavakava

Of all the carved wooden figures produced by the islanders the most common, and perhaps the most grotesque, are the moai kavakava, or the 'statues of ribs'. Each has a human figure with a large, thin, and markedly aquiline nose, protruding cheekbones which accentuate their hollow cheeks, long extended earlobes, and a goatee beard that curls back on the chin. The abdomen recedes, and the ribs and backbone protrude like that of a person suffering from starvation.

At least one story goes that King Tuu ko ihu discovered two sleeping ghosts (aku aku) at the foot of the cliff in the topknot quarry. Both ghosts had pendulant ear-lobes reaching down to their necks, beards, and long hooked noses, and were so thin that their ribs stood out. Tuu ko ihu returned home and carved their portrait in wood before he forgot what they looked like, and from then on the people of the island have always carved these statues.

The Rongo-Rongo Tablets

If there is one thing on Easter Island which is likely to defy explanation for all time then it's the rongo-rongo script. The first European to become aware of the existence of a native script on the island was Eugene Eyraud, who recorded in 1864 that tablets or staffs of wood covered in some form of writing or hieroglyphics could be found in all the houses on the island. The figures were carved into these tablets with sharp stones, but by the time Eyraud came across them the islanders appear to have lost or forgotten their meaning.

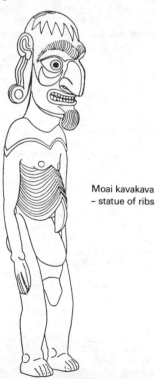

Moai kavakava – statue of ribs

The old and complete name of the tablets was *ko hau motu mo rongorongo*, which literally means 'lines of script for recitation'. It is said that Hotu Matua brought a number of these tablets with him, along with learned men who knew the art of writing and reciting the inscriptions. Most of the tablets are rather irregular, flat wooden boards with rounded edges, each about 30 to 50 cm long. They are covered in neat rows of tiny incised symbols which include birds, animals, possibly plants and celestial objects, and geometric forms. There are hundreds of different signs – too many to suggest that this writing is some form of alphabet.

Tradition says that there are three separate classes of tablets. One type recorded hymns in honour of Makemake and other divine beings. The second type recorded crimes or the other deeds of individuals. And the third type recorded those who had fallen in war or other conflicts. It is also said that tablets recording genealogies also existed. Only a few rongo-rongo tablets survive today, although it's probable that at one time thousands were in existence.

The first attempt to translate the tablets was made in Tahiti by Bishop Jaussen in 1866 using an Easter Islander living there who was said to be able to read the tablets. This and other similar attempts failed. It generally appeared that the natives were either reciting memorised texts, or merely describing the figures, rather than actually reading them. It seems that by this time the last truly literate Easter Islanders who could read the tablets were dead, either as a result of the slave raid in 1862 or the subsequent smallpox epidemic when the survivors returned to the island.

There are various theories concerning the nature of the script. One is that the script may not be a readable script at all, but simply a memory jogger for reciting memorised verse. Another is that the characters are ideographs, similar in

Rongo-rongo script

principle to those of the Chinese script. One person has even suggested a connection between the rongo-rongo script and a script used by a 3000-year-old civilisation in the Indus River Valley, in what is now Pakistan.

Index

MAPS

Dear traveller

Prices go up, good places go bad, bad places go bankrupt ... and every guide book is inevitably outdated in places. Fortunately, many travellers write to us about their experiences, telling us when things have changed. If we reprint a book between editions, we try to include as much of this information as possible in a Stop Press section. Most of this information has not been verified by our own writers.

We really enjoy hearing from people out on the road, and apart from guaranteeing that others will benefit from your good and bad experiences, we're prepared to bribe you with the offer of a free book for sending us substantial useful information.

Thank you to everyone who has written, and to those who haven't, I hope you do find this book useful – and that you let us know when it isn't.

Tony Wheeler

The recent elections in Chile were held too late to be included in the text, but just in time for a last minute Stop Press.

To the surprise of more cynical observers, Chile held elections on 14 December 1989 for the President and seats in the two legislative houses. Mr Patricio Aylwin was elected President with 55% of the vote.

Aylwin, himself a Christian Democrat, heads a coalition of 17 opposition parties called the Coalition for Democracy. In the Senate the Coalition's candidates won 22 seats, 16 went to right and centre candidates while 10 are occupied by Pinochet appointees, including Pinochet himself. In the House of Deputies the Coalition took 69 of the 120 seats.

This might seem to be a substantial victory for Aylwin and the Coalition, but it is by no means overwhelming. Pinochet and his appointees hold the balance of power in the Senate and the Coalition's majority in the Lower House is short of the two-thirds needed for constitutional amendments. This puts Aylwin in the same position as other reformist leaders of Chile — he leads an uneasy coalition which is demanding reforms that may not be achievable without antagonising entrenched economic and political interests, both domestic and foreign. Pinochet remains the commander of the army until 1998, and any loss of economic or political stability may become a pretext for him to seize power again.

One sensitive issue is the prosecution of those responsible for human rights abuses during Pinochet's regime, a key demand of left-wing elements in the Coalition. Such prosecutions are prohibited by a 1978 Amnesty Law. The military leadership has virtually promised another coup if this law is repealed by the new legislature.

The following Stop Press section was compiled using information sent to us by these travellers: Helga Schmidbauer (D), Robert A Raguso (USA).

Money & Costs
The current exchange rate is US$1 to Ch$318. The economy has experienced strong growth and an expanding export industry. It seems that this trend might continue as the business community showed it had confidence in the newly elected government by the almost unchanged economic indicators like currency exchange rates and interest rates. The unemployment rate is quite high, and there is a 20% inflation rate. Chile's economic future looks bright but

there are some weaknesses, like a large foreign debt and interest bill.

Getting There & Border Formalities

The train between Calama (Chile) and La Paz (Peru) is operating again, but there is only one class. The best tickets to obtain are for the three-seat benches, as you can stretch out on them. The other two-seat benches are not long enough to stretch out on.

The border formalities at Calama can take four to eight hours to complete. Most of the time is wasted waiting for the office to open, or while your passport circulates from building to building.

At the border, when you leave the train for immigration formalities, reserve your seat by leaving a blanket on your seat like the locals do. Otherwise, you will lose the seat. The locals reserve all vacant seats with their blankets, and do not give them up without a fight.

La Serena

La Serena is an aptly named semitropical city in the transverse mountain ranges about eight hours north of Santiago, near Coquimbo. It's the second oldest city in Chile and still boasts many examples of colonial architecture not destroyed by earthquakes or tidal waves.

The people are very relaxed and although it's not a town with riveting nightlife (the casinos are popular) it's well worth a few days if you're covering the entire northern arm of Chile. The La Recova market on Cienfuegos and Cantournet has a variety of musical instruments, llama wool and products of the local Chilean papaya industry.

The local archaeological museum, featuring the multicoloured pottery of the various Diaguitas traditions, is only a notch below that of San Pedro and worth a visit. Some fine examples of colonial buildings are the Iglesia Sto Domingo (Matta and Cordovez), the Iglesia Catedral (Carrera and Cordovez) and the Casa de la Providencia (on Justo Donoso and Cantournet).

A good place to stay is the *Residencial Chile* on Avenida Matta, and it costs US$5 per night. There is an inner courtyard with a beautiful garden, and the host will change US dollars.

Travellers' Tips & Comments

Armada de Chile, Barcena 150, runs boats to the Antarctica. Women are not accepted. The *Empresa Maritima de Estado, Empremar* and the *Edificion Comapa* are other possibilities.

You can also take flights from the military airport. Go to the airport and ask around.

Helga Schmidbauer – West Germany

The best rates were available through the securities outfits in the Bolsa (stock exchange) in Santiago. The Bolsa is the ornate building at 75 Nueva York, located on a pedestrian mall, near the Chile metro stop. You give the guard your passport and then ascend to the appropriate office. Explain that you are there to sell dólares.

Jill Yesko – USA

Guides to the Americas

Alaska - a travel survival kit
Jim DuFresne has travelled extensively through Alaska by foot, road, rail, barge and kayak, and tells how to make the most of one of the world's great wilderness areas.

Argentina - a travel survival kit
This guide gives independent travellers all the essential information on Argentina — a land of intriguing cultures, 'wild west' overtones and spectacular scenery.

Baja California - a travel survival kit
For centuries, Mexico's Baja peninsula — with its beautiful coastline, raucous border towns and crumbling Spanish missions — has been a land of escapes and escapades. This book describes how and where to escape in Baja.

Bolivia - a travel survival kit
From lonely villages in the Andes to ancient ruined cities and the spectacular city of La Paz, Bolivia is a magnificent blend of everything that inspires travellers. Discover safe and intriguing travel options in this comprehensive guide.

Brazil - a travel survival kit
From the mad passion of Carnival to the Amazon — home of the richest and most diverse ecosystem on earth — Brazil is a country of mythical proportions. This guide has all the essential travel information.

Canada - a travel survival kit
This comprehensive guidebook has all the facts on the USA's huge neighbour — the Rocky Mountains, Niagara Falls, ultra-modern Toronto, remote villages in Nova Scotia, and much more.

Central America on a shoestring
Practical information on travel in Belize, Guatemala, Costa Rica, Honduras, El Salvador, Nicaragua and Panama. A team of experienced Lonely Planet authors reveals the secrets of this culturally rich, geographically diverse and breathtakingly beautiful region.

Colombia - a travel survival kit
Colombia is a land of myths — from the ancient legends of El Dorado to the modern tales of Gabriel Garcia Marquez. The reality is beauty and violence, wealth and poverty, tradition and change. This guide shows how to travel independently and safely in this exotic country.

Costa Rica - a travel survival kit
This practical guide gives the low down on exceptional opportunities for fishing and water sports, and the best ways to experience Costa Rica's vivid natural beauty.

Ecuador & the Galápagos Islands - a travel survival kit
Ecuador offers a wide variety of travel experiences, from the high cordilleras to the Amazon plains — and 600 miles west, the fascinating Galápagos Islands. Everything you need to know about travelling around this enchanting country.

Hawaii - a travel survival kit
Share in the delights of this island paradise — and avoid its high prices — both on and off the beaten track. Full details on Hawaii's best-known attractions, plus plenty of uncrowded sights and activities.

La Ruta Maya: Yucatán, Guatemala & Belize - a travel survival kit
Invaluable background information on the cultural and environmental riches of La Ruta Maya (The Mayan Route), plus practical advice on how best to minimise the impact of travellers on this sensitive region.

Mexico - a travel survival kit
A unique blend of Indian and Spanish culture, fascinating history, and hospitable people, make Mexico a travellers' paradise.

Peru - a travel survival kit
The lost city of Machu Picchu, the Andean altiplano and the magnificent Amazon rainforests are just some of Peru's many attractions. All the travel facts you'll need can be found in this comprehensive guide.

South America on a shoestring
This practical guide provides concise information for budget travellers and covers South America from the Darien Gap to Tierra del Fuego. By the author the *New York Times* nominated 'the patron saint of travellers in the third world'.

Also available:
Brazilian phrasebook, **Latin American Spanish** phrasebook and **Quechua** phrasebook.

Lonely Planet Guidebooks

Lonely Planet guidebooks cover every accessible part of Asia as well as Australia, the Pacific, South America, Africa, the Middle East and parts of North America and Europe. There are four series: *travel survival kits*, covering a country for a range of budgets; *shoestring guides* with compact information for low-budget travel in a major region; *walking guides*; and *phrasebooks*.

Australia & the Pacific
Australia
Bushwalking in Australia
Islands of Australia's Great Barrier Reef
Fiji
Micronesia
New Caledonia
New Zealand
Tramping in New Zealand
Papua New Guinea
Papua New Guinea phrasebook
Rarotonga & the Cook Islands
Samoa
Solomon Islands
Sydney
Tahiti & French Polynesia
Tonga
Vanuatu

South-East Asia
Bali & Lombok
Burma
Burmese phrasebook
Indonesia
Indonesia phrasebook
Malaysia, Singapore & Brunei
Philippines
Pilipino phrasebook
Singapore
South-East Asia on a shoestring
Thai Hill Tribes phrasebook
Thailand
Thai phrasebook
Vietnam, Laos & Cambodia

North-East Asia
China
Mandarin Chinese phrasebook
Hong Kong, Macau & Canton
Japan
Japanese phrasebook
Korea
Korean phrasebook
North-East Asia on a shoestring
Taiwan
Tibet
Tibet phrasebook

West Asia
Trekking in Turkey
Turkey
Turkish phrasebook
West Asia on a shoestring

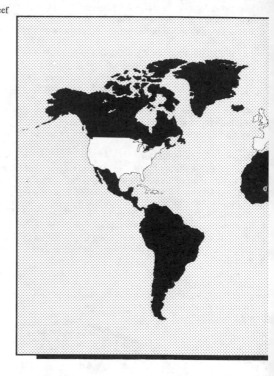

Indian Ocean
Madagascar & Comoros
Maldives & Islands of the East Indian Ocean
Mauritius, Réunion & Seychelles

Mail Order

Lonely Planet guidebooks are distributed worldwide and are sold by good bookshops everywhere. They are also available by mail order from Lonely Planet, so if you have difficulty finding a title please write to us. US and Canadian residents should write to Embarcadero West, 112 Linden St, Oakland CA 94607, USA and residents of other countries to PO Box 617, Hawthorn, Victoria 3122, Australia.

Europe
Eastern Europe on a shoestring
Iceland, Greenland & the Faroe Islands
Trekking in Spain
USSR
Russian phrasebook

Indian Subcontinent
Bangladesh
India
Hindi/Urdu phrasebook
Trekking in the Indian Himalaya
Karakoram Highway
Kashmir, Ladakh & Zanskar
Nepal
Trekking in the Nepal Himalaya
Nepal phrasebook
Pakistan
Sri Lanka
Sri Lanka phrasebook

Africa
Africa on a shoestring
Central Africa
East Africa
Kenya
Swahili phrasebook
Morocco, Algeria & Tunisia
Moroccan Arabic phrasebook
Zimbabwe, Botswana & Namibia
West Africa

North America
Alaska
Canada
Hawaii

Mexico
Baja California
Mexico

South America
Argentina
Bolivia
Brazil
Brazilian phrasebook
Chile & Easter Island
Colombia
Ecuador & the Galápagos Islands
Latin American Spanish phrasebook
Peru
Quechua phrasebook
South America on a shoestring

Central America
Central America
Costa Rica
La Ruta Maya

Middle East
Egypt & the Sudan
Egyptian Arabic phrasebook
Israel
Jordan & Syria
Yemen

The Lonely Planet Story

Lonely Planet published its first book in 1973 in response to the numerous 'How did you do it?' questions Maureen and Tony Wheeler were asked after driving, bussing, hitching, sailing and railing their way from England to Australia.

Written at a kitchen table and hand collated, trimmed and stapled, *Across Asia on the Cheap* became an instant local bestseller, inspiring thoughts of another book.

Eighteen months in South-East Asia resulted in their second guide, *South-East Asia on a shoestring*, which they put together in a backstreet Chinese hotel in Singapore in 1975. The 'yellow bible' as it quickly became known to backpackers around the world, soon became *the* guide to the region. It has sold well over half a million copies and is now in its 7th edition, still retaining its familiar yellow cover.

Today there are over 80 Lonely Planet titles – books that have that same adventurous approach to travel as those early guides; books that 'assume you know how to get your luggage off the carousel' as one reviewer put it.

Although Lonely Planet initially specialised in guides to Asia, they now cover most regions of the world, including the Pacific, South America, Africa, the Middle East and Eastern Europe. The list of *walking guides* and *phrasebooks* (for 'unusual' languages such as Quechua, Swahili, Nepalese and Egyptian Arabic) is also growing rapidly.

The emphasis continues to be on travel for independent travellers. Tony and Maureen still travel for several months of each year and play an active part in the writing, updating and quality control of Lonely Planet's guides.

They have been joined by over 50 authors, 40 staff – mainly editors, cartographers, & designers – at our office in Melbourne, Australia, and another 10 at our US office in Oakland, California. Travellers themselves also make a valuable contribution to the guides through the feedback we receive in thousands of letters each year.

The people at Lonely Planet strongly believe that travellers can make a positive contribution to the countries they visit, both through their appreciation of the countries' culture, wildlife and natural features, and through the money they spend. In addition, the company makes a direct contribution to the countries and regions it covers. Since 1986 a percentage of the income from each book has been donated to ventures such as famine relief in Africa; aid projects in India; agricultural projects in Central America; Greenpeace's efforts to halt French nuclear testing in the Pacific and Amnesty International. In 1991 $68,000 was donated to these causes.

Lonely Planet's basic travel philosophy is summed up in Tony Wheeler's comment, 'Don't worry about whether your trip will work out. Just go!'

Tetnus–Diptheria 5/9/90

Polio Booster

– Gamma Globulin

280–4100

Med records